Everything You Think You Know About Politics . . .

And Why You're Wrong

Everything You Think You Know About Politics . . .

And Why You're Wrong

Kathleen Hall Jamieson

A New Republic Book

BASIC
BOOKS

A Member of the Perseus Books Group

Published by Basic Books,
A Member of the Perseus Books Group

Designed by Rachel Hegarty

Library of Congress Cataloging-in-Publication Data
Jamieson, Kathleen Hall.
    Everything you think you know about politics— and why you're wrong / Kathleen Hall Jamieson.
        p. cm.
    Includes bibliographical references and index.
    ISBN 0-465-03627-9
    1. Electioneering—United States.   2. Advertising, Political—United States. 3. Campaign debates—United States. I. Title.
JK2281 .J35 2000
324.7'0973—dc21   00-027905

First Edition

00 01 02 03 / 10 9 8 7 6 5 4 3 2

To the memory of Robert Squier,
who produced a
get-out-the-vote television spot
reminding viewers of the legacy of
Susan B. Anthony
and
Rosa Parks

Contents

Contents

Preface

November 30, 1999. The face on the screen is that of George W. Bush, Republican, governor of Texas, son of a former president, and presidential aspirant. On the issue of U.S. trade policy, the Texas Republican says, "China will find in America a confident and willing trade partner." He adds, "Trade freely with China, and time is on our side." Arizona Senator John McCain appears next. Same issue. "I don't believe in walls," he notes. "If I were president, I would negotiate a free trade agreement with almost any country willing to negotiate with us."

There is, however, dissent in the ranks of the Republican contenders for president. Former Reagan administration official Gary Bauer, who opposes China's entry into the World Trade Organization (WTO), declares, "My party needs to listen to Main Street, not to Wall Street on this issue." Businessman Steve Forbes agrees. "No more turning a blind eye to Chinese spies in our nuclear labs," he says, "no more keeping silent about Chinese slave labor camps."

And what of the former Republican contender who is now seeking the spot at the head of the Reform Party ticket, Pat Buchanan? His position too is clear and concise. "Global economy must call into existence a global government, and globalism is at war with patriotism," he intones. These six statements, averaging sixteen and a half words and 6.83 seconds each, digest the substance of the agreement between Bush and McCain and the crux of the disagreement between those two and Bauer and Forbes on the issue of China's admission to the WTO. Taken together, the statements profile with dispatch the stands of the Republican contenders.

CNN's Brooks Jackson weaves the soundbites into a narrative that includes context and skillful paraphrase of related candidate beliefs. From him we learn that Al Gore is "for fast-track negotiating theory, for China's entry into the World Trade Organization. . . And the same for Bill Bradley. Here he is at the signing of NAFTA." Note the efficiency of Jackson's closing sentence: "So, unless there's a huge upset, the next president of the U.S. will be a strong free trader, just like the incumbent."

The candidates' positions are as clear here as in their extended answers to questions about trade in the first townhall forums of the primary season. Note, for example, George W. Bush's answer December 7, 1999, in the Arizona townhall to a question from Gary Bauer asking why he had embraced the Clinton-Gore policy of giving China most-favored-nation status and membership in the World Trade Organization?

Bush: I appreciate that, but you know how to insult a guy by saying [I] follow the policies of Clinton-Gore. I don't. They believe in what's called a strategic partnership. I believe in redefining the relationship to one of competitor. But I believe competitors can find common ground. I think it's in our nation's best interests to open up Chinese markets to Arizona farm products, to Iowa farm products, to high-tech manufactured goods. It's in our best interests to sell to the Chinese. It's also in our best interests to make sure that the entrepreneurial class in China flourishes. I think we make China an enemy, they'll end up being an enemy. I think if we trade with China, and trade with the entrepreneurial class, and give people a breath of freedom, give them a taste of freedom, I think you'll be amazed, Gary, at how soon democracy will come. And so, I also believe . . . China ought to be in the World Trade Organization. I also believe that Taiwan ought to be in the World Trade Organization. But let me make this clear to you and to the Chinese. I will enforce the Taiwan relations law if I'm the president. If the Chinese get aggressive with the Taiwanese, we'll help them defend themselves.

Bauer: Governor, we would have never made the argument that you just made if we were talking about Nazi Germany. Is there no atrocity that you can think of, the labor camps doubling in their slave labor, a bigger crackdown, more priests disappearing in the middle of the night, is there anything that would tell you to put trade on the back burner?

Bush: Gary, I agree with you that forced abortion is abhorrent. And I agree with you when leaders try to snuff out religion. But I think if we turn our back on China and isolate China, things will get worse. Imagine if the Internet took hold in China. Imagine how freedom would spread. In my earlier answer, I said our greatest export to the world has been, is, and always will be the incredible freedom we understand in America. And that's why it's important for us to trade with China to encourage the growth of an entrepreneurial class. It gets that taste of freedom, it gets that breath of freedom, in the marketplace.

Taken together, the soundbites from the two candidates and their townhall answers paint a more complete picture of their positions than either response alone. There is obvious merit in paying attention to both. But if time is of the essence, Jackson's report can serve as a telegraphic substitute for the townhall exchange. The reason is simple. Whereas candidates take time to get to the point, Jackson has cut to the chase. In boiling their positions down to essentials, he has confirmed that soundbites can be substantive, that there is nothing inherently vacuous about brief candidate statements, and that his investment in finding these core statements has made it possible for us to learn in less than three minutes what otherwise would have taken an hour and a half. Soundbites can be superficial or substantive. Substantive soundbites are the stuff of which the best news stories are made.

If that is the case, why is the brevity of candidate statements in news taken as prima facie evidence that the discourse of democracy has decayed? What accounts for the casual assumption that a soundbite is by definition superficial?

My theory goes like this. Someone created a neutral word to describe the selection of a brief section of a candidate's speech for a newscast. Soundbite. Someone else—someone who had forgotten that "I love you," "Will you marry me?" "It's a healthy baby girl," "I will go to Korea," "Ask not what your country can do for you," and "We have nothing to fear but fear itself" meet the definition of soundbite—appropriated the word to describe a superficial, crafted candidate statement designed to be excerpted into news. If asked to use the word in a sentence, a student might now write, "That's a great soundbite, but where's the substance?" "Soundbite" came to function as a synonym for superficial.

Other phrases, such as "negative ad" or "negative campaign," have been so variously defined as to be meaningless. Like a soundbite, a negative campaign is presumed to be bad for democracy. This is an instance of what rhetorical critic Kenneth Burke meant when he noted that language does our thinking for us. The thinking done by soundbite and negative campaigning leads reformers to call for longer soundbites, unmindful that length and substance are not synonyms, and for less negativity, apparently unaware that without attack we would lack the information needed to differentiate the candidates. I have been as guilty of this as others.

Misapplied concepts are not the only problem. Listen to the pundits during a campaign and you will hear suspect assumptions treated as dogma. They include such "truisms" as attack is bad for the public; attack drives voters from the polls; debates are boring; there is nothing to

be learned from paying attention to debates; and politicians break most of their campaign promises. If such notions are the scaffolding on which the indictment of the discourse of politics is built, the structure is shaky.

It is often difficult to know whether a book is worth reading, particularly a book whose title is an unabashed provocation. How, after all, do I know what you know about politics? And even if I could read your mind, your mail, your magazines, and your ballot, by what breach of strategic sense would I want to announce to the world (or to you) that you are wrong?

Of course, I don't know that you personally are wrong. What I do know is that many of the students in my classes, friends in the neighborhood, and reporters on the phone make assumptions about the way U.S. politics works that just don't check out against the record as I see it.

You may be the exception. To save you the trouble of reading a book that tells you what you already know, I've concocted a quiz. No time limit. Open book. No penalty for consulting with the political junkies in your life. Before you begin, however, a caution. Read the questions from the assumption that they are claims about what happens most of the time. There are exceptions. I will note them in the book. Read the questions armed with a sense of irony. After all, the conflict I am trying to set up between what you think you know and what the data reveal is employing a norm that I will later argue should accompany and not replace one that values consensus. In the same vein, reducing complex questions to true or false answers and you to being wrong with the implication that I am right is as simplistic as some of the assumptions I am challenging. You might say that I am using conflict, simplified narratives, and manipulative devices just as news and ads do—to entice you into watching and reading. You'd be right about that.

⤝ Here's the quiz.

1. In 1992, the phrase "the economy, stupid" and not the communication surrounding the campaign deserves full credit for the election of Bill Clinton.

    A. TRUE   B. FALSE

2. Most presidents make a strong effort to keep most of their campaign promises.

    A. TRUE   B. FALSE

3. Over a third of the typical general-election speech by a major-party presidential candidate is devoted to attacking the other party's nominee.

    A. TRUE   B. FALSE

4. General-election presidential political ads spend more than half of their air time attacking.

    A. TRUE   B. FALSE

5. When candidates make statements in speeches, they usually expect us to take them at their word and so provide no supporting evidence.

    A. TRUE   B. FALSE

6. Most candidate ads lie most of the time.

    A. TRUE   B. FALSE

7. The quality of presidential general-election campaigns has steadily worsened over the years.

    A. TRUE   B. FALSE

8. Campaign discourse in speeches and debates has become steadily more negative over the years.

    A. TRUE   B. FALSE

9. Reporters pretty accurately represent the content and level of attack in their stories about candidate speeches.

    A. TRUE   B. FALSE

10. Voters make a distinction between attack that is accurate and attack that is inaccurate, between attack that is personal and attack

that is issue based, and between attack that is histrionic and attack that is stated in a neutral fashion.

A. TRUE   B. FALSE

11. Voters prefer ads that contrast the records of the candidates to ads that simply attack.

A. TRUE   B. FALSE

12. There isn't very much useful information in campaigns; it's all mainly hype.

A. TRUE   B. FALSE

13. Attack turns off voters. The high level of attack in the general-election presidential campaign of 1996 was a main reason that voter turnout was down.

A. TRUE   B. FALSE

14. Attack benefits the sponsor and hurts the person attacked.

A. TRUE   B. FALSE

15. Political advertising turns off voters and they stay away from the polls as a result.

A. TRUE   B. FALSE

16. There is no useful information for voters in reporting about campaign strategy and tactics.

A. TRUE   B. FALSE

17. Women know less than men about politics.

A. TRUE   B. FALSE

18. The *New York Times* gave Dole less coverage in 1996 than Clinton.

A. TRUE   B. FALSE

19. The person who is ahead in the polls gets more strategic coverage than the underdog.

A. TRUE   B. FALSE

20. Reporters are right when they say there isn't much that can be learned from watching debates.

A. TRUE   B. FALSE

For the correct answers, see the opposite page.

⇒ Answers

1. In 1992, the phrase "the economy, stupid" and not the communication surrounding the campaign deserves full credit for the election of Bill Clinton.

   FALSE

2. Most presidents make a strong effort to keep most of their campaign promises.

   TRUE

3. Over a third of the typical general-election speech by a major-party presidential candidate is devoted to attacking the other party's nominee.

   FALSE

4. General-election presidential political ads spend more than half of their air time attacking.

   FALSE

5. When candidates make statements in speeches, they usually expect us to take them at their word and so provide no supporting evidence.

   FALSE

6. Most candidate ads lie most of the time.

   FALSE

7. The quality of presidential general-election campaigns has steadily worsened over the years.

   FALSE

8. Campaign discourse in speeches, ads, and debates has become steadily more negative over the years.

   FALSE

9. Reporters pretty accurately represent the content and level of attack in their stories about candidate speeches.

   FALSE

10. Voters make a distinction between attack that is accurate and attack that is inaccurate, between attack that is personal and attack that is issue based, and between attack that is histrionic and attack that is stated in a neutral fashion.

    TRUE

11. Voters prefer ads that contrast the records of the candidates to ads that simply attack.

    TRUE

12. There isn't very much useful information in campaigns; it's all mainly hype.

FALSE

13. Attack turns off voters. The high level of attack in the general-election presidential campaign of 1996 was a main reason that voter turnout was down.

FALSE

14. Attack benefits the sponsor and hurts the person attacked.

FALSE

15. Political advertising turns off voters and they stay away from the polls as a result.

FALSE

16. There is no useful information for voters in reporting about campaign strategy and tactics.

FALSE

17. Women know less than men about politics.

TRUE   and   FALSE

18. The *New York Times* gave Dole less coverage in 1996 than Clinton.

FALSE

19. The person who is ahead in the polls gets more strategic coverage than the underdog.

FALSE

20. Reporters are right when they say there isn't much that can be learned from watching debates.

FALSE

Scoring:

18–20 correct—Top of the class. Exceptional.

16–18 correct—Not bad.

14–16 correct—Still above average.

12–14 correct—Approaching the danger zone.

10–12 correct—You could almost reach this level by sheer chance.

0–10 correct—You have the instincts of some working pundits.

If your answers differ from mine and you are growling that you know you are right and I'm wrong, I invite you to read on.

A Note on Research

A decade ago a research team at the Annenberg School for Communication of the University of Pennsylvania began a comprehensive study of the effects of campaign communication. The project was massive, involving the efforts of faculty, staff, and students at the Annenberg School. Individuals who worked intensively on one topic or another are listed at the end the relevant chapter. The undergraduate and graduate research assistants who provided support are identified in the Acknowledgments. This book is, in other words, a collaborative effort.

We wanted to answer the question, What does the public know about politics, and how does it know it? Our answers are drawn from the presidential campaigns of 1952–1996, the debate over the McCain tobacco bill, the gubernatorial elections in California and Illinois in 1998, and the Philadelphia mayoral campaign of 1999.

First, we wanted to know what candidates say in the forms of communication over which they exercise the greatest control. The problem in doing this is straightforward. The materials were scattered across archives and collections throughout the United States. Some existed only in attics of speechwriters and admakers. With the support of the Ford Foundation and the Carnegie Corporation of New York, we collected and analyzed the extant presidential campaign ads, speeches, and debates from 1960, 1980, 1988, 1992, and 1996. This phase of the Campaign Mapping Project was a collaborative effort with a parallel research team at the University of Texas headed by Roderick P. Hart. The work of that group is reported in a separate book. With support from the Pew Charitable Trusts, the materials from the other 1952–1996 presidential contests were assembled and examined as well. When we report data from the Annenberg Campaign Mapping Project (ACMP), we are referring to 2,525 presidential general-election speeches, 880 ads, and 23 debates.

Since issue-advocacy advertising is an increasingly expensive and visible form of communication, we also gathered all of the issue ads aired in the health care reform debate of 1993–1994, in the debate over the McCain tobacco bill, and in the 1994, 1996, and 1998 election cycles. In the process, we examined over 400 issue ads. Much of this research was supported by a grant from the Pew Charitable Trusts.

To assess the impact of news, ads, and debates, we interviewed 8,850 respondents in five large-scale surveys. Some of our polls were single one-time snapshots; others watched the public over time. Support from the Annenberg Public Policy Center made this examination possible. A description of each of our surveys appears in Appendix III. A description of the more technical analyses we conducted appears in Appendix II.

Surveys and analysis of content are powerful tools. To them we added a complete map of the 1996 general-election advertising by Dole, Clinton, the AFL-CIO, and the Business Coalition in over a thousand counties. We draw on that information to determine the effects of attack, advocacy, and contrast in the ads.

Taken together, these materials provide the most complete profile ever assembled of presidential general-election campaigns and their impact. Some of the results surprised us. Many ran counter to conventional wisdom about campaigns and elections. In this book, we share our findings.

Acknowledgments

The contributors to chapters in the book include Christopher Adasiewicz, Sean Aday, Deborah Beck, Joseph Cappella, Veronica Davison, James Devitt, David Dutwin, Michael Hagen, Richard Johnston, Kate Kenski, Mary McIntosh, Mark Mendoza, Suzanne Morse, Ned Nurick, Dan Romer, Susan Sherr, Lesley Sillaman, Paul Waldman, Stacy Benjamin Wood, and Eric Zimmer. Their names appear at the ends of the chapters on which they worked.

The research reported in this book was funded by the Ford Foundation, the Carnegie Corporation of New York, and the Pew Charitable Trusts. We are grateful to Marcia Smith and June Zeitlin at Ford, Geri Mannion at Carnegie, and Paul Light, Sean Treglia, and Michael Delli Carpini at Pew for championing the project.

For his important role in framing the Campaign Mapping Project, we are indebted to Rod Hart of the University of Texas. (For another more or less compatible view of how campaigns work, see his book *Campaign Talk*.) At late hours and in odd places, John Zaller and Larry Bartels helped us sort out methodological issues. Thank you. Dan Romer helped the graduate students and me make sense of oceans of data. Joe Cappella was the project's utility infielder. Deborah Stinnett held the undertaking together with remarkable sanity and good humor. Josh Gesell fended off distractions with mighty efficiency. Debra Williams, Leslie Atik, Deborah Porter, and Donna Burdumy provided heroic staff support.

I also gratefully acknowledge the research assistance of the following individuals:

Project Manager
Deborah Stinnett

Staff

Timothy Blake

Richard Cardona

David Graper

Deborah Porter

Ellen Reynolds

Sue Roberts

Archivist

Sharon Black

Acknowledgments

Researchers	Research Assistants
Megin Adams	Kristina Alvarez
Stacy Benjamin	Erin Carstensen
Courtney Bennett	Candice Chia
Fernando Bermejo	Bruce Evans
Amy Branner	Tatiana Garcia-Granados
Rona Buchalter	Jordana Harris
Elaine Casey	Melissa James
Jessica Davis	Lisa Jellinek
Natalia Gridina	Robert Kanapka
Benjamin de Guzman	Jean Kwon
Isabel Molina-Guzman	Rachel Pomerance
Paula Lazli	Shannon Richardson
Brigette Rouson	Lance Rogers
Melinda Schwenk	Laura Rosenberg
Laura Segal	Pallavi Sharma
Jeffrey Stanger	Debra Shiau
Kirsten Stewart	Ann Tracey
Jeffrey Tancil	Lynda Tran
Eric Zimmer	Tiffany Zientz

At Basic Books, Tim Barlett, Vanessa Mobley, and Felicity Tucker counseled and cajoled with grace and insight. Paul Taylor provided a helpful critique of the work in progress. Bill Knapp and Alex Castellanos provided political perspective. Many of the cartoons scattered throughout the book were created for us by Pulitzer Prize winner Signe Wilkinson. Rob (a.k.a. Jamie) and Pat no longer add laundry to my life but continue to add love, as does Bob.

Everything You Think You Know About Politics . . . and Why You're Wrong is dedicated to the memory of documentary film producer and political consultant Bob Squier, a good friend and irrepressible tease who by crafting the title increased the likelihood that I would write this book. Great soundbite, Bob. Thank you.

Kathleen Hall Jamieson
Philadelphia, March 2000

Everything You Think You Know About Politics . . .

And Why You're Wrong

PART I

The Content and Effects of Campaigns

⇒ Did You Know?

In the general election of 1996, the ads for Clinton-Gore made 312 different claims. Of ads. The Dole-Kemp ads made 128 claims and, of those, recycled 9. In other words, the level of redundancy in the Democratic ads was substantially higher than in the Republican ones.

In addition, of the 440 claims made by the two campaigns' ads, 160 were misleading by the standards set in chapter five.

Chapter One

Do Campaigns Matter?

I N RETROSPECT, the eventual winner of a presidential contest
seems to have run the better race, with a more efficient organization, better advertising, and a more consistent message. But does
this analysis indicate causality, coincidence, or merely 20-20 hindsight?
Journalists see campaigns as important, especially key campaign events.[1]
But if they did not see things this way, the value of their work would be
called into question. After all, if campaigns don't matter, why do we
need political reporters?

Many scholars, on the other hand, reach a different conclusion. Election studies seek to answer two basic questions: What determines whom
an individual decides to vote for, and what determines which candidate
will emerge victorious? The prevailing view from both individual-level
and macro-level analyses is that campaigns have little effect; preexisting
conditions are far more effective predictors of outcomes. Campaigns are
merely theatrical exercises that provide entertainment and reinforcement of partisan dispositions but in most instances do not determine the
electoral outcome.

This conclusion comes not only from political scientists but also from
communication experts. The "minimal effects" model proposed by
media scholar Joseph Klapper in 1960 posited that mass communication
has relatively little power to change attitudes and behaviors and that
media effects are of marginal significance in explaining important decisions such as vote choice.[2] This perspective has, to a great extent, held
sway ever since.

Election campaign studies in 1944 and 1948 found that campaigns
were far more likely to reinforce existing dispositions than to alter them.
Individuals whose demographic characteristics predicted that they were
likely to vote for the Democratic candidate, for example, moved toward

that vote as the campaign progressed. Those who concentrated most on politics were the most likely to retain the preferences they held at the outset of the race.[3]

From the perspective of the minimal-effects model, political attitudes and party allegiances are formed early and are generally stable. Indeed, voters behave in ways that make reinforcement rather than change of attitudes more likely. So, for example, those disposed to the candidates of one party are more likely to pay attention to messages from that source. Voters are also more likely to talk about politics to those of like mind. And opinion leaders, a category of politically interested individuals we would identify as active communication participants, are likely to depict politics in ways consistent with their own biases.

A variant of this view holds that although the potential for substantial campaign effects exists, only in rare cases will that potential be realized. If a campaign is to produce an unexpected outcome, large numbers of voters must adopt views incompatible with their initial vote preference. With a model using only the respondents' race and June data on presidential approval and party identification, Finkel predicted 81 percent of eventual votes.[4] Since presidential approval and vote intent are likely to be highly correlated, this result is in part a confirmation that few voters switch from one party to the other during the course of a campaign.

Patterson and McClure also argue that voters are usually not persuaded by campaigns.[5] News and political ads provide some information (ads more so than news, in their most surprising finding), but voters are able to use that information without being hoodwinked by the candidates' manipulation.

These individual-level analyses assume that most voters make up their minds long before the campaign begins in earnest. If this is the case, other factors must be determining voters' decisions. Because these factors are structural rather than message-based, election results can be accurately forecast before the campaign begins.

In the "referendum" model of campaigns, the outcome of the election is determined primarily by the state of the economy: If the economy is healthy, the incumbent is reelected; in a recession or downturn, the challenger wins. When making their decision, voters evaluate the state of the economy, assign the president credit or blame, and vote accordingly. Other factors such as the relative number of registrants in each party will fill out a predictive model, but the state of the economy is central. This finding has been replicated, and has come to be accepted not only as internally valid but as strong support for the conclusion that campaigns in general have minimal, if any, measurable effects.[6]

An alternative explanation is articulated by political scientist Thomas Holbrook, who shows that significant changes in support for candidates do occur during the course of campaigns, and that these shifts can be attributed in large part to campaign events such as conventions and debates.[7] He also argues that there exists an "equilibrium" level of support for candidates that can be attributed to national conditions. Actual candidate support can stray far from this equilibrium at various stages during the campaign but tends to move back toward equilibrium by the campaign's end.

Taken together, this body of research (of which a small portion is discussed in this book) points to the conclusion that in the end, campaigns have little effect. They are valuable as a means of reinforcing voter expectations but not as a significant source of original political outcomes.

We propose an alternative set of questions to use in assessing whether campaigns matter. First, can the predictive models determine who will become president? Second, do they provide voters with useful information about the past, present, and future? Third, does the performance of the media during campaigns have measurable effects? Our answer to these questions is "yes." Campaigns in general and campaign communication in particular do matter. The question is how closely this information is followed by television and print media audiences. Without data to describe the scope of political messages, any determination of the effectiveness of campaigns is conjecture.

Predicting Electoral Outcomes

The majority of voters decides how to vote fairly early in the campaign, by the time the party conventions are over (usually in August). National Election Study reports from 1952 to 1996 indicate, however, that a substantial number reserve judgment until later in the race. In addition, there is variation in the percentage of early deciders from year to year, ranging from a low of 54 percent in 1992 to a high of 79 percent in 1956. The candidates spend their greatest energy trying to persuade these initially undecided voters. It is axiomatic among campaign professionals that presidential races involve a 40-40-20 equation: Forty percent of the people will always vote for your party, 40 percent will never vote for your party, and the remaining 20 percent are up for grabs. As is often the case, the practitioner's rule of thumb based on experience turns out to be remarkably close to the academic's conclusion based on scholarly analysis—recall that Finkel was able to predict 81 percent of individual votes.

At the core of nearly all predictive models is the power of economic conditions to predict voting outcomes. Economic conditions will inevitably be central to vote choice, since individuals perceive that the president has power over the economy and therefore some measure of accountability for the individual's economic fortunes, and the economy is an issue that is both national and personal, affecting everyone. As a result, the economy will always be high on the list of vote considerations. Occasionally, however, other issues intrude to the point of greater importance—as did competition with the Soviets in 1960, or the Vietnam War in the 1968 election.

But is the economy itself shaping votes, or does the campaign rhetoric about the economy perform this function? In most elections, at least one of the candidates will spend a great deal of time and energy attempting to increase the salience of economic considerations in the minds of voters. The famous sign on the wall of Bill Clinton's 1992 campaign headquarters ("It's the economy, stupid") reminding the staff to focus on economic issues was but one example of a principle that has guided many candidates. The question Ronald Reagan asked in 1980, "Are you better off now than you were four years ago?" is now a staple of presidential campaigning. The Campaign Discourse Mapping Project has identified the economy as by far the most common topic of candidate speeches in every presidential election, from 1952 to 1996. There is also empirical evidence that campaigning focuses voters' attention on the economy, leading them to consider it more seriously when casting their vote.[8]

The bulk of knowledge voters have about the economy comes from the media. By the time November arrives, voters have been receiving communication from the incumbent, the challenger, and competitors in the primaries as well as from the news media about the present state and future prospects of the economy. As a consequence, they have been primed to consider it when voting.[9] Research has also shown that individuals' personal economic situations are of less consequence in determining their vote than their assessment of the country's economic situation.[10] When voters judge how well the president has "handled" the economy, they use what they know of general economic circumstances, looking beyond their own fortunes.

Another critical problem in most predictive models is that they include measurements, either of opinions of the economy or of the president or both, taken late in the year. Although the end of the party conventions (which usually take place in July and August) may mark the formal start of the general election, the campaign actually begins far earlier. Bill Clinton began airing campaign ads in mid-1995, over a year before the election. Primary campaigning always begins well in advance of the Iowa and New Hampshire contests, which take place in January and February of the election year. In most election years, the likely party nominees are determined by April (even earlier in some cases), and those nominees certainly don't wait until their conventions to begin campaigning. To say that measurements of presidential approval or economic perceptions taken in July are "precampaign" and unaffected by campaign communication is simply false.

Even if we assume that July is an appropriate time to measure independent variables among voters, the observed correlation between economic conditions and electoral outcomes is not incompatible with a model that takes into account some campaign effects. After all, it would be odd to assert that a well-run campaign could make voters completely forget their experiences in the labor market, the mortgage market, and the supermarket in the previous four years. By using presidential approval ratings (which correlate highly with vote choice) as an independent variable, predictive models stack the deck in their favor by ensuring that only sudden reversals in preference will be unexplained.

Even if campaigns are able to change a relatively small number of votes, these votes could, in a close election, determine the outcome of the race. Here it is important to note that even the most accurate aggregate models have in some cases predicted the wrong outcome. In fact, one common feature of the most often cited and most accurate aggregate models is that they all incorrectly predicted a victory for Richard Nixon in the 1960 election.[11] The point here is not simply that the margin of victory for Kennedy was smaller than the amount of variance left unexplained by the models, and that the models predicted only a slim advantage for Nixon in any case. If these were the only relevant factors, then we could expect at least some of the models to have predicted a Kennedy victory. Rather, in an election decided by less than one vote per precinct, there were apparently effects of the campaign that overcame the economic factors favoring Nixon.

The other race that predictive models most often get wrong is 1992. As political scientist Mark Hetherington shows, voters' opinions of the economy during that year were strongly predicted by their media use; those exposed to more news were more likely to think that the economy was doing poorly. Those perceptions, in turn, influenced vote choice, which worked against George Bush.[12] Unfortunately for Bush, the media portrayed the economy negatively, even as the country was moving out of recession. This evidence points to the conclusion that it is not the economy itself but rather perceptions of the economy, which are shaped by the media, that determine voting patterns.

Scholars who use deterministic models in which voter decisions are preordained assume that the election is a competition between structural conditions on the one hand and the campaign on the other. This portrayal is accurate only if we understand the campaign to be an inherent deception, supplying voters with information that contradicts the actual facts of the country's situation. As political scientist Samuel Popkin argues, campaigns provide voters, particularly those who pay little attention to politics in noncampaign periods, with needed information, much of which is factually accurate.[13] Gelman and King also conclude that the role of the campaign "is to enlighten the voters—to give them sufficient information in a timely fashion so they can make up their minds relatively easily."[14] A campaign will not be able to convince voters that red is blue and night day, but it can persuade them to look out the window. As V. O. Key noted, "Voters are not fools."[15] One need not believe them foolish in order to hold that campaigns matter.

Campaigns and Information

Although there is much to criticize in both campaign news and candidate advertisements, the fact remains that in a presidential campaign, a wealth of information is available. For most voters, particularly those whose attention to politics at other times is minimal, the increased focus on the election in the press and in conversations among citizens will inevitably result in some information gain. Although these Americans may need only a few critical pieces of information in order to make a rational vote choice, the campaign will afford them the opportunity to learn more, to check what they already know against other sources, and perhaps most important, to make connections between politics and their own lives.[16] Although many studies have shown Americans' level of general political knowledge to be surprisingly low,[17] our survey during the 1996 election indicates that by the end of a campaign, voters were able to accurately place the candidates on a wide variety of issue positions.

We must be wary of assuming that in order to "matter," a campaign must deceive, driving voters away from the candidate whom they would otherwise support. The "reactivation" process demonstrated by Lazarsfeld, Berelson, and Gaudet as well as by Finkel posits that voters whose original candidate preference is at odds with their predispositions switch to the candidate more in line with those predispositions. If communication drives such changes, then campaigns do matter. For these voters, the campaign has offered important information that may reveal distinctions and show where true self-interest resides.

During the campaign, each side will tell a story about the state of the country and argue that conditions warrant that side's election. To a great extent, the more plausible story will be the one that better accords with the information people hold, whether obtained from personal experience or from the mass media. If we define a campaign from the start as obfuscation, then effects are less evident. However, if we understand the campaign to be a forum in which voters navigate the candidates' selective use of facts and evidence to form accurate, useful conclusions, campaign effects are more apparent.

Another critical function of campaigns is prompting candidates to go on the record on a wide variety of issues. Those seeking high office are expected not only to state their positions in debates, ads, and speeches but also to offer plans for future action. In doing so, they provide a wealth of information of use to citizens, journalists, and others to forecast and then evaluate each presidency. As Chapter 2 notes, presidential candidates do in fact attempt to keep the majority of the promises they make during the campaign. It follows that the campaign will not only inform voters about the substance of a potential presidency but will also provide criteria by which to judge each president. For example, when George Bush pledged not to raise taxes in his 1988 race, he provided voters with a clear criterion by which to judge his performance. When he broke the promise, his opponents in the 1992 primaries, specifically Pat Buchanan, held him accountable.

This is not to say that had Bush kept the promise he would have won in 1992. The same sort of problem plagued incumbent Democrat Jimmy Carter in 1980 when Republican challenger Ronald Reagan used against Carter the same "misery index" Carter had constructed four years earlier to attack the record of Gerald Ford. In each case the earlier statements were remembered and used by voters four years later. By forecasting the presidency to come, each campaign arms voters with information and a context through which to view later events and decisions. The fact that voters penalize candidates for not keeping promises also induces presidents to work to deliver on them.

In addition to previewing the four years to come, campaigns offer the nation a chance to assess the performance of the incumbent and his party. Despite the presence of distracting issues, important questions are asked during the course of a campaign, not only by journalists but also by citizens in conversation with each other. By the campaign's conclusion, many voters have probably clarified or confirmed their impression of the conduct of those who have held power in the preceding years.

Like many effects of campaigns, this one is more likely to occur among those who pay closer attention. Even voters who are "tuning out," however, may be drawn to campaign events that provide opportunities for learning. Candidate debates are particularly rich sources of information that tend to draw the attention of large numbers of voters. For example, 97 million people watched a single debate in 1992. Included in this group were not just political junkies but also a large number of otherwise inattentive viewers. Another critical effect of debates is that debate watchers tend to emerge with improved opinions of *both* candidates.[18] As a consequence, those who see their favored candidate lose the election are encouraged to retain their faith in the system.

Campaigns and the Media

A persistent, and for many researchers disappointing, finding is that direct, powerful effects of media are elusive, if they exist at all. Study after study has found media exposure to at best have minimal effects on attitudes, cognitions, and behaviors.[19] This is no less true in politics than in other arenas. Notwithstanding that the communication literature is rich with research on the interplay of media and politics, many political scientists have until the past decade or so dismissed or ignored the media as a source of political influence. For example, one recent work summarizing decades of research on voting behavior contains no discussion of the media in more than 600 pages of analysis.[20]

However, a number of studies suggest that gross exposure variables are not sufficiently tailored to locate the powerful effects of media that may in fact exist. Media effects on presidential vote choice are not nonexistent; they are merely hidden. John Zaller makes the obvious but largely ignored observation that presidential campaigns are characterized by roughly equivalent amounts of opposing communication.[21] Thus, the effect of each side may cancel the other out. Or, as Bartels puts it, "In a world where most campaigns make reasonably effective use of reasonably similar resources and technologies most of the time, much of their effort will necessarily be without visible impact, simply because every campaigner's efforts are balanced against more or less equally effective efforts to produce the opposite effect."[22] Although the advent of issue advocacy has made it possible for one side to air substantially more messages than the others in an election campaign or policy debate (see Chapter 16), both of the most-watched forms of communication in a campaign, debates and news, have balance as a norm.

Campaigns in the United States are characterized by roughly equal amounts of candidate communication, and by news that prides itself on adherence to the norm of balance. Despite the claims of many that the news media as a whole are biased (see Chapter 24), the norms of objectivity and balance dictate that political stories present both sides of any policy debate or electoral contest. Some observers are quick to note, of course, that there are usually more than two sides to an issue. But for our purposes here, that is beside the point. The norm of balance helps blunt the effect of either of the balanced views.

With an understanding of this dynamic, Zaller has been able to provide strong evidence of media effects. Using data from House races and the Mondale-Hart primaries in 1984, he argues persuasively that the critical independent variable is not the total amount of media exposure but the "reception gap" between competing messages. Since this gap appears at different levels of exposure in different cases, linear models are not equipped to capture its effects, which can be substantial. Zaller's model is one of the few that ask what the content of media messages is, and whether that content encourages change or stability in vote choices. His results isolate dramatic effects of news coverage on support for candidates in certain situations, particularly during primary campaigns.

Primary campaigns demonstrate the power of the news media in two distinct ways. First, as Zaller shows, when a candidate's visibility in the media increases, support for the candidate rises. For heavy consumers of media, this effect is more pronounced. Second, decisions made by reporters have an impact on who ultimately becomes president. The time of reporters' greatest influence is the preprimary period, the months leading up to the critical Iowa caucus and New Hampshire primary. During this time, a relatively small group of political reporters will come to a consensus on which of the candidates are worthy of attention; the others, whatever their qualifications, will be given less press attention. Although its arrival in August 1999 was decried by pundits, the Iowa straw vote produced a kind of braking effect on the media's rush to anoint Texas Governor George W. Bush with the Republican nomination. The straw poll also threw chaff at the assumption that former Christian Coalition organizer Gary Bauer was not a viable candidate and bolstered the fortunes of millionaire publisher Steve Forbes, who came in second, and Elizabeth Dole, who finished third. As every candidate knows, without press coverage in the early stages, a campaign is at risk. The Iowa straw poll tilted the spotlight a bit more in the direction of three other candidates and, at the same time, prompted Lamar Alexander to announce his withdrawal from the race.

Ironically, the two principal criteria used by the press to determine who the contenders are—fundraising success and performance in early polls—are themselves a function of prior exposure in the press. As soon as the New Hampshire primary takes place, the press tends to define the race as a contest between two major contenders, in a process known as "winnowing."[23]

Watching their funding dry up as backers shift to those more likely to take the nomination, some candidates drop out, and others begin to downsize their operations. Those who have personal wealth, such as Steve Forbes (in 1996), hang on, as do those whose base is sufficiently strong to sustain a resource-poor campaign, which was the case with Jesse Jackson in 1984. Others whose ascetic style of campaigning means that they can persevere as long as debates give them a forum for reaching an audience (for example, Jerry Brown in 1992) will also stay on the campaign trail. But those examples have been the exceptions, and no one who fell into any of these three categories (self-financed, solid small base that one party cannot afford to alienate, or able to run a Zen-like campaign) has yet to win the nomination of a major party.

Pushed by the need to allocate scarce resources (money, space, and reporters' time) and to write clear, dramatic stories about a pair of antagonists, reporters and editors essentially help determine who will be allowed to compete for each party's nomination. As columnist David Broder put it:

> Neither the television networks, nor newspapers nor magazines, have the resources of people, space and time to describe and analyze the dynamics of two simultaneous half-national elections among Republicans and Democrats. That task is simply beyond us. Since we cannot reduce the number of states voting on Super Tuesday, we have to reduce the number of candidates treated as serious contenders. Those news judgments will be arbitrary—but not subject to appeal.[24]

To paraphrase Bernard Cohen, the media may not be successful in telling us for whom to vote, but they are stunningly successful in telling us whom we may choose between.[25] This facet of the party nominating process is a clear example of media influence.

Various other media effects operate in the campaign context just as in other times. An extensive body of scholarship shows that although the news media do not tell people what to think, they can tell their audience what topics to think about.[26] This agenda-setting function may be understood as a campaign effect that can influence elections through priming of issues. Other kinds of agenda-setting occur during campaigns as well; for instance, Roberts and McCombs found that candidate advertising can set an agenda for news coverage. That process too could be described as a campaign effect.[27]

"Priming" is a notion drawn from psychology that posits that certain behaviors or messages can increase the importance a person attaches to some factor in making a decision. Campaigns focus on their assets and downplay their liabilities in ways that suggest that instead of changing opinions, campaigns are changing "the very basis of choice." For example, in the 1988 election, the Bush campaign successfully magnified the importance the public attached to a little-known prison furlough program in Massachusetts that had given a "weekend pass" to Willie Horton. As Richard Johnston notes, priming in campaigns is not a new concept. It was articulated in 1954 by Berelson and his colleagues, who found that as a result of the campaign, some voters "may have kept the *same evaluation* of the candidates but shifted to *different standards* (e.g., from judging 'the man' to judging 'the issues')."[28] Shanto Iyengar and Donald Kinder offer experimental evidence that even noncampaign news can prime voters to consider certain issues when evaluating the president.[29]

Voters are also influenced by the way news frames events. Every news story can be understood to have a particular frame, which can be defined as an organizing theme that determines what information is included and excluded.[30] News frames can affect people's opinions on policy issues.[31] As Patterson and Jamieson have argued, campaign news is primarily presented through a "strategy," or "horse-race," frame.[32] This type of coverage casts campaign discourse and events as strategic moves designed to win votes, and discusses issues primarily as vehicles manipulated by the candidates in search of votes.

In a study of the 1994 election in the Netherlands, Kleinnijehuis and Ridder found that for politically unsophisticated voters, "Horse race news amplifies the prevailing trends in opinion polls."[33] Patterson and McClure found that when asked to discuss the campaign, respondents volunteered mostly horse-race information.[34] Using content analysis and a series of field experiments, Cappella and Jamieson showed not only that the strategy frame had migrated from campaigns to coverage of policy debates, but also that this frame activated voter cynicism and depressed learning.[35] The activation of cynicism is seen from this perspective as a consequential media effect.

Why Are More Scholars Finding Media Effects in Campaigns Now Than in the Past?

One explanation of the recent evidence of campaign effects is that the media have more opportunity to influence voters in an era of reduced party impact and presence. The decline of political parties in the United

FIGURE 1.1   Party identification, 1952–1996.

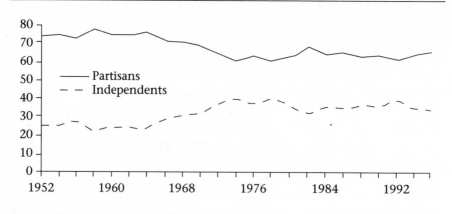

SOURCE: National Election Studies

States has been well documented and much lamented by political scientists since the 1970s.[36] In 1975, Kirkpatrick, Lyons, and Fitzgerald described a trend beginning in 1952 in which voters saw the centrality of individual candidates as increasingly important in making a vote choice, whereas the centrality of parties waned as a predictor.[37] During the mid-1970s, scholars forecast that the downward trend would continue. As Nie, Verba, and Petrocik wrote, "Perhaps the most dramatic change in the American public over the past two decades has been the decline of partisanship."[38]

After the 1970s, party identification leveled off and has remained stable for the past twenty years (see Figure 1.1). Although at least one group of researchers has argued that partisanship continues to be more influential than is commonly thought, some continue to blame the decline of the parties for all manner of political ills.[39]

Regardless of how many voters will identify themselves as affiliated with one of the two major parties or what those identifications may predict, there is no question that the parties themselves have been transformed. Whereas parties formerly had a substantial presence in people's lives and communities, they now exist at a distance. Although the narrow election of Democrat John Street in the Philadelphia mayoral election of 1999 demonstrates that in close contests party organization can be decisive, gone are the days when powerful political machines in cities such as Chicago could mobilize precincts whose residents (both living and dead) would cast virtually identical votes. A 1986 survey found only 14 percent agreeing that "I always support the candidates of just one party."[40] Although voters still use candidates' party identification as a shortcut or heuristic, the parties themselves provide less information for making electoral choices. In their absence, the mass media have become the predominant source of candidate information.

As Ithiel de Sola Pool noted in 1971, "With the decline of the political party as an influence on the voter, the voter has become more independent."[41] The advent of the mass medium of television has made it possible for candidates to communicate directly even to low-involvement voters, thus sidestepping the effects of selective exposure and attention and minimizing the power of the two-step flow of information from elite opinion leaders to more passive opinion followers. So, for example, in the first televised campaigns of the electronic age, a Republican general attracted the votes of Democrats who continued to identify themselves with the party of Roosevelt but who "defected" and voted for the Republican at the top of the ticket.

Importantly, the first sign in decades of the revival of party importance came because parties found a way to create influence through advertising. Although blamed for circumventing the caps on spending set up as part of the quid pro quo of public financing of presidential campaigns, and condemned as well for its capacity to shield the identity of the source of advertising, issue-advocacy advertising has been the vehicle through which parties have begun to recover their influence. For example, in the first twenty months of the 1998 election cycle (January 1997 through August 1998), the Democratic and Republican parties accounted for a mere 9.9 percent of all the issue ads produced. However, in the final two months of the cycle (September 1998 through Election Day), the two parties produced 70.8 percent of the issue ads.

We hypothesize that the power of parties is being revived precisely because of their ability to produce media effects for candidates through their use of issue advocacy. This speculation is premised on an assumption that some would challenge: that advertising can change attitudes. In Part II we will offer our evidence for that conclusion.

If media effects have become more apparent in recent years, it may be not only because researchers have improved their techniques but also because the magnitude of those effects is growing. With each passing election, American politics is increasingly defined by its mediated nature. The more powerful the media's role in disseminating campaign information, the more motivated candidates will be to tailor their messages and images to the media's requirements. As an example, consider candidate style. It is often noted that the great statesmen of our nation's early history would not have performed well on television, but one need only compare today's politicians to those of a few years ago to see how much has changed. When viewed today, Eisenhower's delivery in his campaign advertisements seems stilted. Even John F. Kennedy, considered in the memory of many to be a master of the televised medium, appears stiff in his delivery compared with our last few presidents.

Presidential candidates are now expected not only to be fluent and conversational in their delivery but also to reveal intimate details of their lives. The clash between the new and old models was evident when Bob Dole, who will perhaps be the last presidential candidate to have started his career in the pretelevision age, sat uncomfortably as his wife told Larry King of his private struggles with his disability. Voters today expect to be supplied with such personal information about candidates, and the candidates comply, however reluctantly. Details of the personal lives and personalities of the candidates are transmitted vividly by television. Not only have the news media supplanted the parties in providing information, but they also discourage party-line thinking during the campaign. By focusing intensely on the personalities of candidates and not their issue positions or party ties, the media prime voters to focus on the individuals seeking office, not on the parties.[42]

The second explanation for increased sightings of media effects is that the techniques used by early researchers were incapable of finding them. The persuasive effects of media have been lurking unnoticed not simply because balanced messages of comparable salience cancel each other out but also because, as Carl Hovland noted forty years ago, cross-sectional surveys are unlikely to produce evidence of short-term persuasion and opinion change.[43] The majority of audience research on campaign effects has been conducted using cross-sectional surveys, which capture public opinion at one point in time. If an event—such as a debate—produces an effect and there is no survey in the field at the time, the ability to detect the effect will be limited to the somewhat unreliable self-reports of those who are asked long after the event to assess the effect the debate had on them. One further weakness in this research is that survey work is often conducted without addressing the content of informative messages, mediated or otherwise. By contrast, more recent work manipulating or analyzing media content has provided evidence of significant media effects.[44]

A final explanation is that media effects in the early election studies were overlooked by the researchers. For example, Becker, McCombs, and McLeod showed that the Columbia researchers overlooked the fact that among voters who were exposed to media messages in opposition to their predispositions, substantial degrees of persuasion occurred. In addition, the early studies showed an agenda-setting effect, although they did not interpret it as such. In fact, media exposure increased the salience of certain issues in the vote choices of the 1948 subjects.[45]

Conclusion

In sum, campaigns have important effects on the electorate both in terms of the conduct of the candidates who become officeholders and the citizens who watch them. In order to assess how campaigns matter on the individual level, we must first capture the differences in how the campaign is received and understood by different individuals. As campaigns grow more sophisticated, voters will increasingly be the focus of particularized messages. As an example, in the 1992 and 1996 presidential elections, candidates eschewed national advertising in favor of local time-buys targeted to specific areas and specific types of voters. Not only did different localities receive different messages, some received none at all. If we seek to understand the effects of the campaign, knowledge of the information environment in which voters find themselves is essential. Because they have until recently assumed a homogeneous communication environment over the entire country, surveys such as the National Election Studies may be unable to capture important effects. On the societal level, we must expand our definition of campaign effects beyond changing votes. Campaigns are a means of choosing leaders, but they are also a way for the governors and the governed to connect with each other. They tell us what we should expect from our leaders, how we should evaluate them, which actions are good and which bad, and what constitutes success or failure. In this sense, among others, campaigns matter.

The increasingly complex informational environment, combined with a wider array of techniques at the disposal of contemporary researchers, calls for scholarship that sheds light on the nuances of both media messages and voter reactions. This book will address this challenge through the use of content analysis and survey data, combining the two where possible to paint a fuller picture of electoral campaigns and their effects on individual voters and our democracy as a whole.

Paul Waldman and Kathleen Hall Jamieson

Chapter Two

The Morning After:
Do Politicians Keep
Their Promises?

V OTERS HAVE ALWAYS INDULGED a certain amount of hy-
perbole and rhetorical excess from their politicians," wrote a reporter for *Newsweek* in 1991. "Campaign promises lifted hearts
and hopes, even if the promises later went unfulfilled. . . . But will
[politicians] really tell the truth? Don't count on it. Politicians are well
aware of the dirty little secret behind all the popular demands for
straight talk: Americans say they want truth, but they don't like what
they hear when they get it."[1] Disagreeing on the cause, but concurring
on the symptom, *U.S. News and World Report* said of the 1992 election:
"Despite the signs that America wants honest answers, George Bush and
Bill Clinton are sinking into the old rut of attack politics, avoiding tough
issues . . . and calling each other scoundrels, wastrels and worse."[2]

Was the following off-year election any better? Of the 1994 campaign,
James M. Perry of the *Wall Street Journal* noted, "Lost in the rush to win,
sometimes at any cost, is the quaint notion of a thoughtful candidate
willing to take time to explain, slowly and wisely, his or her positions on
major policy issues."[3]

What of 1996? A commentary by Paul Magnusson in *Business Week*
said of the "vacuous" 1996 election: "The opportunity to engage the
public in a serious debate about real-world solutions is being squandered
while the two candidates blather about the best method to prevent flag-
burning or pander shamelessly with pledges of tax cuts."[4] Earlier in the
election, Michael Lerner predicted in *Tikkun* that Clinton was "far more
likely to run his campaign based on manipulation of images and vacuous sound bites."[5] And when all was said and done, a piece in *Time* had
this to say of the 1996 election: "Out go the lights on the '96 campaign,

and it's time to ask what we've learned. The voters couldn't have learned a lot, unless they were unaware that education is good and drugs are bad. . . . By all means smile. The candidate sporting a silly grin beats the one wearing a scowl."[6]

Bland, boring, unhelpful, lacking substance, the campaign of 1996 was accused of failing to provide one of the basic requirements of electoral democracy: a reasonable and forthright dialogue between candidates for the presidency and voters—in other words, an opportunity for voters to influence the course of government. Candidates, the argument goes, dodge important issues and embrace uncontroversial goals, while substituting platitudes for proposals and soundbites for substance. As a result, campaigns lack the steady stream of specific information most voters need to understand the issues, assess the candidates' pasts and plans, and reach a reasoned projection of the impact of the election of one candidate over the others on the country as a whole as well as closer to home.

The questions we address in this chapter are central to the notion of electoral democracy. First, do elections offer voters clear policy choices? And if so, are those choices related to governance? Are the promises candidates make during the campaign honored by the eventual victors? Finally, did candidate communication in the 1996 campaign forecast enough of the policymaking of 1997 to justify a voter's attention to the campaign? After exploring the distinct answers offered by academics, the press, and the public, we will argue that those who condemn the campaigns of 1992 and 1996 for exceptional vacuity are off the mark.

We will begin by reviewing some positions in the controversy over what some call "prospective policy choice"—a belief that the campaign is an opportunity for voters to compare and contrast specific policy stands of candidates and to choose the candidate who best represents their views.

The notion that a politician's promises are untrustworthy is commonplace. "There are two major kinds of promises in politics," wrote comedian and social activist Dick Gregory in 1972, promises made to "persons or groups able to deliver the vote," and called patronage, and "promises made by candidates to the voters," which are "most frequently called 'lies.'"[7] Even Abraham Lincoln subscribed to the notion that "taken as a mass" politicians are "at least one big step removed from honest men." To that he added, "I say this with the greater freedom, because being a politician myself none can regard it as personal."[8]

A contemporary critic of prospective policy choice, political theorist Benjamin Page, writes: "Specific policy stands [by candidates] are uncommon. . . . The infrequency with which candidates discuss policy is a major factor preventing most Americans from learning what the stands are. This problem, in turn, is compounded by the fact that the most specific stands are often taken in inconspicuous places and go virtually unreported by the media."[9] In a later chapter we will agree with Page's second point—that the media underreport the policy substance of campaigns. But we take issue with his conclusion that candidates infrequently take specific policy stands.

In Page's view, this defect of American democracy is long-standing. Though focusing on the elections of 1960 and 1968, he also points to the election of 1932 to cite Roosevelt's failure to provide specifics on major policy proposals. The example is not an isolated one: "Dewey in 1948 was either silent or very general about most social welfare programs. . . . Adlai Stevenson . . . was not very specific in proposing policy. . . . Jimmy Carter in 1976 followed the same pattern. . . . Although noted for unusual specificity early in their campaigns, both Goldwater in 1964 and McGovern in 1972 gradually retreated to more ambiguous stands."

More recently, political scientist Richard Joslyn looked at several presidential elections to determine what type of appeals candidates made. He distinguished the prospective policy-choice appeal from three other appeals: retrospective policy-satisfaction, benevolent leader, and ritualistic. After examining over 800 televised spot ads and the two 1988 televised presidential debates, consistent with Page's argument, Joslyn found little evidence for the prospective policy-choice approach. The advertising consisted largely of retrospective (which reward or punish a candidate for past performance) and benevolent-leader appeals (which assure voters that a candidate means well, identifies with them, and is trustworthy), while the debates contained mainly ritualistic ones.[10]

Although prospective policy stands were not totally absent, they appeared too infrequently to constitute a significant aspect of the candidate's rhetoric. In Joslyn's words, "candidate appeals make unlikely the kind of intended, prospective policy choices that are usually valued by electoral scholars. Candidates make it difficult for voters to know what their future intentions are beyond the support for consensually held values and policy goals." Joslyn does grant the possibility that "electoral choices have prospective but *unintended* policy consequences. That is, we may select a public official for non-policy reasons and, in the process, also get an officeholder who holds certain (to us previously unknown) policy preferences." What seems clear to Joslyn is that there simply isn't enough substantive discussion for voters to make a thoughtful decision based on the issues. Whatever the candidate ads are specifying, they are not specifying the stuff of governance.

The absence of substantive policy proposals in presidential campaigning is often interpreted as a calculated effort to alienate as few voters as possible. As Marjorie Randon Hershey pointed out in an examination of the 1988 contest between George Bush and Michael Dukakis, "To address a huge audience, a speaker needs a simple and compelling message. It is much simpler and more compelling to focus on the murderous Willie Horton than to discuss the complexities of balancing safety against the need to rehabilitate criminals."[11] In this view, issue stands are downplayed in favor of the simplified symbols to which voters are perceived to be susceptible.

The view that candidates fail to address voters' central concerns extends beyond some academic circles. Though not uniformly, the press commonly suggests that candidates and campaigns do not speak to the issues. For example, by most accounts the 1996 campaign fell short of providing an informative campaign dialogue. The candidates pandered, many said. The voters were inclined to concur. In a postelection survey for the Annenberg Public Policy Center conducted by Chilton Research, 76 percent of respondents agreed that "candidates tell public what it wants to hear, not what is best for country." Additionally, 42 percent thought Clinton and Dole either ducked or were not talking about issues.[12]

There are other views. Chief among them is the notion that elections provide the information voters need to distinguish one candidate's positions from another's and choose those best for the voter and the country. The support for this position is, in fact, quite compelling. In his argument that election outcomes are affected by the candidates' stands on issues, political scientist John Petrocik stresses what he calls "issue-ownership," a theory describing successful candidate framing of the vote choice as a decision to be made in terms of a problem facing the nation that the candidate and his party are better able to resolve. We discussed such agenda setting and priming attempts in the previous chapter.

In this analysis, the campaign is seen as a marketing effort to define the meaning of the election in terms of the issues most closely identified with the party, on the assumption that, for instance, a voter concerned most with Democratic issues should vote for a Democratic candidate. This view stresses the capacity of campaigns to swing votes on the basis of issue appeals. From this perspective, one could argue that in 1980 it was the Republican Ronald Reagan who successfully promoted Republican-owned issues. Although Reagan trailed Carter in the polls early in the campaign, Petrocik demonstrated that of those who changed their vote intention, 77 percent of the voters concerned with Republican-owned issues who did not originally support Reagan shifted to him, while 56 percent of shifters with a Democratic agenda moved to Carter. Petrocik's findings suggest not only the decisive role campaigns can play in elections but also the importance voters place on candidates' stands on issues.[13]

Along the same lines, Pomper's earlier work shows that party platforms and campaigns are ways by which candidates and parties court voters and convince groups that their concerns and those of the party coincide. Whether the issue is a minimum wage increase, balancing the budget, or equal rights for minority groups, the candidate's focus on issues is an attempt to attract blocs of voters. "The writers of the campaign manifesto will act to win this support, even anticipating group demands before they arise," notes Pomper. "Moreover, an organized interest group is likely to exist, making explicit demands on the party's platform drafters, who in turn are quite receptive to any group with a plausible claim on voter loyalties."[14]

The simple presumption that parties are making is this: Voters have rational identifiable interests and will respond favorably to a party that pledges to pursue them. Lower taxes, civil rights, pro-life legislation, welfare reform—any number of issues and stands that a party takes are calculated to appeal to the interests of defined voter blocs. Candidates may pursue other strategies but not to the substantial exclusion of issue-based appeals.

Past performance and preferred plans do broadly distinguish Democrats from Republicans. As Polsby and Wildavsky argued in the 1996 edition of *Presidential Elections*, "American parties do indeed differ—more so now than in the recent past—and . . . much of the time, they respond to changes in voter sentiment."[15]

Even when the nominees are moderates, as was the case in 1996, clear differences persist. Consistent with the expectations created by their party identification in 1996, Clinton favored and Dole opposed FDA regulation of cigarettes as a drug delivery system; Clinton favored and Dole opposed family medical leave and its extension. Clinton was pro-choice on abortion rights; Dole was pro-life. Although both favored reductions in the rate of increase in Medicare spending, Dole favored deeper cuts. Dole's proposed 15 percent tax cut was across the board and as a result carried disproportionate benefits for the well-to-do; Clinton's tax cuts were targeted to benefit those of more modest means.

Parties do resemble each other more nearly at some times than at others, but these similarities are part of a process of cyclical adjustment, the incorporation by one party of the other's successful innovations. Periods of similarity give rise to dissimilarity as segments of the populace press the parties to address unmet concerns. The minority party, eager for the advantage, steps in. If it prevails and sustains the advantage, the other party incorporates the resonant planks into its platform, causing the parties to more closely resemble one another again.

As important as the persistence of differences between parties and their nominees is the fact that the victors actually work to enact most of their promises. An extensive study by political scientist Jeff Fishel looked at the promises made by candidates Kennedy, Johnson, Nixon, Carter, and Reagan and the action each took to fulfill them. What Fishel discovered is telling. He identified various types of action, defined as executive orders and proposed legislation, a president could take on campaign promises: fully comparable action ("[t]he president's proposal met the requirements of the pledge in a complete and comprehensive manner"); partially comparable action ("[t]he president's proposal did not meet the full requirements of the pledge, but still contained large and similar components or represented action that was similar in purpose"); token action (the "proposal represented a gesture, and little more, to the pledge"); contradictory action (the "proposal represented the opposite of what was suggested by the pledge"); no action, mixed action (the "proposal simultaneously met some requirements of the pledge, but went in opposite directions on other parts"); and indeterminate.[16]

Working with this framework, Fishel concluded that 67 percent of Kennedy's promises were met by either fully or partially comparable action, as were 63 percent of Johnson's, 60 percent of Nixon's, 65 percent of Carter's, and 53 percent of Reagan's. Such figures raise questions about views such as that of Columbia University professor of government David Truman that "[t]he platform is generally regarded as a document that says little, binds no one, and is forgotten by politicians as quickly as possible after it is adopted. . . . Considered as a pledge of future action, the party platform is almost meaningless and is properly so regarded by the voters."[17] Pomper's analysis of party platform pledges and subsequent action from 1944 through 1976 confirms that "pledges are indeed redeemed."[18]

In Clinton's case, this correlation translated into multiple actions: a cut in the number of federal workers (with an increase in work to contractors); an increase in the minimum wage; funding, albeit short-term, for 100,000 new police officers; funding for empowerment zones; the assault weapons ban; a national service program, Americorps; and an executive order safeguarding abortion rights. Indeed, in some ways, Clinton proved to be an overachiever. With help from the Federal Reserve, Silicon Valley, Bill Gates, and a gutsy tax increase, Clinton did not merely cut the deficit in half as he had promised, but he even produced balanced budgets. Where Clinton had promised an economy "second to none," he delivered: jobs, low inflation, and low unemployment.

Often lost in the discussion of promises of major party nominees is the fact that in most campaigns there are as many areas of agreement between candidates, if not more, as of disagreement. When the nominees of both major parties take a common stand on an issue, the likelihood that it will be translated into action increases. Both Clinton and Bush supported the North American Free Trade Agreement (NAFTA) in 1992; it became U.S. policy despite opposition from key Democrats. The budget passed in 1997 included the drop in the capital-gains tax rate that both Dole and Clinton had favored in 1996 but also included tax breaks for education on which they had concurred. Also, the capital-gains exemption on sale of a home by a married couple was raised, as both candidates had pledged to do. Both men promised to work to balance the budget, and this consensus was reflected in the budget discussions. Each agreed that a commission should be appointed to make recommendations on preserving Medicare; that commission has been appointed.

In addition, action that might be categorized as a failed attempt early in a presidency may be revisited. For example, the most visible failure of Clinton's first term was his inability to secure passage of health care reform that would have provided universal insurance coverage. With the help of the Republican Congress in the closing year of his first term, Clinton did achieve two of the goals of his earlier plan—providing portability of coverage between jobs and barring use of preexisting conditions as a basis for denying insurance to workers. Early in his second term, Clinton revisited the issue with a proposal to make it possible for individuals aged 55–65 who were not yet eligible for Medicare to buy into that system.

Finally, when the federal government is divided, a president should not be blamed when his initiatives are compromised into a less desirable form or are rebuffed entirely by the opposition party. Clinton, for example, did try to keep his promise to rebuild the country with a program of jobs and public works. The Republicans in Congress were philosophically opposed and thwarted the effort. At other times, presidents keep their promises despite themselves. Clinton's 1992 promise to end welfare as we know it was used by the Republicans to call his bluff and secure his signature on a plan of their own.

Campaign discourse can also be important because it helps alter the way an issue is framed. In 1996, Clinton joined the state attorneys general in taking on the tobacco companies. Specifically, he argued that the tobacco companies had been advertising to kids with the result that one in three who started smoking in youth would die of lung cancer or a tobacco-related cause. Clinton favored a widespread ban on advertising that might reach or influence those under the legal age to purchase cigarettes. Under pressure, Camel cigarettes retired its popular icon Joe Camel. But to focus only on whether Clinton secured the advertising ban would be to miss an important byproduct of his rhetoric. In an environment in which documents were being released showing that the tobacco industry was aware that nicotine was addictive and deadly, Clinton's rhetoric helped focus on the evils of tobacco. Whereas in the 1993–1994 legislative session, proponents of health care reform in Congress failed to secure adoption of an increased tax on cigarettes as a means of paying for insurance coverage, in 1997 an increase on the tax on each pack of cigarettes was passed by the Republican Congress and signed by Clinton to provide health insurance to children without it.

None of this means that the presidency is not paved with at least some neglected promises. In regard to Haiti and China, what Clinton forecast and what he delivered were two different plans of action. The earnings limit on Social Security recipients remained, despite his promise to end it; and instead of opposing a gas tax, Clinton proposed one. But overall, Clinton fits the historical pattern. In most cases, he at least tried to make good on his promises.

If the promises of the victors forecast their actions in office, and if the positions shared by the major-party nominees are even more likely to be enacted, there is good reason for voters and the media to pay attention to what the candidates say in their speeches, ads, and debates. Attention to candidate discourse is important for a second reason. Those areas of social need that are left unaddressed by the eventual victor are unlikely to be addressed once that person is elected. For example, the general election of 1996 focused in part on the Democratic claim that the Republicans wanted to cut Medicare by $270 billion and on the response by Republicans that they opposed cuts but favored a reduction in the rate of growth. Lost in this squabble was the fact that Clinton had proposed cuts in the rate of growth as well, but more important, while both candidates promised to preserve Medicare, neither was willing to explain how. The absence of specific discussion accurately predicted that the impending insolvency of this important social program would be unaddressed by either Clinton or the Republicans in Congress soon after the 1996 election. Indeed, one could argue that the joint promise to preserve Medicare without a corresponding explanation of the exact mechanisms of implementation—which could include raising the age of entitlement, means testing, increasing taxes, or cutting benefits—made it more difficult for either party to take the initiative in solving the problem.

The failure to grapple with Medicare in the 1996 election is but one instance in which an issue of consequence was inadequately discussed. Other examples can be cited in which campaigns ignored major issues facing the country. In 1988, for example, neither Bush nor Dukakis saw an advantage in discussing the savings and loan crisis, Bush because it occurred under a Republican administration and could be attributed to Republican deregulation, Dukakis because influential Democrats in Congress

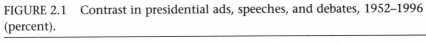

FIGURE 2.1 Contrast in presidential ads, speeches, and debates, 1952–1996 (percent).

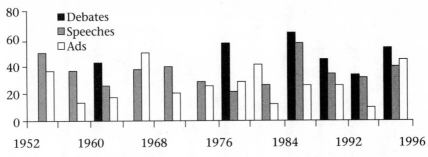

were implicated. These sorts of instances provide a justification for the claim that candidates do not address the issues. But as we have argued, the failure to address some issues does not justify the conclusion that all or even most issues are sidestepped. Instead the opposite is the case.

A related notion holds that the candidates fail to engage each other on the central issues. The complaint is a long-lived one. Writing in *The American Commonwealth* in 1890, James Bryce observed that "the aim of each party is to force on its antagonist certain issues which the antagonist rarely accepts, so that although there is a vast deal of discussion and declamation on political topics, there are few on which either party directly traverses the doctrines of the other. Each pummels, not his true enemy, but a stuffed figure set up to represent that enemy."[19] Berelson and his colleagues observed the same lack of engagement in the 1948 election: "The opposing candidates tended to 'talk past each other' almost as if they were participating in two different elections.... Each candidate stressed the matters considered most strategic and effective in his own propaganda."[20]

Contrary to this view, evidence from the Campaign Mapping Project suggests that although there is variability from year to year, most arguments are supported by evidence, and overall there is a high level of argumentative engagement. Most significantly in debates, but also in speeches and even ads, candidates contrast their views with those of their opponents (Figure 2.1). Moreover, the claims inherent in such contrasts are explicitly defended by reference to evidence (Figure 2.2). The basic framework of "He supports X, but I support Y" frequently extends to include an illuminating and significant "because" clause.

Despite evidence that candidates offer at least some consequential promises and, once elected, work to deliver on them, there is a percep-

FIGURE 2.2   Contrastive statements containing evidence, 1952–1996 (percent).

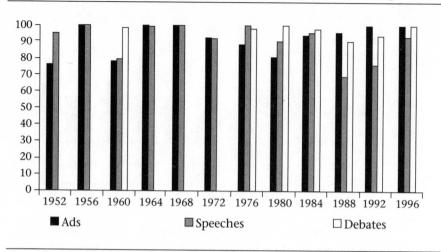

tion among reporters that candidates in general, and Bill Clinton in particular, will say anything to get elected. For example, in an evaluation of tax-cut proposals offered by Bob Dole and Bill Clinton, *Investor's Business Daily* breezily remarked: "Clinton's tax-cut promises have many flaws. First off they are Clinton promises—easily made and even more easily broken."[21] A few months later, the publication reiterated the complaint: "To win the White House in 1992, candidate Bill Clinton promised anything and everything. But President Clinton broke his word, and then complained that the public took his campaign talk too literally."[22] Why, the editors asked, should voters in 1996 trust a man who violated their trust in 1992? To bolster the argument, *Investor's Business Daily* supplied a list of Clinton's top ten broken promises, which ranged from the number-one middle-class tax cut to the number-ten campaign finance reform. Though the list is a short one, the publication reminds its readers, it goes on and on. The conclusion? "It's clear that our president views governing not as honoring his vows or believing in something, but as getting past the next election."

In a similar vein, *Time* writer Michael Duffy noted that Clinton's retreat on a middle-class tax cut was evidence for the lingering perception that he was a "'pander bear' who would say anything to get elected."[23] A concurring view by another *Time* writer, Nancy Gibbs, explained: "Voters are now being treated to a lavish round of political pandering. . . . The moment one candidate makes a bid, his rival tops it. The immediate goal on both sides is simply to control the news cycle: there is no reasoned discourse, just strikes and counter strikes. . . . By the time he ran in 1992, Clinton had learned that brazen replies were key to political success."[24] Clinton was enticing voters, it seemed to some observers, to enter a realm of hopeful promises and sunny tomorrows, a realm in which he had either no chance or no intention of converting his words into action.

In a postelection panel discussion, assembled by *Editor and Publisher* in December 1996 and attended by Associated Press Vice President Walter R. Mears and *Dallas Morning News* Washington correspondent Susan Feeney, Mears remarked that the president had "had no substance."[25] Said Feeney, "A lot of Clinton promises were dumped overboard before he ever took office in 1992. The promises Clinton made and kept is a very short list indeed." Stacey Jones decried "a common post-election malady: broken promises." President Clinton, some reports suggested, suffered acutely from this malady: "Were there any campaign promises," asked one reporter on January 14, "which the new president would not break?"[26]

The early characterization of the Clinton presidency as one beset by discarded pledges was captured a few days later in a *New York Times* headline: "An Impatient Public; Letting Go of Hope as Clinton Softens Pledges." The piece began, "Without any prompting in conversations over the last four days, voters here cited the campaign pledges that Mr. Clinton already seemed to be pulling back on, like a tax cut for the middle class and easing the immigration of Haitians. Some people were angry about that. But most seemed resigned, with looks that said, 'What else did you expect?'"[27] If one did expect the president to backpedal on his promises, the following excerpts from other stories in the *New York Times* would have confirmed suspicion: "But there was no way to get around the fact that Mr. Clinton was not prepared to fulfill his campaign promise to abandon the Bush Administration policy of forcibly returning Haitians picked up at sea."[28] "President Clinton is on the verge of doing a grave disservice to American women by betraying his campaign promise to defend abortion rights."[29] "Mr. Clinton was elected on the campaign promise to cut the taxes of the middle class. Of course, he reneged and actually proposed an across-the-board energy tax."[30] "Since he won office 25 months ago, Mr. Clinton has been regularly accused of upending policies and campaign promises to accommodate a new poll or fresh advice, but few much doubted that the switch was his, and that for better or worse, it set the nation's agenda."[31]

Often the implicit reason suggested for Bill Clinton's promise breaking was self-interest and weakness. In this vein, *The Nation* remarked, "After Clinton's backpedaling on ending the military gay ban, his abandoned campaign promise to free imprisoned Haitian refugees and his appointment of a Reagan mouthpiece to remake his image, his cave-in on the Lani Guinier appointment ignited a broader sense of betrayal."[32]

The *National Review* attributed Clinton's promise breaking, at least to some extent, to overreaching. "Mr. Clinton came to power burdened by far more, and more specific, promises than any President in recent memory. He found it necessary to start breaking them even before he took office." Worse, in some instances, Clinton tried "to claim he hadn't made the promises."[33] That Clinton started breaking his promises before he took office was also noted by *Time*, which in an article titled "Bent Promises: Bill Clinton Backs Down on Campaign Promises to Cut Taxes, Reduce the Budget and Reform Welfare" listed his prominent early broken promises. Consistent with late New York Mayor Fiorello La Guardia's quip that the first task of a statesman is to disappoint supporters and break campaign promises, the article said, "Bill Clinton was off to a flying start."[34]

The improbability of many of Clinton's promises was repeatedly noted in the press. "The truth, of course," as Michael Ruby of *U.S. News and World Report* noted, "is that trimming middle-class income taxes is antithetical to deficit reduction even with major spending cuts."[35] Another observer noted that "[l]ately, not even the people who pledge to do the impossible take their vows seriously."[36] *Nation's Cities Weekly* began a piece on the early Clinton presidency: "A heavy dose of reality was served up along with President Clinton's first budget proposal, as campaign promises and high expectations have given way to fiscal practicality."[37] Lawrence Klein, writing in *Challenge*, saw Clinton's behavior in a broader context: "It is useful, however, to look at the campaign statements and to compare them with present realities—both in terms of performance and intentions—and to recognize, of course, that campaign statements must be heavily discounted."[38]

If campaign promises must be heavily discounted, it follows that they are not worth much to begin with. The "improbability" of some of Clinton's promises lends support to the claim that either his campaign in particular or presidential campaigns in general offer little guide to governance. Although Michael Kelly does not explicitly make this claim, his argument does so implicitly: "The bad thing, as Clinton found out after he was elected, was that it is difficult to actually deliver on pledges of the sun and the moon. . . . This is over-promising on a scale that would give God pause."[39]

It may also have given voters pause. At the outset of Clinton's first term, respondents in a CBS News/*New York Times* poll were pessimistic about his intention to follow through on campaign promises. Asked whether they thought Clinton would try to keep all, most, some, or

TABLE 2.1   Voter perception of Clinton's effort to keep campaign promises during his first term.

All	7%
Most	28%
Some	44%
Hardly Any	13%
None	1%
Don't Know/No Answer	7%

SOURCE: CBS News/*New York Times* poll, August 16–18, 1996.

hardly any of his campaign promises, only 7 percent said all; 36 percent allowed that he would try to keep most, with 46 percent indicating some, and 11 percent hardly any.[40] Voters appear to take account of candidate intentions when considering promises in general versus important promises. Whereas this poll suggested that only 43 percent of respondents believed Clinton would try to keep all or most of his promises, an ABC News/*Washington Post* poll taken at about the same time revealed that 64 percent believed Clinton would try to keep most of his important campaign promises.[41] There seems to be a tacit understanding that not all promises are created equal.

When polling questions shift from whether a candidate intends to fulfill his promises to whether promises have actually been kept, the numbers drop precipitously. Asked a year into his first term "Is President Clinton keeping most of his campaign promises or not?" only 37 percent of respondents said yes.[42] The figure is consistent with the results of a series of polls taken near the end of Clinton's first term, which asked, "How many of his 1992 campaign promises has Bill Clinton tried to keep—all of them, most of them, some of them, or hardly any of them?"[43] The results appear in Table 2.1.

Comparing polling information on Clinton with that on some of his recent predecessors reveals that voters had similar expectations of George Bush. An ABC News poll conducted in April 1989 discovered that 65 percent of respondents believed Bush would try to keep most of his important campaign promises during his term as president, the same as the percentage for Clinton.[44] At the start of Reagan's second term, a poll revealed that 58 percent thought he would keep most of his important campaign promises.[45]

And as with Clinton, fewer voters tend to think presidents actually fulfill promises than think they will try. Only 9 percent thought Bush was able to keep all or most of his 1988 campaign promises.[46] It was perhaps reflection on such figures that prompted GOP strategist John Sears to comment, "Trouble is, people just don't believe anything George Bush says anymore."[47] Asked about the Reagan record, 55 percent thought he had kept most of his campaign promises,[48] and 40 percent thought the same was true for Nixon.[49]

Though a pattern might be difficult to discern in these figures, it is clear that a substantial segment of voters perceives that presidential promises go unfulfilled. Such a belief by a large number of voters is troubling in a democracy. The legitimacy of democracy rests in part on the role citizens are presumed to play in shaping governance, a role that has them elect candidates who distinguish themselves from each other by distinct policy proposals. Policy proposals are, in turn, seen as pledges or promises. By dismissing campaign promises, citizens underestimate their own influence on policy.

National Election Studies (NES) data ranging from 1964 to 1992 analyzed by political scientist Stephen Craig reveal a long-term drop in the importance voters attach to their role in elections. When asked "How much do you feel that having elections makes the government pay attention to what the people think?" 64.6 percent of respondents in 1964 replied, "A good deal." The percent of respondents giving that answer declined steadily over the years, then rallied with a 10 percent increase in 1992 to a modest 46.7 percent.[50]

Although large segments of the press and public share the view that there is a political disconnect between candidates and voters, year after year the behavior of presidents supports the opposite view. As we have noted, work by Pomper and Fishel demonstrates that there is fidelity between candidate words and presidential deeds. Political scientists Quirk and Matheson noted this and also the danger of infidelity: "The rhetoric of the campaign, especially that of the winning presidential candidate, creates commitments that carry weight after the election. Such commitments may help establish a popular mandate for the president's program. They may also, however, bind the president to an unworkable strategy for governing. After making an unusually categorical campaign promise to oppose new taxes when he was running for president in 1988, George Bush was politically devastated by having to reverse his position."[51] If for no other reason than the penalty that lack of performance can exact in the polls, presidents are under pressure to follow through on their promises. Since vice presidents regularly seek the presidency, the electorate can express its approval of the administration of a past incumbent by voting, for example, for Bush in 1988 or against Mondale in 1984.

Is a record of perfect fulfillment of campaign promises possible? Can a president fail to fulfill some of his promises without undermining his credibility? Frankly, these matters don't seem to be the perceived problems. As public opinion polls and a sampling of press reports suggest, presidents are seen not as defaulting on a few or even some promises but as failing to fulfill *many* of them. Clinton is seen to be a particularly egregious offender. A 1996 postelection survey for the Annenberg Public Policy Center showed that 42 percent thought Clinton's word was no good.[52]

Clinton's record of promise keeping, however, is comparable to his predecessors' pattern. After examining Clinton's record on his 1992 pledges, Carolyn M. Shaw from the Department of Government at the University of Texas concluded: "Clinton's record is largely comparable to those of his recent predecessors. Sixty-nine percent of his proposals are fully or partially comparable to his campaign promises." The figures for Kennedy were 67 percent, for Johnson 63 percent, for Nixon 60 percent, for Carter 65 percent, and for Reagan 63 percent. Shaw added: "This examination of the content and quality of campaign promises shows that Clinton's pledges were not merely empty rhetoric."[53]

Yet, as we saw, the first year into his presidency, only 37 percent of voters said they thought he was keeping most of his campaign promises. By the end of his first term, 35 percent thought Clinton had tried to keep all or most of his promises; only 15 percent thought he had succeeded in doing so. The media seemed to agree. But there were notable exceptions. A systematic look at the Clinton record leads to an inevitable conclusion: Clinton largely delivered on his promises. In a story assessing in modest detail what Clinton pledged and what he delivered, Kimberly Crockett of the *Phoenix Gazette* concluded: "Bill Clinton won't be remembered as a man who means what he says and says what he means. However, he will be regarded for his ability not only to get things done, but to deliver more than he promised."[54] In August 1996, Knight-Ridder Newspapers reviewed 160 Clinton promises of the 1992 campaign to determine what action, if any, the president had taken. Analysts found that Clinton had delivered on 106, or 66 percent, of them. When they added those promises that he tried unsuccessfully to keep, they found "Clinton fairly could be credited with trying hard to keep 81 percent of his 1992 campaign promises."[55] Further and detailed support of the Clinton record on campaign promises came in another Knight-Ridder report in the *St. Petersburg Times*. Working from a list of 134 promises, researchers identified 105 as kept, 25 not kept (regardless of presidential effort), and 4 pending.[56]

The problem with such long-term assessments may simply be that they occur too late. After four years of featuring the president's failure to deliver on campaign promises, including lists of top-ten broken promises, and breezy characterizations of Clinton as a classic promise-breaker, the media's occasional catalogue of the long-term record may simply be too weak an antidote. Citizens seem to derive the mistaken impression that Clinton and other presidents fail miserably to live up to their word.

Depressing our sense of how many promises are kept is a retrospective magnification of the centrality of those promises left unfulfilled. According to Bruce Buchanan, University of Texas at Austin professor of government, George Bush repeated his "read my lips—no new taxes" pledge "in every speech."[57] Yet, in the Annenberg Campaign Mapping Project archives, we located only eight instances in the general-election speeches in which Bush invoked his "read my lips" pledge. A search of the two debates revealed only one reference to it, and no mention appeared in his ads. That Bush was punished for his reversal on taxes is all the more interesting when one looks at polls conducted shortly after his election victory. In a Gallup survey, 68 percent thought that the Bush administration would not be able to avoid raising taxes.[58] In another survey, 44 percent thought it highly likely and 35 percent somewhat likely that "federal taxes will be raised to help balance the budget during Bush's term in office (as President)."[59] And in another survey, 66 percent said they thought Bush would ask Congress to increase taxes.[60]

After going back on his campaign pledge "read my lips—no new taxes," President George Bush paid the price in lost popular support. When only 9 percent of those polled in June 1992 agreed that Bush had kept most of his promises, what portion owed its unfavorable view of him to his retreat on this one issue and the attention it received?

The public perception of Clinton's promise keeping, while not as low as Bush's 9 percent, also seems unjustified in light of his record. The problem may be that it is the nature of the evaluation—a focus on individual broken promises rather than comprehensive assessments of the record—that leads the press to create an inaccurate and unfavorable impression among citizens. A piece such as Jacob Weisberg's, which appeared in *New York* magazine, was uncommon: "Bill Clinton has been more faithful to his word than any other chief executive in recent memory. . . . The irony is that Americans are oblivious to most of his kept promises."[61]

Perhaps Americans underestimate the reliability of a candidate's pledges because journalists tend to focus on promises broken but not on those kept. For example, Chinese President Jiang Zemin's 1997 visit to the United States was an occasion for Ted Koppel to remind *Nightline* viewers of Clinton's delinking of the annual extension of China's most-favored-nation trading status and its human rights record, despite a disingenuous campaign promise to the contrary. Koppel concluded: "President Clinton is much closer to the mark today with his policy of engaging China than he was five years ago with that cheap shot about President Bush coddling dictators."[62] There can be little objection to such analysis: A president's broken promises should be pointed out. But when proportionate emphasis does not fall on honored promises, misperception on the part of citizens is likely.

An example that highlights this point involves Clinton and welfare reform. As part of his 1992 campaign, Clinton promised to end welfare as we know it. Although there were skeptics, in 1996, prodded by a Republican Congress, Clinton signed legislation that significantly overhauled welfare. In fact, the reform was so far-reaching that some of his supporters and particularly those on the left denounced the plan as excessively harsh and unfair. In response to such criticism, Clinton pledged that if reelected, he would "fix" welfare reform.

Many commentators dismissed that promise. "He promised to do five impossible things before breakfast—balance the budget, provide tax breaks for education, promote family values, avoid deep cuts in Medicare and 'fix' welfare reform, all without more government intrusion."[63] "Here's how the Clinton record may look in January 2001: Welfare: Clinton promised during the 1996 campaign that in his second term he would fix the problems and cruelties in the welfare reform legislation he bragged about signing. But he hasn't."[64] "On the other hand, President Clinton probably will not be able to 'fix' the new welfare-reform law that he knows is terribly unfair to millions of poor Americans and legal immigrants."[65] Among the 1997 predictions of the *Orlando Sentinel*: "Welfare. Liberal Democrats who believed that Clinton would 'fix' welfare reform will be sorely disappointed. He might try, and maybe even let Hillary take a crack at it. The GOP Congress has no intention of weakening its hard-fought crusade to get the federal government out of welfare."[66] "The only item worth noting on Mr. Clinton's domestic agenda is his vow to 'fix' the Republican welfare-reform bill he himself signed into law this summer. Of course, the Clinton 'fix,' designed to bring back 'welfare as we know it,' won't sail in Congress. So scratch that one."[67]

Parallel comments came from the opposite side of the political spectrum as well: "I always had my doubts that President Clinton ever intended to 'fix' the dreadful 'welfare reform' bill. . . . And Clinton's radio address to the nation last Saturday indicates that he doesn't want to, and is already trying to justify reneging on his promise."[68] Similarly, "For those to whom this Clintonese is unintelligible, it means: For the record, I'd like to say it'd be nice to restore eligibility. Even though I won't fight for it, I don't want you to think that I don't care."[69]

But in fact, Clinton did secure changes. In the 1997 budget agreement, Clinton won concessions from the Republican Congress, including restoration of benefits to legal immigrants, $3 billion over five years to help welfare recipients move into jobs, tax credits to businesses that hire long-term welfare recipients, and $1.5 billion over five years for the partial restoration of food stamp benefits cut in 1996.[70] Some reporters did credit these accomplishments. Michael Kelly, for one, viewed these concessions as a significant fulfillment of earlier promises: "Well, [Clinton] did [fix it]. In the recent budget deal between the White House and Congress, the president accomplished the restoration of SSI benefits to all immigrants who were legal before August 22, 1996. . . . This and other measures, including funding to provide work for unemployed Food Stamp recipients, that were negotiated into the budget agreement have, in [Urban Institute policy analyst] Zedlewski's words, 'gone a long way toward fixing the problem.'"[71] When the details of the budget deal became known, Clinton received a rare acknowledgment from *Newsweek* writer Jonathan Alter: "With the help of a Republican Congress, Bill Clinton has now fulfilled just about all of his major campaign promises."[72] However, the amount of space devoted to forecasting that he would break his word was not matched by space crediting him with keeping it.

In short, politicians are caught in the juggernaut created by a media corps that preemptively keeps score of the nonfulfillment of presidential promises before voters can solidify their own—perhaps more balanced—impression.

Mark Mendoza and Kathleen Hall Jamieson

Chapter Three

Who's to Blame?
Is the Perception Gap
in the Campaigns,
Media Coverage,
or Both?

AS EARLY AS AUGUST 1996, media commentators were characterizing the U.S. presidential election as "boring."[1] With incumbent Bill Clinton securely ahead in the tracking polls and Republican nominee Bob Dole failing to gain "momentum" from his August nominating convention, the race lacked the critical dramatic element of an uncertain outcome. With the election-day result in little doubt, the news media were faced with a choice of three courses of action: They could have fabricated dramatic tension where little existed; they could have covered the campaign by asking a set of questions having less to do with who would win and more to do with the issues facing the country; or they could have simply ignored the campaign and filled the news void with other matters.

To a great extent, they chose the latter course. Compared with earlier general-election years, there was a striking drop in the amount of coverage given to the 1996 U.S. presidential election. With funding from the Carnegie Corporation of New York and the Ford Foundation, the Annenberg Public Policy Center of the University of Pennsylvania undertook a comprehensive analysis of the discourse of the 1996 presidential campaign. Our analysis of broadcast news during the last two months of the campaign showed that network coverage of the election declined by

55 percent from 1992. Coverage in major newspapers dropped by over 40 percent. If the purpose of news coverage is to forecast a winner and loser and to analyze the tactics one candidate is using well and the other poorly, this drop in coverage was unsurprising.

In the second week of September, our research team reported the decline in front-page newspaper coverage and in reporting on the evening news. When CNN asked an editor for the *New York Times* for a comment on our finding, he said that if it were true, it reflected the fact that the campaign was boring. This rationale raises a provocative question: Were reporters simply reflecting the view of the electorate, or were they creating a self-fulfilling prophecy? Whatever the case, it was not difficult to find reporters commenting that the conventions were staged photo opportunities devoid of useful information and that the debates contained "nothing new." These comments coincided with a drop of about 4 million viewers in the convention-watching television audience from 1992 and a 25 million decline from 1992 in the average number of viewers for each debate. Consistent with plummeting viewership for major campaign events, voter turnout on election day was down from 1992.

A prominent U.S. media perspective in 1996, as in previous elections, cast the purpose of the campaign not as a means of educating the citizenry or setting a programmatic agenda but rather as a contest between two tacticians bent on winning the election rather than governing. With the result evident, coverage fell. Only within this cynical paradigm would one even ask whether the election was "boring."

Overreporting of Tactics and Strategy

A national survey on voters and media conducted by the Media Studies Center/Roper Center in September 1996 found 46 percent of respondents reporting that the media were paying too little attention to issues and 50 percent saying that there was too much attention being given to who was ahead and who behind.[2] As was noted in Chapter 1, strategy coverage in news assesses campaign events and statements by their likely influence on the outcome of the contest. The strategic frame is marked by several features: winning and losing as the central concern; metaphors of war and sports; mention of performers (candidates), critics (journalists), and audience (voters); emphasis on candidate style and perceptions; and a reliance on polls to evaluate campaigns and candidates.[3] As many observers have noted, strategy coverage is the dominant form of campaign news. In the past few years, this strategic frame has infiltrated coverage of policy debates as well.[4]

This kind of focus on the campaign process serves a number of purposes for journalists. First, it allows them to engage in interpretation, offering opinions unconstrained by "objectivity." Second, it reinforces their privileged position by focusing on "inside" information to which only they have access. Third, it fulfills a dramatic imperative by portraying the campaign as a contest for power between two antagonists who battle toward an exciting climax in which the winner is confirmed. Finally, it cannot be falsified. Whereas an article on the substantive similarities and differences between candidates can contain errors, one cannot argue conclusively about whether or not a specific campaign statement is designed to serve a revealed tactical end.

The reporting on the two presidential debates and one vice-presidential debate showed the strategic frame in action. On ABC, Peter Jennings began his report after the first debate by saying, "Well, if you look to the polls as a guide, the overnight polls tell us that very few minds were changed last night."[5] This conclusion would hardly be noteworthy, as U.S. history has not recorded a single instance in which a televised debate has had an incontrovertible impact on electoral outcome. This fact, however, is forgotten by journalists every four years as they search to find a "winner" for each debate. On the other networks, the commonly asked questions were the same: Who won? Was anyone's vote changed?

Debates are the best opportunity U.S. voters have to assess the qualifications and agendas of those who would lead. Our research indicates that in the relatively extended format of debates, candidates are more likely to compare their positions than simply to attack. In addition, debates often feature information about candidate positions unavailable from other sources.

It is ironic that the one consistently substantive forum is discussed in the least informative terms. Press coverage of debates is, if anything, even more focused on strategy than the rest of campaign coverage. In 1996, a guiding question of coverage of the debates was whether Dole could do something sufficiently dramatic to change the outcome of the race. In the phrase used by countless media commentators, Dole had to "hit a home run." When the debates featured no vitriolic exchanges or embarrassing gaffes, their importance was downplayed. None of the three commercial broadcast networks aired a story about the final debate the following evening.

Because it produces stories focused on who is ahead and why, the strategic frame disadvantages the person behind in the polls. Here, too, the possibility of self-fulfilling prophecy comes into play particularly since, with a single exception, the major polls dramatically underestimated Dole's likely percent of the vote. In the campaign's final days, major media polls had Clinton defeating Dole by margins much higher than his eventual eight-point victory. One, a CBS News/*New York Times* poll, gave Clinton an eighteen-point advantage. Had reporters known that the likely vote was much closer than the polls indicated, would coverage have increased and strategic coverage of Dole decreased, and with these changes, would Dole's prospects have changed?

All this being said, it is important to note that when taken as a whole, 1996 showed a slight improvement over previous recent elections in the proportion of strategy coverage. Our content analysis divided campaign stories into those focused on strategy, those concentrating on issue distinctions, and those composing a miscellaneous category. Whereas in previous years, the proportion of strategy stories on broadcast news had reached 64 percent (in 1988), in 1996 only 47 percent of campaign stories focused on tactics. This was a slight drop from 1992, when 50 percent of the news reports emphasized the strategic element.

Overrepresentation of Attack

Even with the absence of substantive coverage of campaign forums such as debates, the media continue to emphasize one particular facet of the "horse race": attack. The evening after the last presidential debate of 1996, two of the three commercial broadcast networks featured a heckler calling Clinton "a draft-dodging, yellow-bellied liar" at a campaign event that day. That reported moment is symptomatic of a tendency in campaign coverage to report attack rather than advocacy, and conflict rather than consensus. For every presidential general election since 1960, anyone relying on news reports for information about the campaign would conclude that it contained a far higher level of attack than was in fact the case.

The candidates' discourse is also more complex and varied than news coverage suggests. Their speeches, debates, and ads include claims advocating the sponsor's candidacy (self-promotional arguments), claims attacking the opponent (oppositional arguments), and claims that both advocate and attack (comparative arguments or contrast).

The press's emphasis on attack may reflect something other than the journalistic norm that focuses on conflict.[6] In previous campaigns, the reporters' focus on attack reflected one type of candidate communication:

advertising. In 1980, 1988, and 1992, broadcast news coverage of all candidates' discourse generally reflected the proportion of attack found in candidates' advertising claims. For example, in 1988, 38 percent of candidates' advertisements were self-promotional, and 40 percent were oppositional. Broadcast news coverage of all types of candidates' discourse (speeches, ads, and debates) revealed similar proportions: 41 percent self-promotional arguments and 45 percent oppositional arguments.

In short, the proportion of reported attack in discourse in broadcast news has reflected the proportion in advertising, not that in speeches and debates. Because advertising tends to be more attack-driven than speeches and debates (which are more advocacy- and contrast-driven, respectively), this dynamic probably heightens the public perception of the amount of attack in presidential campaigns.

As in previous years, in 1996 broadcast news overreported attacks in candidates' speeches and debates. But unlike in previous years, it also overreported attacks in candidates' advertising. Fewer than 25 percent of candidates' advertisements were oppositional in 1996, whereas 42 percent of quotes from ads reported in broadcast news took that form. What accounts for the discrepancy?

The most likely explanation is the rise of a type of argument that both attacked and advocated in the same ad. In 1996, nearly half of all ads were contrastive, more than double the proportion in previous years. This type of discourse also increased in speeches and debates, though not as dramatically. At the same time, the proportion of pure attack ads declined by nearly half from 1980, 1988, and 1992. The proportion of attack dropped in speeches as well, but remained the same in debates. In sum, in 1996 candidates sought to contrast their agendas with those of their opponents rather than simply to attack; this emphasis appeared even in advertising.

But the networks' coverage did not reflect this change. Broadcast news downplayed the contrastive claims candidates made between themselves and their opponents; instead, it either reported candidates praising their own candidacies or attacking their opponents. Forty-nine percent of reported candidate arguments were self-promotional, 42 percent were oppositional, and only 9 percent were comparative.

It is possible that one candidate was responsible for single-handedly raising the overall level of attack in the campaign. Because Dole was generally viewed as the attacker in the race, he may have been the culprit. But our data do not support this conclusion. Over half of Dole's arguments in speeches and debates were contrastive, double the rate of his oppositional arguments. Though 46 percent of his advertising claims were oppositional, over half were either contrastive or self-promotional.

Clinton does not appear to be responsible either, as he attacked even less than did Dole. Only about 1 percent of his debate and speech claims attacked, compared with 17 percent of his ads. Unlike previous years, it appears that candidate advertising in 1996 was not the index by which we could predict the reporting of attack.

Why is this finding significant? First, as in previous years, 1996 broadcast network coverage made it appear that candidates were much more likely to attack than they really were. Second, by underreporting comparative claims, news prevented viewers from learning where both candidates stood on a variety of issues. When Clinton gave a speech attacking Dole's tax plan and outlining his own, the networks were likely to report only Clinton's attack on Dole's plan or only his advocacy of his own proposal. This either-or focus deprived the electorate of contrastive—though certainly biased—views of where the candidates stood.

Interestingly, according to a survey by the Pew Research Center for the People and the Press, 65 percent of those surveyed said there was less discussion of issues in 1996 than in previous years.[7] By contrast, in 1992, 59 percent said there had been more discussion of the issues than in earlier years. It is likely that the public drew this conclusion from the drop in overall reporting about the campaign and from the press's tendency to feature attack rather than advocacy and seldom report contrastive claims. When contrastive arguments are not reported, candidates may appear less concerned about the issues than their actual discourse would suggest.

Substance Appeared in Speeches and Debates but Was Undercovered

Not only have the networks overreported attack in candidate discourse, but perhaps more important is that they historically have underreported its substance. Nearly all candidate claims in speeches and debates are backed by evidence—data or reasoning to support the speaker's position. Most candidate statements take the following form: "I know that our policy to control missiles is poorly administered (claim), for in the entire U.S. government, only three people are working on this problem (evidence)." Claims supported by evidence provide discourse more useful to voters because the supporting evidence provides justification for them to accept the claim. By employing evidence, candidates also give the voters a fuller understanding of the pros and cons of national issues.

However, if voters do not watch debates or listen to speeches, in news they are likely to hear only candidates' claims, not the evidence supporting them. In pre-1996 campaigns, network news stripped the evidence from arguments, thus reducing them to simple assertions. The 1996 campaign was not much different. Whereas 95 percent of Clinton's and Dole's claims in their speeches were backed by evidence, only 40 percent reported by the commercial networks included proof. However, compared with earlier campaigns, this measure actually marked an improvement in network coverage. In 1980, only 26 percent of candidates' speech arguments in news contained evidence, compared with 20 percent in 1988 and 39 percent in 1992.

By omitting the evidence when reporting candidate arguments, network coverage suggests candidates are trafficking in unfounded claims, when in fact they almost always offer support or reasons for their views. In U.S. presidential campaigns, the media not only distort candidate discourse by overreporting attack, but they also shortchange candidates and voters by underreporting the evidence candidates offer for their claims.

Accuracy in Ads

In 1992 the major networks instituted a new form of press coverage called the "adwatch." In adwatches, reporters evaluated the content of broadcast political ads. Pioneered in newspapers in the 1990 off-year elections, some adwatches scrutinized political ads for accuracy, others analyzed their strategy, and some looked at both. In 1992 the majority of adwatches assessed accuracy; by contrast, in 1996 not a single broadcast network adwatch exposed the inaccuracies in ads. In 1992, 14 percent of the ads for George Bush and Bill Clinton contained at least one misleading claim; in 1996 that percentage soared to more than 50 percent—an all-time high in the history of the modern presidency.

The misleading statement most often made in the Democratic ads was that the Republicans wanted to cut Medicare by $270 billion. Unstated were four facts: The Democrats also wanted to cut, so the implication that if one voted for Clinton there would be no changes was wrong; the "cut" was not an absolute one but rather a decrease in the rate of growth;

under the Republican plan, the dollars spent per beneficiary would continue to rise but at a slower than otherwise anticipated rate; finally, neither the Republican nor the Democratic plan would ensure that Medicare would survive long enough to provide benefits for the baby-boom generation that will begin retiring in 2010.

The most-repeated Republican deception said or implied that the Clinton tax increase was assessed on the middle class. In fact, the Democratic plan raised taxes on the upper 1.5 percent of income earners. Some of the Dole ads made the middle-class claim outright. Others talked about "the largest tax increase in history" while showing photos of blue-collar workers. Whether the tax increase was the largest was a matter of definition. Adjusted for inflation, the tax increase of the Reagan era—an increase Dole supported—was larger.

Ducking the Issues

The level of uncorrected and unchallenged inaccuracy, largely unreported by the media, was not the only significant problem with the discourse of the 1996 campaign. An additional flaw was the extent to which the major-party candidates sinned by omission.

In 1995 the trust fund for the part of Medicare that covers in-patient hospital care (Part A) began drawing down its reserves. At the current rate, the trust fund itself will be exhausted by 2001.[8] Neither candidate indicated what he would propose to ensure the solvency of Medicare. Instead, both favored turning the problem over to a bipartisan commission. Neither specified how he would address the forthcoming shortfall in Social Security either. These problems are of special concern because, as a poll of Americans by the American Association of Retired Persons (AARP) indicates, "only 35 percent have confidence in Social Security's future—46 percent of retirees and 27 percent of non-retirees; 51 percent have confidence in Medicare." Also unaddressed was the need for massive investment in the nation's highways, water systems, and school buildings. In other words, significant social problems were simply sidestepped. And voters were skeptical of the promises the candidates did make. Two-thirds doubted that Clinton could both balance the budget and increase spending for new programs, and the same proportion doubted that Dole could reduce the deficit while cutting taxes by 15 percent.[9]

The candidates minimized the likelihood that they would be asked about these omissions by setting up rules for the debates that prohibited the moderator, PBS's Jim Lehrer, from asking follow-up questions, and that specified the candidates would not address questions to each other. Outside the debates, the two major-party candidates minimized their accountability by ducking press contact. Apparently fearful that he would be asked about an alleged mistress with whom he may have been involved in the final years of his first marriage, Dole deviated from traditional campaign strategy that dictates that the person behind in the polls becomes increasingly accessible to reporters. Conversely, the person ahead in the polls typically minimizes press contact throughout the campaign. Clinton was no exception in this respect; the first time he answered press questions about possible illegalities in his fundraising was the end of the week after his reelection.

In sum, in the 1996 election, the candidates ducked key issues, distorted others, and avoided the accountability that comes with follow-up questioning in debates and national press conferences. When not dismissing the campaign as boring, reporters too often stressed tactics over substance, overreporting candidate attack, underreporting candidate comparison and argument, and ignoring misleading ads. By shunning the conventions, the debates, and the voting booth, the citizenry gave the politicians and the press little incentive to change their ways. Of course, these assessments presuppose that citizens are aware of the backgrounds, dispositions, and promises of the major-party candidates.

An alternative and more minimalist test would ask whether citizens learned what they needed to cast an informed vote. In 1996, the Annenberg Public Policy Center (APPC) commissioned four cross-sectional surveys that were conducted by Chilton Research. Among other things, the surveys were designed to assess what the electorate knew about the candidates for president.

Voters' Knowledge About Candidates

By mid-October 1996, most Americans could recall most of the major candidates for president and vice president. Over 90 percent of registered voters could name each of the two major-party presidential candidates, and approximately three-quarters could name each of the vice-presidential contenders. Less than two-thirds could name the Reform Party's presidential candidate, although 93 percent knew, when asked directly, that Ross Perot was a candidate for president.

Between 80 and 90 percent were able to identify correctly whether Dole, Clinton, neither, or both favored expanding family leave, supported increased funding for job training, favored making it harder for women to obtain abortions, and supported a 15 percent across-the-board tax cut. The level of knowledge with regard to Clinton's policies was slightly greater, on average, than with regard to Dole's; 85 percent knew the incumbent favored a ban on cigarette advertising to children and opposed eliminating the Department of Education, for example, while 72 percent knew the challenger's position.

On only one policy—targeted tax cuts—did a majority fail to identify the positions of either candidate correctly. This finding is easily explained by the fact that both candidates favored tax cuts. There was similar confusion about support for vouchers, a finding probably attributable to Clinton's support for "choice" in the form of charter schools. In these two cases, the cognitive shortcuts on which voters would ordinarily rely were an unreliable guide. Republicans should be expected to cut taxes; Clinton was promising this as well. Republicans are expected to support vouchers—but Clinton's support of "choice" probably blurred the party distinction. There were also low levels of knowledge about which candidate favored a constitutional amendment requiring a balanced budget. Heuristics would ordinarily have guided voters to choose Dole, but Clinton's repeated support in ads and debates for a balanced budget—although not a balanced-budget amendment—probably confused those paying some but not a great deal of attention.

The remaining cases in which knowledge was less widespread—Dole's support for guaranteeing immigrants access to public schools, Clinton's support of the death penalty and opposition to same-sex marriages—involved positions contrary to the ones deduced from party labels, which suggests that policy questions may assess voters' capacity to divine the liberal and conservative positions on an issue in general more than their familiarity with particular candidates. This drop-off in accuracy suggests as well the failure of the press to communicate these kinds of policy distinctions. However, if the inferences the electorate draws as a result are generally reliable, that can be taken as a good sign for communication between those who aspire to lead and those considering a vote.

The bottom line in 1996, then, was that even in a campaign in which candidates kept information from the electorate, and in which candidates who sinned by omission were covered in less than exhaustive fashion by the press, voters learned a great deal about the central issues that mattered in their lives. They did so in large part because the campaign and media coverage of these issues helped voters link candidates to parties; this linkage led to accurate inferences about where the candidates stood on many issues but confused voters about candidate stands on those issues less reliably forecast by party identification.

Kathleen Hall Jamieson, James Devitt,
Paul Waldman, and Michael Hagen

Chapter Four

What Is Happening Now? The Quality of Campaign Discourse

BY DRAWING ON THE SPEECHES, ads, and news of the 1952–1996 general elections, we will debunk some widely held beliefs about presidential campaign discourse, including that it has become more negative—both in terms of the news reports and the stump speeches of the major-party presidential candidates.[1]

More Negative Campaigns?

A common misconception about U.S. politics is that presidential campaigns have grown more "negative" over the years. The content analysis conducted by the Annenberg Campaign Mapping Project (ACMP) researchers found that this is not, in fact, the case. Candidate discourse was divided into *advocacy* (arguments in favor of the speaker's position), *attack* (arguments critical of the opponent or his position), and *contrast* (arguments contrasting the speaker and the opponent).

As we noted earlier, different genres display different patterns: Ads feature relatively more attack, debates tend to produce more contrast, and speeches are marked by advocacy. However, the amount of attack has not increased dramatically in any of the genres. In short, the notion that campaigns have grown more negative is mistaken. Candidates' discourse has not become dramatically more adversarial through the modern era of televised campaigns. In fact, 1996 featured less attack than had previously been the norm.

How does one account for the perception that attack is up? Some observers have argued that press coverage has become more negative over time. If this were true, it might explain a more general conclusion that campaigns themselves have become more negative. Our study, however, reaches a different conclusion.

More Negative Press Coverage?

In addition to analyzing candidate discourse in speeches, ads, and debates, the ACMP also examined candidate discourse reported in the news. Although indicating problematic characteristics of campaign news, the results here do not show a significant change over time. On this measure, at least, campaign news has not featured increasing amounts of attack in recent elections. On the contrary, attack has been reported at a relatively steady level since 1960. Although, as we argued in the last chapter, news does overrepresent the attack in campaign discourse, it does not do so to a greater degree today than it did in past years.

Accenting the Negative

Although there has not been a change over time, the press does in fact have a tendency to highlight attack and simplify complex arguments. As the following example from the 1992 election shows, reporters, particularly those on television, tend to report the more inflammatory part of a candidate's speech in the news.

Section of Original Speech by President Bush:

> Now there's been some bad news. There's been some very bad news for Clinton and Gore. It comes out that we are not in a deep recession. We grew at 2.7 percent and these guys are weeping tears. The only way they can win is to tell everybody that everything isn't worth a darn. They criticize our country and say we are less than Germany and slightly better than Sri Lanka. My dog Millie knows more about foreign affairs than these two bozos. It's crazy. Let them tear down the country. Let's us all build it up by getting this economy moving. . . And look—if you listen to Governor Clinton and Ozone Man—if you listen to them—you know why I call him Ozone Man? This guy is so far off in the environmental extreme we'll be up to our neck in owls and out of work for every American. This guy's crazy. He is way out, far out, man. Wait 'til he—hey, listen—you think you're going to save General Motors by slapping more regulations on 'em? Less regulation, less taxes.[2]

Section of NBC Report:

Reporter: Bush also includes Al Gore in his attacks, when he accuses both Democrats of knowing nothing about foreign policy.

Bush: My dog Millie knows more about foreign affairs than these two bozos.

Reporter: Bush has also taken to calling environmentalist Gore "Mr. Ozone."

Bush: You know why I call him Ozone Man? This guy is so far off in the environmental extreme we'll be up to our neck in owls and out of work for every American. This guy's crazy. He is way out, far out, man. Wait 'til he—hey, listen—you think you're going to save General Motors by slapping more regulations on 'em? Less regulation, less taxes. Bring that back.

Reporter: Here, Bush was campaigning in the heart of the hard-hit auto industry and trying to win the so-called Reagan Democrats. Later in Grand Rapids, Bush was trying to hold the Republican vote with the help of Gerald Ford, the last Republican incumbent to lose in a presidential race. The Ford campaign is the one that haunts the Bush campaign. In the home stretch, Ford came from far behind, only to lose in a photo finish to a southern governor.[3]

Section of CBS Report:

Reporter: On the Bush campaign these days, you are upbeat or else. The Michigan poll [is] adding ammo to the claim that the president is on the move, although Democrats heartily dispute it. Many people are undecided, and Mr. Bush could hardly contain himself today when warning them against the Democrats, calling them at one point "bozos."

Bush: If you listen to Governor Clinton and Ozone Man—if you listen to them—you know why I call him Ozone Man? This guy is so far off in the environmental extreme we'll be up to our neck in owls and out of work for every American. This guy's crazy. He is way out, far out, man.

Reporter: But in economically strapped Michigan, hecklers tried to spoil the fun. The state's governor says it doesn't mean a thing.

Governor Engler: We've seen the Republican vote coming home very solidly, and then in recent days—two or three days now—we're starting to see the independent vote.

Reporter: Michigan is another one of those states Mr. Bush won in '88 and badly needs now. Certainly he's going all out to show confidence.

Bush: The American people know what the Arkansas record was. They know what waffling in character means, and I am going to win election on November third.

Reporter: Well, perhaps it was the mood of the day, perhaps it's a sign of how much trouble Mr. Bush may be in. In any case, he has now decided to do an interview with MTV, something he laughed at a few months ago when Governor Clinton did it.[4]

Section of ABC Report:

Reporter: The president, getting into the spirit, called his opponents "two bozos" and then let fly at Clinton running mate Al Gore's passionate environmental views. He called Gore, as he has for days, "the Ozone Man."

Bush: You know why I call him Ozone Man? This guy is so far off in the environmental extreme we'll be up to our neck in owls and out of work for every American. This guy's crazy. He is way out, far out, man.

Reporter: The partisan crowd loved it all, and the president, seeming to feed on that, worked himself up even more in his finale.

Bush: And let's lead the world to new heights of prosperity for every single American. Don't let them tear it down. God bless America. Thank you all very much.[5]

This example of the same speech covered by three media outlets shows that even in an address that could hardly be called eloquent or well organized, substantive arguments with evidence nonetheless do exist, but those arguments don't make it into the network news reports. Bush makes two arguments in this excerpt. He asserts that the economy is not in recession and offers a figure on economic growth as evidence. He also claims that Clinton and Gore are environmental extremists and contrasts his own position, which is that businesses should be subject to less regulation. Whatever the merits of his arguments, news viewers never hear them in full. Instead, viewers are left with the impression of a candidate simply attacking, when in fact he offered an indictment supported by evidence. This pattern is repeated in news stories: Candidates' arguments are simplified by removing evidence and justification, leaving only what appear to be unsubstantiated attacks. The news thus portrays candidate discourse that is meaner, simpler—and leaner in content—than it actually is.

The Same Story? Or Not?

Another myth about presidential campaigns is that candidates deliver the same speech again and again, varying their discourse only marginally. As a result, goes the argument, candidate speeches are not presumed to be particularly useful sources of new information.

In fact, candidate speeches vary both in the topics discussed and in the arguments used. Each candidate's speeches, when understood as a group, show a common pattern. The candidate will discuss a small number (usually one or two) of core issues in all or most of his speeches. In addition, each speech will cover a number of other topics, which will vary from speech to speech. In the study, the presidential candidates averaged between four and nine topic areas per speech during the general election. Some focused on foreign policy and defense, others on domestic policy, others on economic policy, and so on. This was true for every candidate in the study.

If candidates were giving the same speech repeatedly, each speech would produce a similar list of arguments. That isn't the case. Every candidate in the study had speeches with few extended arguments and speeches with many shorter arguments, speeches that primarily advocated and speeches that primarily attacked. In other words, candidates often discuss the same issue in different ways. A qualitative reading of speeches bears out this conclusion. Candidate speeches can in fact be a useful source of information for voters, offering a wide range of candidates' issue positions, arguments, and rationales in addition to a restatement of their principal themes.

The three examples indicate the value of investigating the traditional assumptions we make about political campaigning and political communication. By overreporting candidate attack, underreporting the evidence candidates marshal, and implying that there is little variety in the general-election speeches of presidential candidates, reporters invite us to conclude that campaigns have less substance than is in fact the case.

Susan Sherr, Paul Waldman, David Dutwin,
and Kathleen Hall Jamieson

Chapter Five

What Should We Really Expect? How They Talk to Us

THERE HAS BEEN EXTENSIVE ANALYSIS of how leaders communicate with citizens and what audiences can expect from them in that regard.[1] Writing at the end of the McCarthy era of the early 1950s, rhetoric scholar Karl Wallace defined four "moralities of communication" that remain today. In an article entitled "An Ethical Basis for Communication," Wallace noted that speakers have the obligation to search and inquire, to be accurate, fair, and just in their use of argument, to be willing to submit private motivations to public scrutiny, and to tolerate dissent.[2] Rather than simply tolerating dissent, a model of deliberation built on argument, engagement, and civility would embrace it. It would do so because the goal of this process is not winning the argument but making the best case on all sides as a vehicle for a kind of deliberative collaboration, an understanding of where the best solution resides.

The size of the United States, the heterogeneity of its population, and the complexity of its role in the international community mean that the kind of deliberative discourse envisioned by Aristotle is beyond our reach. Any whisper of Aristotle or Athens invites the charge of polis envy. But that does not mean we can't aspire to an Athenian ideal characterized by argument and engagement. Just as there are tendencies in candidate speeches, ads, and debates that we ought to deplore, there are certain characteristics we ought to consider indispensable to effective democratic discourse.

At the core of this model is a belief that democratic deliberation must be practiced if use of it is to become habitual. As rhetoric scholar Thomas Nilsen noted in an essay published in the aftermath of McCarthyism:

"Most of the average citizen's political actions consist of making choices between alternatives presented to him. When we determine how he makes his choices, we determine to a large extent the kind of person he is and the kind of citizen he is, whether he is a person who grows in his ability to make rational choices and develops [those] . . . capacities that make him truly human."[3] Henry David Thoreau voiced a similar concern when he wrote "I believe that the mind can be permanently profaned by the habit of attending to trivial things, so that all our thoughts shall be tinged with triviality."[4] So too did Francis Bacon in the *New Organon:* "For it is by discourse that men associate, and words are imposed according to the apprehension of the vulgar. And therefore the ill and unfit choice of words wonderfully obstructs the understanding."[5]

There has been a long-standing tension between confidence in the deliberations of the community and fear that in the heat of passion the public will embrace a course of action not in its own interest. "[A]s the cool and deliberate sense of the community ought, in all governments and actually will, in all free governments, ultimately prevail over the view of its rulers," noted Madison in *The Federalist No. 63,* "so there are particular moments in public affairs when the people, stimulated by some irregular passion or some illicit advantage, or misled by the artful misrepresentations of interested men, may call for measures which they themselves will afterwards be the most ready to lament and condemn."

The likelihood that the public will be misled is minimized if the competing views are available and tested by advocates, audiences, and the press, if all sides engage in warranted argument, and if they accept responsibility for defending their own claims and the claims others offer on their behalf. This concept sounds idealistic, but unless a certain critical degree of substantive interchange is preserved among candidates, the people, and the media that control their encounters, the possibility of a critical information deficit will exist.

Civility

When one's purpose is polemical, the construction of venomous prose may serve to mobilize partisans and vent the loathing of the author. For example, Walt Whitman spared few pejoratives in describing those who participated in the Democratic nominating conventions before the Civil War as

> the meanest kind of brawling and blowing officeholders, office-seekers, pimps, malignant conspirators, murderers, fancy-men, custom-house

clerks, contractors, kept-editors, spaniels well-train'd to carry and fetch, jobbers, infidels, disunionists, terrorists, mail-riflers, slave-catchers, pushers of slavery . . . spies, bribers, compromisers, lobbyers, sponges, ruin'd sports, expell'd gamblers . . . pimpled men, scarr'd inside with vile disease, gaudy outside with gold chains made from the people's money and harlots' money twisted together; crawling, serpentine men, the . . . born freedom-sellers of the earth.[6]

To those of like mind, this outpouring is the justified rhetoric of moral outrage over slavery; to those being described, it is ad hominem; to us, without this context, it reads as parody. Regardless of the interpretation, this is not the sort of discourse productively addressed to those one wishes to engage in deliberation.

Confronted with immoral action, one might well argue that Whitman's diatribe is a more fitting rhetorical response than reasoned invitation to dialogue. All of those options should, of course, be available to the citizen exercising the rights guaranteed under the First Amendment. The reasons are straightforward. As Justice William Brennan wrote in *New York Times v. Sullivan* (1964), "Debate on public issues should be uninhibited, robust, and wide open, and that . . . may well include vehement, caustic, and sometimes unpleasantly sharp attacks on government and public officials."

When focusing on the rhetorical exchanges that occur among parties in an ongoing relationship and on those individuals who have come together as a community to address problems, it simply makes practical sense to embrace civility as a norm. When one is engaged in an ongoing relationship with an interlocutor, the costs of incivility can be high. Inventive invective invites payback, and the consequences may be felt years or even decades later. When Republican Senator Roscoe Conkling of New York and Republican James Blaine "excoriat[ed] each other in unmerciful terms" one day, with Blaine describing Conkling's gait as "the turkey-gobbler strut," the "blast created a gulf between them that was never bridged, though Blaine often tried to reach across the chasm." Payback occurred in 1884. Blaine was the Republican nominee for president. Conkling refused to campaign for him, saying, "I am not in the criminal practice." When Conkling's heavily Republican county voted against Blaine, he lost New York by under a thousand votes and with that the state and the presidency.[7]

Enmity engendered by injudicious attack can persist even after the offender has died. Just after the turn of the twentieth century, a member of Congress was described as having "spun vitriolic stuff out of his own inner consciousness, and it burned and scorched his victims like molten lava. His merciless sarcasm made for him mortal enemies, who hated him while alive and some of whom hate him in his grave."

Communities are sets of relationships writ large. When communities deliberate, they often do so in a rule-governed environment. By adopting rules of deliberation at the beginning of a new U.S. Congress, the membership voluntarily limits the range of rhetoric acceptable on the floor. When a member wonders why he can't call another member a liar or a hypocrite even if the evidence justifies the label, the answer is not simply that the rules of the House forbid it but also that the membership has voluntarily agreed by vote that these are the rules under which the House will operate during that Congress. Among other things, the rules caution a member not to call another a liar even if he is not telling the truth, to not impugn his integrity even if his actions invite it, and to not call him a hypocrite even if he is hypocritical. These circumscriptions are designed to create a climate conducive to deliberation. And central to the ability to deliberate is the presumption of mutual respect.

The founders recognized the importance of civility to deliberation. In the debates at the Constitutional Convention, liberality "as well as prudence induced the delegates to treat each other's opinions with tenderness," recalled John Jay, "to argue without asperity, and to endeavor to convince the judgment without hurting the feelings of each other. Although many weeks were passed in these discussions, some points remained on which a unison of opinions could not be effected. Here again that same happy disposition to unite and conciliate induced them to meet each other; and enable them, by mutual concessions, finally to complete and agree to the plan they have recommended."[8]

In the debate over representation, argument grew heated as delegates favoring a weaker national government pressed the advocates of a strong federal system for assurances that groups of states would not combine to abuse the rights of smaller states. John Lansing, Jr., of New York, spoke on behalf of perfectly equal representation among the states, regardless of size. James Madison, architect of the Virginia proposal, lost patience and replied heatedly. "Can any of the lesser States be endangered by an adequate representation?" he asked. "Where is the probability of a combination? What the inducements? Where is the similarity of customs, manners or religion? If there possibly can be a diversity of interest it is the case of the three large States. Their situation is remote, their trade different. The staple of Massachusetts is fish, and the carrying trade; of Pennsylvania, wheat and flour; of Virginia, tobacco. Can States thus situated in trade ever form a combination?"[9]

Delegates were accustomed to attacks on positions, such as the claim illustrated in Alexander Hamilton's subsequent support of Madison's argument. He pointed to problems with the reasoning rather than deficiencies of the reasoner. "He deduces from these principles the necessity that states entering into a confederacy must retain the equality of votes. This position cannot be correct."[10] The advocate is insulated from direct attack by Hamilton's emphasis on the claim.

Madison violated the implicit rule by specifying slovenly habits of mind and attributing them to the thinkers rather than focusing on the argument: "Those gentlemen who oppose the Virginia plan do not sufficiently analyze the subject. Their remarks, in general, are vague and inconclusive."[11] Sensitive to the prospect of insult and disruption, Benjamin Franklin rose to propose reflection on the uniqueness of the problem and the need to seek divine grace. He suggested prayer.[12] A later commentator observed that "this timely and gracious advice of the aged diplomat produced its desired effect, and the debate resumed the highly impersonal tone of its early stages."[13] Lansing eventually left the convention, but by staying long enough to press his case many times, he bolstered its authority.

The lessons learned in such clashes were shared in memoirs and autobiographies. Ben Franklin recalled:

> When another asserted something that I thought an error I deny'd myself the pleasure of contradicting him abruptly, and of showing immediately some absurdity in his proposition; and in answering I began by observing that in certain cases of circumstances his opinion would be right, but in the present case there appear'd or seem'd to me some difference, etc. I soon found the advantage of this change in my manner; the conversations I engag'd in went on more pleasantly. The modest way in which I propos'd my opinions procur'd them a readier reception and less contradiction; I had less mortification when I was found to be in the wrong and I more easily prevail'd with others to give up their mistakes and join with me when I happened to be in the right.[14]

In public deliberation, civility should work in service of an agenda. Making the case for one agenda over others is best accomplished in engaged argument.

Engaged Argument

Aristotle prized argument; yet argument has a double meaning. On the one hand, it means reasoned discourse, or "the organizing process of disciplined thought."[15] On the other, it signals a clash between two sets of reasoned claims. The first is an "utterance of a sort of communicative act," the second "a particular kind of interaction."[16] For the sake of clarity here, the first is called "argument," and the second "engagement."

Engagement is a process of comparison that enables audiences to determine which argument has the greater force. It emanates from what debate theorists call "clash" and "extension." Clash pits competing argumentative positions against each other in a fashion that invites the audience to select the more persuasive. It carries the argument forward, clarifying in the process the implications of the cases built for each side.

Five decades of scholarship about communication have confirmed that one can embrace and even expect deliberative norms without sacrificing effectiveness with audiences. Since the time of Aristotle, rhetorical theorists have recognized the importance of evidence in the likelihood that an audience will accept a speaker's position. A substantial body of scholarly work confirms that audiences respond more positively to statements that are accompanied with evidence. As Stiff found in a meta-analysis of thirty-one data sets involving over 4,700 subjects, evidence increases the likelihood that a listener or viewer will find a message persuasive.[17] We also know that argument is preferable to assertion; statement with proof is preferable to statement alone. The reason is straightforward: Evidence forms the "philosophical basis for belief."[18]

We also know that discourse needs to establish its relevance to the audience. The effects of evidence are magnified when the message is perceived to be relevant.[19] At the same time, those who feel involved with the message are more likely to reject poor evidence.[20]

Additionally, evidence should be plausible. Belief change can be predicted by the presence of evidence and its perceived plausibility.[21] By presenting evidence before asking an audience to engage in an action, Cronin increased the likelihood that the audience would perform the requested deed.[22]

There are also advantages for the speaker in offering evidence that has a disclosed source. The communication literature tells us that sourced evidence is more effective than nonsourced.[23] Carefully sourced factual evidence can overcome the prejudices of an audience.[24] An individual's "acceptance of information and ideas is based in part on 'who said it.' Whether it is called ethos or source credibility, research consistently has indicated that the more of 'it' the communicator is perceived to have, the more likely the receiver is to accept the transmitted information."[25]

Evidence also should be representative, typical, and consistent. Audiences seem well equipped to make distinctions about the relative weight different sorts of evidence deserve. Persuasive effects are increased when an anecdote is followed by evidence showing its representativeness and typicality.[26] Inconsistent data are less persuasive than consistent evidence.[27] So, for example, editorials containing evidence such as statistics and relevant studies are more persuasive than those based simply in opinion.[28]

Finally, evidence should be accurate. Postmodernism aside, at some level, political discourse presupposes a set of consensually granted or grantable facts. "Freedom of opinion," as Hannah Arendt notes, "is a farce unless factual information is guaranteed and the facts themselves are not in dispute. In other words, factual truth informs political thought."[29] There either are or are not homeless on our streets. The rate of unemployment, measured in a consensually granted way, has either decreased since 1992 or it has not. William Horton either did or did not kill someone while on furlough from a Massachusetts prison. William Jefferson Clinton's semen either was or was not present on Monica Lewinsky's dress.

To all of this, argument theory adds an additional caution: Proof can be counterfeit. The persuasiveness of fallacies "comes from their superficial resemblance to sound arguments; this similarity lends them an air of plausibility."[30] It was this capacity of discourse that prompted Kant to condemn rhetoric as "the art of deluding by means of fair semblance . . . which borrows from poetry only so much as is necessary to win over men's minds to the side of the speaker before they have weighed the matter, and to rob their verdict of its freedom."[31] Such uses of the available means of persuasion confirm Plato's concern that rhetoric can artfully make the untrue appear true.

In traditional terms, the purpose of argument is to demonstrate the legitimacy of a proposition. This is done by weighing the evidence and determining how well it supports the proposed claim. "Unless [an] assertion was made quite wildly and irresponsibly," notes philosopher Stephen Toulin, "we shall normally have some facts to which we can point in its support: if the claim is challenged, it is up to us to appeal to those facts, and present them as the foundation upon which our claim is based."[32]

Facts and shared beliefs are the substance of argument, and commonly shared norms determine the appropriateness of their use. But facts alone are not the self-sufficient stuff of argument. Argument also builds from such bedrock belief as the fact that education is a social good.

Assumed, as well, is common sense as it relates to the "rules of argument." Testimony from those who are self-interested is deserving of special scrutiny. Evidence must not be sundered from context; relevant evidence must be disclosed, not suppressed; like items should be compared to like. A plan that is offered may legitimately be tested by asking whether it meets a need and whether the advantages that follow from it outweigh the disadvantages.

These assumptions produce both a robust rhetoric and one capable of mobilizing an audience, in part because they place comparable responsibilities on the shoulders of all who enter the deliberative arena. A person who makes a claim has an obligation to defend it with evidence. Evidence should be relevant, consistent, typical, and representative.

The End of Rhetoric Is Judgment

We should recover the classical notion that the end of rhetoric is judgment (*krinate*) and recover as well the notion that one test of deliberative rhetoric should be whether the discourse respects and enhances the audience's faculty of judgment. In the society envisioned by Aristotle, the audience listened to all sides of a case and then judged it justly. Deliberation joined practical wisdom (*phronesis*) and judgment. The "most characteristic function of a man of practical wisdom is to deliberate well. . . . In an unqualified sense, that man is good at deliberating who, by reasoning, can aim at and reach the best thing attainable to man by action."[33]

To arrive at warranted judgment through deliberation requires a focus on the substance of the argument, not the person of the advocate. Vilification and ad hominem arguments get in the way of deliberation by shifting the focus of debate to what congressional rules call "personalities."

In two centuries of political speech, we have developed public norms for appropriate discourse as well as some sense of the ideal to which it should aspire. We assume that both sides have a right to be heard, that argument should be backed by proof, that the fairness and accuracy of the evidence should be subject to scrutiny, that the context from which evidence emerges should not be distorted, that those whose positions are questioned have a right to reply, that in the process of engaging in argument consensus could emerge, and that those making claims should be held responsible for them. The exchanges presuppose that those on opposing sides will grant the goodwill and integrity of their opponents. They assume that those involved in the discussion will not be swayed by specious claims or attacks that appeal to prejudice rather than reason, and that the end of the engagement is a judgment to which each side commits itself and for which it is accountable. An alien viewing this public discussion would assume that all parties disapprove of selective uses of the evidence and resent having statements taken out of context.

When these norms are honored, areas of disagreement and agreement are clarified. The collective understanding of an issue is advanced. The commitment of all participants to the legitimacy of the system is reinforced. The community is better for the experience, and—to the extent possible—reason, not rancor, is the order of the day.

Of course, the foregoing premises resonate of an idealism rarely realized in practice. The effort to impeach President Clinton provides a good case study in how realities overwhelmed such idealism. One troubling aspect of the 1998 debate in the Judiciary Committee over the four articles of impeachment was that both sides violated the rules of deliberative discourse in ways that worked to diminish the audience's capacity to judge. Each side selectively used evidence. A report released by the White House as the deliberations began made that claim: "The referral repeatedly and demonstrably omitted or mischaracterized directly relevant evidence that exonerates the President of the very allegations leveled by the [Office of the Independent Counsel]." As evidence, the report cited such lapses as the referral's omission that Betty Currie responded "none whatsoever" when she was asked if she was pressured by Clinton's statements to her in the Oval Office after his testimony before the grand jury.[34]

What norm was being violated? The report called the referral "not a neutral presentation of the facts. It reflects a careful selection and presentation of the evidence designed to portray the President in the worst possible light. It is being presented as a good faith summary of reliable evidence when it is in fact nothing of the kind." We are accustomed to selective uses of evidence in political campaigns but surprised to see it in deliberations about something as consequential as impeachment of a president.

The Clinton defense team made similar moves. In the same document, the White House argued: "Both the Starr referral and Mr. Schippers' presentation to the committee start from the incorrect premise that the President testified that he was never alone with Ms. Lewinsky. In fact, the President did not deny that he had been alone with Ms. Lewinsky. For example, the President answered 'yes' to the question 'your testimony is that it was possible, then, that you were alone with her?'"[35] The Alice in Wonderland quality of the debate was magnified when a proponent of impeachment told a White House spokesperson that in answer to the question by Paula Jones's attorney (i.e., "At any time were you and Monica Lewinsky alone together in the Oval Office?"), "the President's answer," said the impeachment advocate, "was 'I don't recall.'" He added, "And then he goes on."[36] Neither side's defenders presented Clinton's entire answer in context. If they had, they might have concluded that Clinton's acknowledgment that he had been alone with Lewinsky invited the inference that their time alone was spent transacting business.

The pattern recurred. The impeachment proponent asked, "Now Mr. Craig, did he lie to the American people when he said 'I never had sex with that woman'? Did he lie?" But as Craig pointed out, in that statement Clinton denied not sex but sexual relations. Although some might argue that this is a distinction without a difference, Clinton was nonetheless entitled to be accurately quoted.

The process also violated a basic sense of evenhandedness. During the months of hearings held by the House Judiciary Committee in 1974 to consider the impeachment of President Richard Nixon, the president's lawyer, James St. Clair, was present in the hearing room and free to comment and ask questions.[37] This difference in the two cases led Representative Conyers to claim in the Clinton matter that "The majority have simply rubber stamped the uncross-examined, untested, double hearsay, yes, triple hearsay and conclusions of the independent counsel without conducting any factual investigation of its own."[38] Lost in this environment was the notion expressed by Walter Lippmann in *The Public Philosophy* that "because the purpose of [confronting ideas] . . . is to discern the truth, there are rules of evidence and of parliamentary procedure, there are codes of fair dealing and fair comment, by which a loyal man will consider himself bound when he exercises the right to publish opinions."[39]

Both fair dealing and fair comment were violated in a series of exchanges between Democratic presidential contenders Bill Bradley and Al Gore in December 1999. Bradley told the *Washington Post* that under certain circumstances he would consider *either* cutting *or* raising taxes to pay for his proposed health care plan that would provide vouchers the uninsured, underinsured, and poor could use to buy health insurance. The circumstances? If closing loopholes in the tax code failed to produce projected savings, or if the rate of economic growth dropped below projections. The Gore campaign misleadingly abridged Bradley's statement to allege that "Bradley said he might raise taxes to try to pay for his costly proposals."[40] A chart Gore drew for a reporter then translated future contingencies into current conditions. Under "current circumstances" it said "*AG* No New Taxes!" "*BB* May Raise Taxes to pay for health plan."[41] The deliberative model holds that rhetoric—the art of persuasion—is at its best when it turns citizens into judges, giving them the arguments and information they need to make considered political decisions. It was through rhetoric, the ancients held, that communal identity was created and reinforced. Rhetoric not only illuminated alternative courses of action but also celebrated and enlivened the values upon which the polity was built.

How does contemporary presidential campaign rhetoric measure up to this ideal? Those aspiring to the presidency rarely lie outright. When they mislead, it is by selectively omitting evidence that does not advance their cause, and by doing so invite false inferences. To minimize these tendencies, we need to establish a new set of expectations about campaign discourse. That set of expectations should take the following form: In the speeches, ads, and debates that constitute their discourse, candidates should be unambiguous and fair and should not employ guilt by association. They should also be consistent, accurate, and unbiased and tell the full story, not the partial truth, and establish its relevance to governance. The reason for such a blueprint is straightforward: Judgment is facilitated when civil engaged argument adheres to these principles. It is useful to analyze the 1996 campaign to see how short it fell of this ideal.

Unambiguous

This confusing exchange occurred during the 1996 vice-presidential debate between Al Gore and Jack Kemp:

Gore: We have empowerment zones and enterprise communities, 105 of them, in communities all across the United States of America.

Kemp: Well with all due respect, Jim [moderator Jim Lehrer], there are nine empowerment zones, [and] tinkering with tax credits around the country for inner cities. Los Angeles after the riots did not even get an empowerment zone, believe it or not.

Gore: We did put an empowerment zone in South Central Los Angeles. It is in the form of the largest community development financial institution ever created in the United States or in any other country. And it is creating jobs in South Central Los Angeles right now. The Congress passed an enterprise zone after the Los Angeles riots five years ago. It was vetoed by the prior administration.

Kemp: Well, we've had four years and there's no enterprise zone. There are empowerment zones, but you have to do what Bill Clinton and Al Gore want you to do.

Gore: Well, we have 105 empowerment zones and enterprise communities all across the United States of America. And with all due respect, that's 105 more than were there when we came into the White House.

Part of the confusion in this dialogue is linguistic. In 1980, Kemp proposed enterprise zones—areas in cities and rural regions in which tax incentives would be available to businesses. The Democrats call these "empowerment zones" and "added grants and social programs." In December 1994, six cities and three rural areas were designated empowerment zones (hence Kemp's claim). Each received $100 million in grants and access to $250 million in tax incentives over ten years. Los Angeles was not among the nine (hence Kemp's second claim). However, Los Angeles was given a special designation and awarded a $125 million grant (hence Gore's claim). And many (95) that did not receive empowerment-zone funding were classed as "enterprise communities" and given $3 million grants and a smaller tax-incentive package (hence Gore's carefully worded "empowerment zones and enterprise communities").[42]

Another exchange in the Gore-Kemp debate required a careful look at the meaning of the word "said":

> **Gore:** Bob Dole said in February of this year, this is the strongest economy in thirty years.

The words did appear in a prepared text of Dole's winter speech to the New Hampshire legislature, but in his delivery Dole instead said "some would say" the economy is the strongest it has been in thirty years. He then went on to indict the country's slow economic growth.

Fair and in Context

A Clinton ad in 1996 claimed that "12 million have used medical leave" under Clinton's Family and Medical Leave Act. It is true that 12 million had taken a leave, but 9.5 million of those individuals could have taken it without the protections of Clinton's legislation because their employers were already providing the benefit when the bill was signed into law. Similarly, when the Clinton ads said he would "cut taxes," they failed to mention that the proposed cuts were not available to all families. Specifically, the $500-a-year child tax credit (for each child under 13) was available only to families making less than $75,000.

Clinton wasn't alone in violating basic standards of fairness in 1996. In one of the debates of 1996 Dole said, "Stop scaring the seniors, Mr. President. You've already spent $45 million scaring seniors and tearing me apart." This figure assumed that the entire Clinton/Democratic National Committee advertising budget was focused on attack with an anti-Dole message about Medicare. It wasn't.

Hypotheticals and Estimates Treated As Fact

In one of the debates, Dole reconstructed a hypothetical as fact when he said, "You had a surgeon—or before General McCaffrey, you had a lady who said we ought to consider legalizing drugs." Jocelyn Elders's statement was posed as a hypothetical, which does not qualify as "we ought to consider."

Consistency in Argument

This standard assumes that what is good for the goose is good for the gander. In 1996 a Clinton ad claimed that Dole would have "cut Medicare." The Republicans would have increased funding at a slower rate than the Democrats. If this is a cut, however, then the Democrats should also have defined some of Clinton's actions as cuts (such as freezing the level of funding for safe and drug-free schools).

Similarly, Dole said to Clinton during one of the debates: "The record is pretty clear in Arkansas. When you were governor, drug use doubled." If Clinton, as governor, was responsible for the increase in drug use in Arkansas, then presumably we can extrapolate that the Republican governors were responsible for the rise in teen drug use in their states during Clinton's term as president.

Accuracy

The public believes that Republicans are more likely than Democrats to cut social programs. A Clinton ad capitalized on this assumption by claiming that "Their budget [Republican] would have forced rural hospital closings." What the American Hospital Association actually said was that under the GOP budget, hospitals "could be forced to shut their doors."[43] "Could" is a weaker, more tentative claim than "would."

In 1996, Republican ads repeatedly misstated the effect of the Clinton tax increase by alleging that it increased the taxes of middle-class taxpayers. In an ad focusing on taxes, the Dole-Kemp campaign's announcer said, "But he [Clinton] gave the middle class the largest tax increase in history." The deception was forecast in ads aired early in the general-election campaign that mistakenly reported that the typical family paid more than $1,500 in additional taxes under Clinton. Another Dole ad showed blue-collar workers while noting on the screen the total amount of the Clinton tax increase. In fact, the Clinton tax hike focused on upper-income seniors on Social Security and those Americans in the upper 1.5 percent of income earners.

However, Gore also misstated the administration's record on taxes in the 1996 debate: "That is a record of promises made and promises kept. He [Clinton] promised middle-income tax cuts. We've cut taxes for 15 million families." However, the Clinton "cut" (the earned income tax credit) was for lower-income families, not middle-class ones.

67

Since Republicans favor reduced government, they are prone to focus on increases in the size of the federal workforce that occur under a Democratic president. For example, Dole said in one of the debates: "There are actually more people in government, except for the people in defense-related jobs." However, the Office of Personnel Management described the government payroll as the smallest since the Johnson administration. Proportionately, the payroll was the smallest since before World War II. However, the downsizing in the federal government was accompanied by an increase in use of contractors and subcontractors.

In the vice-presidential debate of 1996, Gore said of the administration-sponsored loan guarantees to Mexico: "We've ended up making a $500 million profit. All of the loans have been paid back." Not true. The *New York Times* reported that at the time of the debate, Mexico still owed $3.5 billion.[44]

Unbiased

A Dole ad said, "Two incomes needed to make ends meet." One source was the *U.S. 1996 Housing and Household Economic Statistics,* which did not contain that claim but did document an increase in two-income households without ascribing a cause. The second source was a quote from Hilda Betterman and H. Todd Van Dellen in the *Minneapolis Star.*[45] Undisclosed was the fact that the two were Republican state representatives.

The Full Story, Not a Partial Truth

In an ad with the theme "preserve," the Clinton-Gore campaign quoted Dole saying, "I was there, fighting the fight, voting against Medicare, one of twelve, because we knew it wouldn't work." The announcer added a standard claim from the Clinton-Gore ads: "Last year Dole/Gingrich tried to cut Medicare $270 billion." However, as the debates and news articles and editorials indicated, this claim told only part of the story: Dole had an alternative plan to Medicare called Eldercare. And as I noted earlier, the Democrats would have cut Medicare too, although less.

A Dole ad claimed "The AARP flatly stated that our plan will increase Medicare spending—7% a year. And they're right." But the AARP also said that "both sides have proposed cuts" and criticized the Republican plan for being too drastic.

Dole said in one of the 1996 debates: "And I may be better off four years from now, but—I don't know—I look at the slowest growth in this century. He [Clinton] inherited a growth of 4.7, 4.8 percent; now it's down to about 2.4 percent." Across fourteen Clinton quarters, the total was 2.5 percent, not a major difference from the 2.4 percent Dole claimed, but that figure was above the 1.2 percent for the same period under George Bush. In other words, the growth under Bush, Clinton's Republican predecessor, was slower than it had been to that point under Clinton.

Direct Relevance to Governance

If attack is used as a tool, the attack should be about something over which the attackee had control or jurisdiction and which the attacker would have changed or done differently. In one of the debates of 1996, Dole claimed that "For the first time in history, you pay about 40 percent of what you earn—more than you spend for food, clothing and shelter combined—for taxes under this administration." However, this figure was an aggregate of federal, state, and local taxes, and Clinton couldn't be held responsible for state and local taxes. Furthermore, the figure was wrong. The Congressional Budget Office put the total at 29 percent, with the federal portion at 19 percent, which was slightly down from previous years.

In addition, an attack should include disclosure of what the candidate making the claim would have done or did do that the opponent did not. In one of the 1996 debates, Clinton stated: "Let me just mention, Senator Dole voted for $900 billion in tax increases." This figure did not include the tax cuts Dole had supported and didn't allow for the fact that some of that money was what "saved" Social Security, something Clinton praised Dole for in one of the debates. Clinton presumably would have cast the same vote had he been in the Senate at the time.

As citizens we should see ourselves and others as the co-makers of argument and co-users of evidence whose task it is to explore alternatives in a spirit open to education and persuasion, a spirit that ennobles those who are members of our audience as well as those who are engaged with us in the process of finding solutions. In such a realm, as Thomas Jefferson recognized, democracy is safe. "We believed," he wrote of his philosophy, "that men, habituated to thinking for themselves, and to follow their reason as guide, would be more easily and safely governed than with minds nourished in error and vitiated and debased."[46]

As long as campaigns employ—if only in part—selective truth telling, and the press and public accept this practice without objection, we tolerate discourse that diminishes the disposition of voters to deliberate at and the capacity of those elected to govern.

Kathleen Hall Jamieson

Chapter Six

Do the Quotes of Scholars Add Anything Different to the News?

S PEND A SHORT TIME at a communication or political science convention and you are likely to hear scholars opining that there is too much talk about campaign strategy in political news coverage and too little about the substantive similarities and differences of the candidates. The not too subtle implication is that if scholars were quoted more and the rest of the sources in the reporters' Rolodexes quoted less, coverage would improve.

But do scholars say anything quotable that distinguishes them from paid political consultants, or, for that matter, from people in the street? The Annenberg research team stripped the identifying context from four weeks of quotes found in the political coverage of the *New York Times*, the NBC evening news, and the *Washington Post* in October 1996. Only quotes that included at least one complete sentence were selected. Before being decontextualized, each of the 274 quotes was identified by source: consultant, scholar in a university, scholar in a think tank (e.g., Brookings Institution or the American Enterprise Institute), or person in the street. (Because the coders were familiar with my ideas and voice, my quoted comments were excluded from the sample.) In each of the four categories, the quoted material was equally likely to focus either on strategy or issues and on ascribing candidate or campaign motive. That finding does not necessarily mean, however, that the academic voice was indistinct.

To see whether it was, ten quotes were randomly drawn from each of the four source categories. Each quote, but not the source, was placed on a white index card and the deck shuffled. Using any cues they could divine, ten coders independently tried to sort the forty cards by source. No coder was able to accurately assign more than three of the ten quotes to the correct source category.

It's possible, of course, that reporters asked questions only about strategy and motive and that scholars responded in kind. Alternatively, reporters may have selectively chosen quotes that featured strategy and motive from a broader menu. However, it is unlikely that the reporters simply made up the quotes.

The press should be able to look to scholars to evaluate contemporary campaigns with an eye toward increasing the amount of substance—and the degree of accountability—provided by candidates and the media that cover them. Universities and think tanks are teeming with highly paid, well-educated professionals who have devoted large numbers of waking hours to understanding social issues from education policy to methods of crime prevention to proposed policies in Bosnia. Scholars who want to decrease the amount of talk about strategy and motives might be well advised not to provide answers that accept the very paradigm that stymies open discussion on the issues that affect the electorate. Were they to adopt this point of view, I suspect that the scholarly voice would become distinguishable from the others in news about politics.

Kathleen Hall Jamieson

Chapter Seven

Are Voters Smarter Than Pundits, the Press, and Scholars About Attack in Politics?

I F A NON-ENGLISH-SPEAKING VISITOR from the Ukraine were to try to learn American English by watching news about our political campaigns, she would assume that something called "negativity" is a form of poison increasingly infecting all forms of political discourse. Also on her list of pejoratives would be the word "attack," and she might conclude that "negativity" and "attack" are synonyms. By listening to the context in which these words are spoken and the tone in which they are uttered, she might well surmise that they are epithets of a sort. And from the fact that they are not usually defined but rather have their meaning assumed, she might infer that there is widespread cultural consensus about their meaning.

Our visitor would be well advised to consult a few of the locals before embracing any of these assumptions. Unlike the press, pundits, and many academics, voters understand that contrast ads (which make a case against the opposing candidate and for the sponsor of the ad) are superior to those that simply attack. The public also sees personal attack as more problematic than attack on issues, inflammatory ads as more problematic than civil ones. And citizens view deceptive attack as more "negative," irresponsible, more of a turnoff, and less informative than truthful attack.

These distinctions—made by the public but not by the press—make sense for a number of reasons. Attack and contrast advertisements actually contain more relevant issue content than those containing no information about the sponsor's opposing candidate. As we will show in a later chapter, using the Annenberg Campaign Mapping Data Base, we coded ads produced for the 1952–1996 presidential campaigns in order to determine the percentage of policy content found among the different categories of political advertisements. Our analysis showed that attack advertisements contained a greater percentage of policy words than did advocacy or contrast ads. This finding is significant because in academic and popular discourse, both attack and contrast ads often fall under the pejorative heading "negative advertising."

Contrast ads are superior to those that simply attack for another reason. By including advocacy, the ads identify the sponsoring candidate, which then makes it possible for those who disapprove of the attack to hold the perpetrator accountable. Finally, by defending the sponsor while attacking the opponent, contrast ads offer voters reassurance that the issue or biographical fact being featured is a legitimate basis for differentiating the two candidates. The likelihood that the opponent is being indicted for actions the sponsor has also supported is dramatically reduced in contrast ads.

Surveyors miss these distinctions when they ask about "negativity" and not about contrast versus attack, or honest versus dishonest attack, or personal versus issue-based attack. In response to polling questions, the American public routinely lists "negative advertising" or "negative campaigning" among complaints about the U.S. electoral system. But what, specifically, do Americans mean by negative advertising?

A 1998 national survey for the Annenberg School for Communication and Annenberg Public Policy Center found that when it comes to political advertising, Americans speak a sophisticated and consistent language. They do not dismiss all advertising critical of an opponent as "negative" or "bad," but rather they make a number of sensible distinctions.

By probing attitudes toward specific advertising formats, this survey expanded on previous ones on "negative advertising." To ensure that respondents had a clear idea of the concepts they were being asked about, they were read hypothetical ads and scenarios and asked for their evaluations of each. Among the findings were these:

- Most survey participants distinguished between one-sided attack ads and two-sided contrast ads.
- Most found contrast ads substantially more responsible and more useful than attack ads. Similarly, most found contrast ads less negative and less of a political turnoff than attack ads.

- Participants disliked attack ads, but were particularly bothered by attack ads that used inflammatory language or attacked an opponent's personal life.
- Participants were least tolerant of misleading attacks.

These evaluations of different ad types largely reflected ad format, whether it can broadly be said that the ad was attack or not, not whether the respondent agreed or disagreed with the content of the ad. Additionally, evaluations of the different ad formats were broadly similar across all demographic groups.

For this survey, 2,000 adults, age eighteen and older, were interviewed nationwide by Princeton Survey Research Associates between August 19 and September 20, 1998. For much of the survey, the sample was split into groups that were read different hypothetical ads and scenarios. By our definition, attack ads were one-sided, only criticizing the opponent; contrast ads were two-sided, pairing criticism with a statement of the sponsor's strengths.

We randomly assigned respondents to hear hypothetical ads on one of two topics, Social Security reform or crime. Within these groups, respondents heard both a one-sided attack ad on the topic and a two-sided contrast version. Respondents rated the ads as responsible (very or somewhat) or irresponsible (very or somewhat) and useful (great deal or somewhat) or not useful (not too or not at all).[1]

Seven in ten respondents said that a two-sided contrast ad about Social Security reform was responsible (65 percent) and useful (75 percent), while four in ten said a one-sided attack about Social Security was responsible (37 percent) and useful (40 percent). Similarly, seven in ten found a two-sided contrast ad about crime responsible (67 percent) and useful (73 percent), but only four in ten found a one-sided attack version responsible (44 percent) and useful (45 percent).

Also by large margins, respondents deemed contrast ads less negative and less likely to turn off voters than attack ads. Respondents rated whether the ads about Social Security or crime were negative (very or somewhat) or not negative (not too or not at all) and how much they would turn people off from politics (great deal or somewhat) or not turn them off (not too much or not at all).

Seven in ten said the one-sided attack about Social Security reform was negative (67 percent) and would turn people from politics (68 percent), compared with four in ten who said the two-sided contrast version was negative (38 percent) and a turnoff (42 percent). Similarly, the attack ad about crime was perceived as more negative (68 percent versus 48 per-

FIGURE 7.1   Contrast ad less negative than attack, less likely to turn off voters.

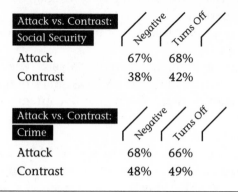

Attack vs. Contrast: Social Security	Negative	Turns Off
Attack	67%	68%
Contrast	38%	42%

Attack vs. Contrast: Crime	Negative	Turns Off
Attack	68%	66%
Contrast	48%	49%

cent) and more likely to turn people off (66 percent versus 49 percent) than the contrast ad on the same topic. (See Figure 7.1.)

Survey respondents gave consistent evaluations of both ads, regardless of format. Those who evaluated contrast ads as responsible also tended to see them as useful, not negative, and not the kind of ad that would turn people off. Attack ads also drew consistent responses. Because these ratings were consistent, they were combined into a single measure of ad quality. Thus, a high-quality ad was deemed responsible, useful, not negative, and not a turnoff for people. Seven in ten respondents judged contrast ads as high quality (76 percent for Social Security, 71 percent for crime), while four in ten judged attack ads as high quality (35 percent for Social Security, 44 percent for crime). Conversely, a low-quality ad was deemed not responsible and not useful, negative, and a turnoff for people. Six in ten respondents perceived attack ads as of low quality (65 percent for Social Security, 56 percent for crime), while only three in ten defined contrast ads the same way (24 percent for Social Security, 29 percent for crime).

For the most part, these evaluations of contrast and attack reflected how respondents felt about the format, not the content, of the ads. In the hypothetical Social Security ads, the sponsor criticized the opponent for wanting to reform Social Security by allowing people to invest their payroll contributions in the stock market. The sponsor wanted to use the budget surplus to shore up the system. In the crime ads, the sponsor criticized the opponent for opposing the death penalty. The sponsor favored the death penalty for those who had engaged in violent acts.

Before asking respondents to evaluate the one-sided attack ad and the two-sided contrast ad, we asked them whether they agreed or disagreed with the two positions for which the ads criticized the opponents: allowing Social Security contributions to be invested in the stock market and thinking the death penalty is wrong.

With the Social Security ads, the respondents' position on how to reform Social Security had little influence on their opinion of the contrast ad and no influence on opinion of the attack ad. Those who favored allowing contributions to be invested in the stock market were only somewhat more likely to judge the contrast ad as high quality (79 percent) than those who opposed allowing contributions to be invested in the stock market (72 percent). Those who favored allowing stock market contributions were as likely to judge the attack as high quality as those who disagreed.

With the crime ads, attitudes toward the death penalty played a similarly small role in shaping opinion. Respondents who favored the death penalty were slightly more likely to judge the contrast ad highly (73 percent) than those who opposed the death penalty (64 percent). Supporters of the death penalty were as likely to judge the attack as high quality as those who disagreed about the death penalty.

For both the Social Security reform and crime ads, majorities favored contrast over attack regardless of their feelings about the positions the ads criticized. In other words, evaluations of these ads focused largely on their format, not content.

Positive assessment of contrast cut across all demographic groups. After we took into account gender, age, race, education, media exposure, political orientation (liberal or conservative), and political involvement, large majorities of respondents still judged contrast ads as high quality and attack ads as low quality.

In sum, compared with contrast advertising, attack ads were seen as more negative, less informative, more irresponsible, and more likely to turn people off from politics. Respondents who were young, who followed politics closely, who were better educated, and who were bothered by the conduct of current campaigns were more likely to prefer contrast to attack. In order to measure this, a "dissatisfaction with campaign conduct" index was constructed from answers about concerns regarding the amount of money politicians spend on campaigns, political advertising on TV and radio, what politicians say to get elected, news coverage of campaigns, the ethics and morals of those running for office, and negative campaigning.

Americans clearly dislike attack ads, but in their view, not all attacks are created equal. The public particularly dislikes attacks that use inflammatory language. It is more tolerant of attack ads that use civil, evenhanded language. The attack ads discussed to this point were civil attacks that used evenhanded language. Inflammatory attack goes beyond straightforward criticism to make hyperbolic claims and to categorically dismiss the opponent.

Recall that four in ten respondents saw civil attack as responsible (37 percent for Social Security, 44 percent for crime), and seven in ten rated it negatively (67 percent for Social Security, 68 percent for crime). But when the same attack contained inflammatory language, it was judged less favorably. Three in ten said an inflammatory attack was responsible (29 percent for Social Security, 33 percent for crime), and fully eight in ten said it was negative (80 percent for Social Security, 78 percent for crime). Inflammatory attack also was judged as more likely than civil attack to turn voters off (79 percent versus 68 percent for Social Security, 71 percent versus 66 percent for crime).

However, attack ads with inflammatory language were thought to be as useful as attacks that were civil and evenhanded. For both formats and both topics, four in ten respondents saw the ads as useful. Because the inflammatory and civil variants presented the same information, that finding makes sense. For many respondents, hyperbolic claims and categorical dismissals of the opponent detracted from an ad's appeal but not its usefulness.

Participants in the survey were less tolerant of attacks on an opponent's personal life and more tolerant of attacks on policy positions. Respondents who heard ads about Social Security were asked to evaluate an attack ad about an opponent's admitted drug experimentation in college. Respondents who heard ads about crime were asked to evaluate an attack ad about an opponent's admitted extramarital affair.

Attacks on an opponent's personal life were judged less favorably than attacks on policy issues. Three in ten said attacking an opponent for trying drugs in college (27 percent) or for admitting an extramarital affair (31 percent) was responsible, compared with four in ten who said attacks on Social Security reform (37 percent) or crime (44 percent) met that test. Similarly, attacks on personal life were perceived as less useful (33 percent for drug experimentation, 37 percent for extramarital affair) than attacks on policy (40 percent for Social Security, 45 percent for crime). And attacks on personal life were perceived as more negative (78 percent for drug experimentation, 75 percent for extramarital affair) than attacks on policy (67 percent for Social Security, 68 percent for crime).

Of all the advertising types we tested, attack advertising that was misleading received the lowest tolerance rating. In the last hypothetical ad scenario, respondents were told that the ads they had heard about Social Security or crime were misleading.

The Social Security ads were misleading because they criticized the opponent for wanting to allow people to invest Social Security contributions in the stock market even though the ad's sponsor also favored this plan. The crime ads were misleading because they criticized the opponent for categorically opposing the death penalty when in fact the opponent supported the death penalty in some cases.

Of all the ad variants we tested, misleading attack was judged to have the lowest quality. For the ads about Social Security, almost eight in ten respondents (78 percent) judged misleading attack as low quality, compared with seven in ten for inflammatory (72 percent) and personal (73 percent) attack and six in ten (65 percent) for attack that was civil, about policy, and presumed accurate. Similarly, for the ads about crime, misleading attack was judged substantially less favorably (71 percent low quality) than civil, policy-related attack that was presumed accurate (56 percent).

Evaluations of inflammatory attack and misleading criticism reflected the ad format, not content. Respondents' evaluations of inflammatory attack and misleading criticism were unrelated to their positions on either Social Security reform or crime policy. Respondents judged inflammatory and misleading attack ads unfavorably regardless of whether they agreed or disagreed with allowing Social Security contributions to be invested in the stock market or with the death penalty.

Pundits and scholars who collapse all attack ads into the catchall category "negative campaigning" are treating the complex world of political ads in a simplistic manner that is not shared by the citizenry at large. This is yet another example of actual campaign conduct being "veiled" in imprecise language that pundits and scholars fail to expose. Perhaps most troubling is the possibility that the opinions of pundits and scholars may at times stand in for the public—thus reinforcing a failure on both sides to engage in public life and political rhetoric as it is really practiced. Finally, voters are smarter than these other voices because they recognize the content of contrast ads as sources of useful campaign information underreported elsewhere.

Kathleen Hall Jamieson, Chris Adasiewicz,
and Mary McIntosh

Chapter Eight

Was Voter Turnout in 1996 the Lowest Since 1924?

I N THE WEEK AFTER THE 1996 ELECTION, many observers expressed concern about the reported 48.8 percent turnout. Pundits worried that the president of the United States had been elected in a contest in which less than half of the eligible electorate cast a ballot. Although low voter participation is cause for concern, the final vote was not as low as those early projections suggested. Indeed, some commentators set the total percent casting a ballot at some level at 54.5 percent, slightly more than 2 percent higher than the low point reached in 1988. Others placed it at 52.8 percent in 1996. Still others pegged it at 51.9 percent.

Those who think that voter turnout is calculated on actual numbers of votes divided by actual numbers of citizens of voting age eligible to vote are likely to be confused when different scholars offer different final-vote percentages.

To understand the differences in projected voting, it is important to ask whether those tallying the votes include absentee ballots and votes cast for offices other than but not for president, and whether everyone counted as part of the denominator is in fact eligible to vote. Because the category "voting-age population," which is calculated by the U.S. Census Bureau, excludes military personnel, their dependents, and eligible voters living outside the United States but includes the much larger population of noncitizens (illegal and legal but not naturalized aliens), those in mental institutions, and those who have lost the franchise through conviction as felons, the voting-age population is larger than the population of voting age that is actually eligible to vote. Since the percent of the population jailed as felons, or on parole or probation, is high and rising, and since in most instances felons are ineligible to vote, including them in the total voting pool swells it with ineligible nonvoters. The result is an artificial drop in turnout.

Moreover, if the proportion of the population that is ineligible to vote is increasing more rapidly than the proportion that is eligible, then comparable levels of voting will look like a dropoff over time. Whether turnout was lower in 1996 than at any time since 1924 is a function of which set of assumptions and which sets of data are used.

This elision of facts as fundamental to a participatory democracy as voter turnout reflects the disinclination of reporters—in the abbreviated format of much contemporary news—to focus on the background information that would make turnout a more useful albeit more complex indicator of the health of the polity. When reporters ask simply "Was turnout up or down? Was it the best turnout, the worst, or somewhere in between?" they are misframing the issue by failing to stipulate a definition of turnout. The complex answer that reflects reality makes a poor soundbite. Accordingly, we are led to believe that there is agreement on the measure and the reported turnout when the scholars who report the figures know that is not the case.

Kathleen Hall Jamieson

Chapter Nine

The Gender Gap in Political Knowledge: Are Women Less Knowledgeable Than Men About Politics?

I N THE AREA OF POLITICAL PARTICIPATION, women are more likely than men to vote. Since 1980, women have voted either at the same or at a higher rate than men.[1] Why then do scholars consistently find that women answer fewer questions correctly about political affairs than do men?[2] Bennett and Bennett reported that the 1986 NES data revealed, for example, that men on average gave more correct answers than did women in response to questions asking if the respondents knew the government positions held by six men.[3] The real answer to this question might lie less in how much women "know" and more in how we account for what they know.

Selected Research Studies
of Political Knowledge

Delli Carpini and Keeter point out that the status of women changed substantially between 1947 and 1989: Educational attainment became comparable between the sexes; a greater female presence developed in the labor force; and the number of women seeking political office rose. Nevertheless, gender differences in political knowledge persisted.[4] Their analysis of responses from 1947 through 1989 revealed gender differences at each level of education, with men more likely than women to answer political questions correctly. Surprisingly, the magnitude of the gender differences in 1989 was similar to that in 1947.

One explanation for the discrepancy might be difference in level of interest. That alternative, however, proved flawed when the knowledge gap persisted even after researchers controlled for level of attention paid to politics. The assumption of lack of interest also falters in the face of the finding that women vote in higher proportions than men.

Another theory suggests that when men aren't sure about an answer, they are more likely to guess and, in the process, to gain the advantage from a scoring system that does not penalize wrong answers and rewards right ones. The plausibility of this hypothesis is increased by the fact that women were more likely than men to give "don't know" responses.[5] There was a net difference in the number of "don't know" responses that women and men gave in answering questions about political knowledge.

Indeed, it is difficult to know what "don't know" means. Sanchez and Morchio explain: "Different respondents use the same words to signify different things—ignorance, indecision, or uncertainty about the meaning of the question asked."[6] So how is someone to sort all this out? Using data from the University of Michigan's Survey Research Center's election studies in 1960, 1964, and 1968, Francis and Busch analyzed patterns in "don't know" and "no opinion" responses, which they termed "nonsubstantive responses," or "NSRs." They concluded that survey researchers should not exclude respondents giving nonsubstantive responses and should not combine them with other categories.[7] Important to note is that "nonsubstantive response" is a phrase coined by researchers and may not reflect how substantive respondents think that their choice is. It is possible that "don't know" responses are perceived to be substantive by some respondents. In either event, it is important to distinguish between a lack of knowledge and an unwillingness to answer based on incomplete knowledge.

Francis and Busch observed that females, nonwhites, low-educated, and noninvolved respondents with feelings of low political efficacy gave the most nonsubstantive responses. Females were more than twice as likely as their male counterparts to give such responses on 15 percent or more of the questions in 1960, 1964, and 1968.[8] In a footnote, however, Francis and Busch suggested that the low NSR rate for males might have been a function of the sex of the interviewers. Most of the interviewers who collected the data were female. Males may have been more likely to give substantive responses to female interviewers.[9]

Sanchez and Morchio arrived at the conclusion that it may not be desirable, when asking knowledge questions, to probe respondents until they give a substantive answer. In their analysis of the American National Election Study of 1984, the results obtained from telephone interviews differed from the results obtained from field interviews because telephone interviewers probed the knowledge questions significantly more than did the field interviewers. Sixty-six percent of those interviewed by telephone gave answers to the four knowledge questions, compared with 43 percent of those interviewed face-to-face. Something other than knowledge appeared to be contributing to the higher average number of correct answers from those interviewed by telephone (2.08) versus those interviewed face-to-face (1.70). Using probability theory, Sanchez and Morchio tested whether the probed answers were due to more than guesswork. Each knowledge question offered a binary choice (Democrat or Republican). Researchers posited that a correct response rate of 50 percent would suggest that the results were the by-product of pure guesswork. They discovered that "[n]one of the percent estimates reflecting correct mentions for probed TEL (telephone) answers is significantly different from the predicted 50 percent."[10]

To better understand the gender gap in political knowledge, we analyzed responses from political-knowledge questions posed to 929 voters after the 1996 election. Twenty-nine questions were asked on topics ranging from which presidential candidate favored a "fifteen percent across the board tax cut" to "permitting late-term abortions using the so-called partial birth abortion procedure when the life or health of the mother is at stake." Answers were limited to "Clinton," "Dole," "both," "neither," and "don't know" responses. Participants answered an average of 14.00 questions correctly and 10.85 incorrectly. On average, respondents gave 4.14 "don't know" responses to the twenty-nine candidate position questions.[11]

We began our analysis by creating political-knowledge scales in three different ways. First, we used the traditional method of giving each correct answer one point; "don't know" responses and incorrect answers received no points. Second, we tallied incorrect responses. Each incorrect response received one point; "don't know" responses and correct answers received no points. Third, "don't know" responses were tallied with each "don't know" response receiving one point; correct and incorrect responses received no points. Using regression models,[12] we analyzed each of these political-knowledge scales as the dependent variable controlling for sex, age, education, income, media use, political interest, amount of political talk with friends or family, race, and party identification.

The gender of the respondent was a significant predictor of correct answers and "don't know" responses. (See Table A9.1 in Appendix IV.) The sex variable accounted for a 2.08 difference in correct answers when we controlled for several other factors. Men gave more correct answers than did women. When it came to predicting "don't know" responses, women gave 1.71 more "don't know" answers than did men. Sex, however, was not a significant predictor of answering questions incorrectly. The significant predictors of giving incorrect answers were age, education, talking politics with family or friends, and race.

We hypothesized that what accounted for the difference in correct responses was that men were guessing more frequently than women. Nadeau and Niemi explain that whereas some individuals simply retrieve information from memory when answering questions, others answer questions regardless of their certainty about their responses.[13] Guesswork is a function of an individual's motivation (interest in the topic) and ability (cognitively able to deduce). In general, individuals who are skilled and motivated overall are more likely to guess than to admit ignorance when asked to answer knowledge questions. Males, those with more education, and those who are interested in a given topic are more likely both to answer questions and to answer them correctly.

We reran the models transforming the "don't know" answers into probability weights for all respondents. An individual who had guessed randomly on any of the questions would have a 25 percent chance of getting it correct. We also tried this method assuming that the individual could successfully eliminate one wrong answer or two wrong answers. Even if individuals had guessed either randomly, by successfully eliminating an answer, or by successfully eliminating two wrong answers, a gender gap in men's favor persisted. (See Table A9.2 in Appendix IV.) When we controlled for age, education, political interest, political talk, and race, sex still predicted answering items correctly even when the "don't knows" were converted under the assumption that individuals were able to eliminate two wrong answers. It appears that the gender gap in political knowledge cannot be explained by a disposition of men to guess.

Each of the twenty-nine items was analyzed using logit regression, controlling for age, education, media use, political interest, and political talk. Sex was a significant predictor of answering the item correctly for fourteen of the twenty-nine items. (See Table A9.3 in Appendix IV.) Women did not perform significantly better than men on any of these items. There was no consistent pattern of response based on policy area.

Graber gives several general explanations for why information may not be recalled. The first is the simplest. Perhaps the person paid no attention to the information in the first place. Second, it's impossible to recall information that was initially stored in short-term memory but not transferred to long-term memory. This can occur when an individual is bombarded with a lot of information or the knowledge item is only briefly mentioned. Third, decay of information in long-term memory may occur. Fourth, the person trying to recall something may fail to access the appropriate storage points in memory. The memory of specific events, for example, decays faster than the memory of attitudes (or tallies) distilled from those events. As for the gender gap in political knowledge, she explains, "Women generally feel less social pressure to retain information and therefore show higher rates of forgetting than men. Women under age 40 had totally forgotten an average of 37 percent of all [news] stories for which we tested recall, compared to 26 percent for their male contemporaries."[14] When women were asked why they had forgotten the information, the primary reason they cited was lack of interest.

Political Knowledge and the 1996 Election

Our data from the 1996 election suggest that the gender gap in political knowledge about presidential candidate positions continues to exist. After we controlled for socioeconomic factors, men answered more questions about candidate positions correctly than did women. Gender, however, was not a significant predictor of answering questions incorrectly. Instead, women were more likely to give "don't know" responses. The difference between the percentage of correct answers and the use of "don't know" responses continues to trouble those trying to account for the gender gap in political knowledge.

To further investigate Graber's explanation, we examined another feature of our 1996 survey. In addition to interviewing voters at various times during the campaign, we also maintained a panel of 309 voters who were interviewed at three points during the campaign: twice before the election and once shortly after. We hypothesized that repeated interviewing would increase sensitivity to the questions we asked and thereby increase motivation to recall information that might have been forgotten even if it had been learned during the campaign. Women tended to report less political discussion with family and friends, and this reduced rehearsal of political information might have minimized their ability to recall issue positions even if they had learned them at some point during the campaign. Because men discussed issues more than women did, repeated interviewing should have had a smaller effect on them. In cases where women remembered less, they might have been expected to show as much learning during the campaign as men but less final recall at the postelection interview.

In this analysis, we still found better recall by men on ten issues. However, we found superior female recall on two: permitting late-term abortions and striving for every child to be able to read by age eight. On two issue questions, women showed learning, which subsequently declined: on cleanup of toxic-waste dumps and targeted tax cuts. The issues on which men still outperformed women could be seen as more traditionally male-oriented, including defense spending, shifting control to the states, and NAFTA. However, some of the issues on which men outperformed women on the single postelection survey no longer elicited a gender difference. These included Medicare spending, school vouchers, voluntary prayer in the schools, expanding family leave, opposing the death penalty, and ending the IRS. Some of these issues affect domains more traditionally defined as women's. Indeed, in a number of cases, the direct effect of the policy underlying the issue is stronger on women than men. For example, because women outlive men and are more likely to take primary responsibility for care of their elderly parents, Medicare spending has a greater influence on their lives. Additionally, although family and medical leave is available to both men and women, it is disproportionately used by women.

In conclusion, our data from the 1996 election suggest that the gender gap in political knowledge about presidential candidate positions is real—a finding that clearly has ramifications for future elections. Even when controls are in place for a variety of factors, men answer more questions about candidate positions correctly than do women. Women are more likely to give "don't know" responses. These "don't know" responses—although difficult to attribute to any one factor—continue to place women behind men in retention of political knowledge. Gender, however, is not a significant predictor of answering questions *incorrectly*. Although men are more likely to guess, the gender gap in knowledge is not due to that disposition. We are left with an intriguing explanation. Our panel results suggest that political discussion may be an opportunity for greater rehearsal of political knowledge by men. Women report less political discussion and therefore may be less able to recall many issue positions. For issues with clear relevance to women (e.g., abortion rights), recall is no weaker and may be stronger for women.

Our year 2000 surveys will investigate differences in political discussion as a contributor to the knowledge gap and examine as well the possibility that women register political information just long enough to determine whether it is consistent with their vote preference, and when that is determined, discard the information. When the information is at odds with their political preference, women may simply tally that fact, adjusting their preference accordingly, and again fail to move that information into long-term memory. In other words, this finding may not signal a deficiency but rather an alternative cognitive strategy that is simply different from the one more generally used by men.

Kate Kenski and Kathleen Hall Jamieson

Part II
Candidate Advertising

⇥ Did You Know?

Whereas in 1992, 14 percent of the general-election presidential ads run by the Democrats and Republicans contained at least one misleading claim, in 1996, 52 percent were vulnerable to this charge.

⇥ ⇤

During the 1996 general election, five major networks—CBS, CNN, FOX, NBC, and PBS—each provided time in which Bill Clinton and Bob Dole (among others in the case of CNN) addressed viewers in recorded minispeeches. We compared the free time to comparable ads by the same candidates and found that the free time contained more advocacy and more accuracy, and was less alarmist. On at least five topics, free time provided more policy detail than did network news stories that ran during the same period. The five topics were education, drugs, health care reform, foreign policy, and Social Security.

Chapter Ten

Does Political Advertising Affect Turnout? If So, How, When, and for Whom?

A DVERTISING CAN AFFECT voter turnout, a candidate's share of the vote, both, or neither. In this chapter, we focus only on the effects of advertising on turnout. In the following chapters, we examine its effects on voters' disposition to favor or oppose a candidate.

The dropoff in the proportion of the population casting a vote has elicited concern from pundits, reporters, and scholars. The explanations for the drop are various and include a diminished belief that a vote makes a difference in the eventual outcome of a race, a drop in the public's sense that balloting is a civic obligation, and a decline in the view that voting, regardless of effect on outcome, is a valued form of ideological expression. Others blame disenhancement with government practices dating from the Watergate era, a loss of interest in politics, the decline of political parties, and the rise of political advertising as a dominant means of communication between those who seek office and the governed.

Although many have written about the effects of political advertising, the information that we gathered about the 1996 presidential campaign was unique. In addition to voting data from the 1,000-plus counties associated with the top fifty media markets, we were able to assemble all the ads aired by the republicans, democrats, the AFL-CIO, and the Business Coalition in the general election presidential campaign. Information on exposure (GRPs) was used to determine how often viewers in each market saw attack and advocacy by the two major party nominees and two powerful interest groups.

We used three sources of information to understand the effect of political advertising on voter turnout during the 1996 general election: voter turnout numbers by county in the top fifty media markets, the reach of advertising from four sources (Clinton and Dole campaigns, AFL-CIO, and Business Coalition), and the proportion of attack, advocacy, and contrast advertising. (Additional details about our method are reported in the appendix.) Although local news coverage of the presidential campaign is difficult to obtain, we do know from an analysis of ten markets that local coverage spikes upward when a candidate visits. We used candidates' visits as a surrogate for local news media coverage and for the mobilizing effect such contact has on supporters.

We analyze total turnout across the top fifty media markets. Using the election of 1992 as a baseline, we first ask whether total advertising in 1996 from the two major candidates increased turnout and whether this effect was linear or exhibited diminishing returns. Finally, we examine the possible effects of advocacy, contrast, and attack advertising to determine their relations to turnout. This procedure allows us to determine whether attack affects the electorate differently from the other types of content and which pattern of effects is activated in each case.

Advertising Is Associated with Increased Voter Turnout

Voter turnout in 1996 was calculated as a percentage: the number of voters voting for president in the county divided by the voting-age population. A statistical procedure called regression was used to analyze the relationship between turnout and advertising reach from the candidates and from issue advocacy ads from the AFL-CIO and the Business Coalition. This technique describes the association between two factors while holding other factors constant. By using this procedure, we can isolate the extent to which the ads of each type for Clinton, Dole, the AFL-CIO, and the Business Coalition have an effect on some other variable, such as turnout or voters' choices among candidates. In all cases we controlled for two other factors. The first was voter turnout in the county's presidential election in 1992. The vote in 1992 controls for a variety of factors that differentiate counties, including such factors as political interest. By controlling on the 1992 county vote, we ask whether advertising predicts 1996 turnout over and above the prediction that would be generated by the 1992 turnout alone. We also controlled for candidates' appearances in the

FIGURE 10.1   Average ad residuals, 1996 vote, controlling for 1992 vote

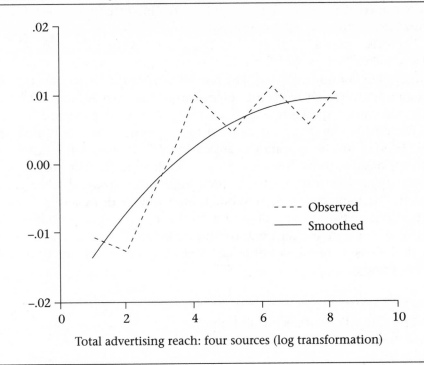

Total advertising reach: four sources (log transformation)

local media market. These appearances tend to generate local media coverage and energize partisans. Controlling for appearances essentially controls for local media coverage and partisan activation on turnout.

All three sources of advertising (the AFL-CIO, the Business Coalition, and the combined advertising of the Clinton and Dole campaigns) show positive effects on voter turnout, although the effects from the Business Coalition are not significant. These results mean that in counties where advertising was higher, so too was voter turnout, even after we controlled for the effects of 1992 turnout and the impact of candidates' visits.

The results seem to suggest that the more political advertising there is in a county, the greater the voter turnout. The effects are fairly similar across counties with a Democratic and Republican history. For example, in all cases, increases in advertising were associated with higher levels of voting. The size of the effects, though, did differ across types of counties. Candidates' advertising was strongest in moderate, Republican, and strong Republican counties and weaker in Democratic counties. Advertising by the AFL-CIO was most strongly linked to voter turnout in Democratic and strongly Democratic counties but not in moderate or Republican counties. Overall, the data for 1996 indicate that advertising is associated with elevated voter turnout.

However, there are real limits to this claim. As the amount of advertising increases to very high levels, voter turnout starts to flatten out rather than continue upward. The best way to see the flattening effect is to group advertising reach into eight categories, each equidistant from the other, using special measures called logarithms. (See Figure 10.1.)

The vertical axis is voter turnout in 1996 after the effects of turnout in 1992 and candidate appearances are subtracted. The horizontal axis is intensity of advertising from low to very high in units that are equally spaced—but the units are the natural logarithms of actual advertising reach. The graph clearly flattens out at intense advertising levels. The relationship between turnout and advertising is best described by a straight line, with a clear trend toward flattening out. In other words, a critical amount of ad exposure enhances the ad's ability to stimulate voter turnout.

Joseph Cappella, Kathleen Hall Jamieson,
Dan Romer, and Ned Nurick

Chapter Eleven

Are Attack Ads Necessarily Negative?

THE PHRASE "NEGATIVE CAMPAIGN" continues to haunt discussions of politics since it became a stock phrase in political discussion in 1988. So pervasive are the phrases "negative ads" and "negative campaign" that more than 1,000 uses appear when the nation's newspapers are searched for the 1996 year. Whereas in 1980 only two national polling questions asked about negativity in presidential campaigns (Figure 11.1), in 1988 that number jumped to thirty-five (Public Opinion Online [Roper Center]). As we discussed earlier, the public is able to discern the value of evidence in attack ads as long as they don't veer into ad hominem attack and false claims.

The phrases "negative campaign" and "negative campaigning" are troubling because it is unclear what they mean. As an earlier chapter noted, academics, pundits, and reporters tend to conflate ads that feature one-sided attack, contrast ads that contain attack, ad hominem attack ads, and ads featuring attacks that deceive. All are grouped under the word "negative." "While both candidates used negative television ads, some political observers suggested that Mr. Weld's relentlessly negative ads in the last week of the campaign backfired," wrote Sara Rimer of the *New York Times* after the close of the Massachusetts Senate race in 1996.[1] "Mr. Dole never overcame the widespread sense that he was waging a negative campaign," noted James Bennet of the *Times* after the 1996 presidential election.[2]

Presidents and presidential candidates are no more precise. "I saw a series the other night about how local campaigns were now becoming also dominated by negative ads," said Bill Clinton.[3] "They're all negative ads," said Republican nominee Bob Dole of the ads aired by the Clinton campaign in 1996.[4]

FIGURE 11.1   Number of poll questions asking about negativity in presidential campaigns.

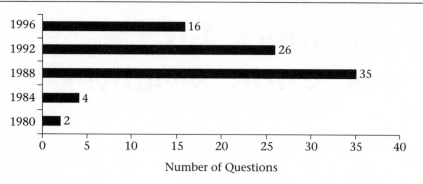

Scholars have perpetuated the confusion. "Fed up with attack ads, negative campaigns and partisan rancor," observed Harvard professor Michael J. Sandel, "Americans are also distressed at the coarsening of everyday life."[5]

The academic literature on advertising contains articles that define an ad as negative if it contains any attack, if more than half of the ad attacks, if "most" of the ad attacks, if the ad is deceptive, and if the ad contains no advocacy other than that in the concluding tag line. So, for example, the widely cited book *Going Negative* by Stephen Ansolabehere and Shanto Iyengar makes no distinction between ads that contain both advocacy and attack and those that simply attack. It also doesn't test to determine whether subjects in its experiments thought the ads being viewed were truthful or deceptive. Without those distinctions and ones provided by viewer impressions, it is difficult to know what is being argued given the proclamation in the book's subtitle *How Political Advertisements Shrink and Polarize the Electorate.*[6]

Whatever the meaning, the context provided in press reports suggests that, consistent with Ansolabehere and Iyengar's subtitle, "negative ads" and "negative campaigning" are bad for democracy. If candidates win after using negative ads or because they used negative ads, then—the logic follows—we have a regrettable situation in which behavior damaging to the body politic is required of those who want to win. "A good percentage of this money is spent on ads," noted Eleanor Randolph in the *Los Angeles Times* in late October 1996, "particularly negative ads. And there were plenty of them this season, eroding the public trust, enhancing public cynicism and winning elections."[7]

In 1998, a task force of academics convened by political scientist Larry Bartels of Princeton University broke from this indiscriminate use of the word "negative": "We believe that the focus on the 'negativity' of campaign advertising is largely misplaced, reflecting and perpetuating a general conflation of the important distinction between ads that are characterized as 'negative' because they are contentious and argumentative, challenging claims about the records, characters and platforms of opponents, and ads that are characterized as 'negative' because they are nasty, inaccurate, or unfair." That report accepts the distinction offered by Annenberg School researchers who distinguish among candidate "advocacy" ads (focusing on the candidate's qualifications), candidate "attack" ads (focusing on the opponent's failings), and candidate "contrast" ads (containing explicit comparisons between the candidate's qualities, record, or proposals and the opponent's).[8]

Imprecise use of the word "negative" is problematic because it combines types of discourse that are actually distinct. The standard use of "negative" in reference to ads also assumes that any attack is illegitimate when, instead, attack-based differentiation is an important way to determine that one candidate is better qualified than others. Finally, "negative" implies that attack ads are more deceptive than ads that simply make a case for a candidate when, it should be noted, the level of inaccuracy in advocacy ads is usually higher.

Since campaigns are increasingly played out in the media and advertising is a central component of political campaigns, determining the effects of attack advertising is important. There is also a significant "crossover" effect when the shelf life of campaign advertising is extended through media coverage of the ads. Today's hand-wringing over the harmful effects of attack advertising comes amid a broader concern about citizen apathy and disengagement from civic life.

Although our focus will largely be with the scholarly evidence, the issue of the effects of attack advertising cuts across layers of American political and intellectual life. Oppositional ads have been the object of censure by politicians, concerned citizens, and members of the media—many of whom cite academic works to bolster their claims. For instance, in *U.S. News & World Report*, Stephen Budiansky noted: "Iyengar and Ansolabehere found that the real problem with negative ads is not that they fool people—they don't—but that they suppress voter turnout. Rather than swaying voters to support one candidate or another, negative advertising reinforces the belief that all politicians are dishonest and cynical. A survey published last week by Arthur Miller, a professor at the University of Iowa, found that 42 percent of likely Republican voters in

Iowa are undecided—up from 34 percent in December—and many are so disgusted by the campaign they probably will not vote in their state's caucuses at all."[9] Similarly, nationally syndicated columnist Jack Germond argued in the *National Journal:* "The trouble [of the low voter turnout in 1996], according to [Curtis] Gans, was not with the candidates but with their greater-than-ever dependence on the negative advertising that was flooding the airwaves. The mudslinging disgusted the public, he suggests, to the point where more than half of the eligible voters simply washed their hands of the whole business and stayed home on Election Day."[10] It is far from clear, however, just what effects attack advertising does have. Despite the broad acceptance of Ansolabehere and Iyengar's findings, some academics and reporters have questioned them.

Studies on the effects of attack advertising have looked at a range of dependent variables. Some, for instance, have examined the effect attack advertising has on evaluations of the ads themselves. Garramone identified general antipathy toward "negative" advertising, finding that three-fourths of her subjects evaluated "negative" political advertising unfavorably.[11] In another study 72 percent of the subjects found such advertising to be "not very" or "not at all informative," with even more disapproving of the ads. However, the study itself suggests the contrary finding that the "negative" ads were more memorable.[12] Christ, Thorson, and Caywood's research suggests that individual responses to "negative" advertising are moderated by such variables as attitudes about the candidates.[13]

Other work has focused on the effects of "negative" advertising on sponsors of the ads. Faber, Tims, and Schmitt note that past research has uncovered both intended and unintended (backlash) effects of "negative" advertising.[14] In an analysis of television advertising, Pinkelton shows that "negative" contrast ads lower the favorable perceptions of the ads' target but do not adversely affect evaluations of the ads' sponsor.[15]

Another area of study that has attempted to tie attack to the decline in voting has reached mixed conclusions. Ansolabehere, Iyengar, Simon, and Valentino and Ansolabehere and Iyengar[16] conducted experimental studies and analyzed aggregate-level data on the effects of attack political advertising. Using a nonrandom subject selection design, they built their studies around actual elections in California and focused on real candidates.

In a laboratory setting designed to approximate a home-viewing environment, viewers were shown a single ad that either attacked or promoted a candidate. Manipulations were performed on television advertisements produced to resemble actual ads. The researchers did not test to determine whether the subjects in the experiment thought they were viewing real ads; thus it is unknown whether respondents granted this assumption. The authors were unable to replicate statistically significant findings when they used actual ads containing positive and negative content.

The ad was shown as part of a lengthier video reel that included other spots and local television news. The results of the study suggested attack advertising depressed intentions to vote by 5 percent compared with the results achieved by self-promotional ads.

The findings of the aggregate-level data are equally problematic. Although the authors concluded that states with attack campaigns witnessed a drop in voter turnout of 2 percent and states with positive campaigns witnessed a 2 percent increase, their study has no direct measure of advertising content. Rather, for an indicator of advertising tone, the authors relied on analysis of news coverage in the thirty-four subject states that held a Senate election in 1992. Consequently, the level of actual advertising attack was not measured. Instead, states were coded as generally positive, mixed, or generally negative based on news reports.

The shortcomings of that study were noted by Finkel and Geer, who investigated the effects of attack advertising on voter turnout by coding the content of ads rather than of news coverage. Using both individual- and aggregate-level data, they analyzed the nine presidential contests from 1960 to 1992. In contrast to Ansolabehere and Iyengar's method of identifying campaign tone by coding news coverage, Finkel and Geer turned to the Julian P. Kanter Political Commercial Archive at the University of Oklahoma for copies of the ads that were produced for those races.[17] To calculate advertising tone, Finkel and Geer subtracted the percentage of an ad's attack appeals from the percentage of its positive appeals. Rather than the description offered by Ansolabehere and Iyengar (negative, mixed, positive), this procedure yielded more refined data by producing a numerical index of the degree of advertising tone. Neither the aggregate- nor individual-level data revealed that negative tone affected voter turnout. However, the authors acknowledge that the archive is incomplete, and as we note elsewhere, it contains ads that never aired.[18] Also affecting the findings is the fact that the authors lacked information on how often the ads aired, or how many persons saw them; thus they reached their conclusions of effect without a reliable indicator of audience exposure.

In response to the absence of exposure data characteristic of the two previous studies, Goldstein turned to Competitive Media Reporting

(CMR) data in an analysis of "negative" advertising's effect on voter turnout.[19] CMR monitors the satellite transmissions of the national networks (ABC, CBS, NBC, and Fox) and twenty-five national cable networks (for example, CNN, ESPN, and TNT). In addition, CMR monitors advertising in the country's top seventy-five media markets. CMR provides data on the content of ads, where they were aired, the day and the time they aired, and the program during which they aired.

Goldstein focused on the 1996 presidential race and the ads run by candidates Clinton and Dole. He coded the ads as all positive, contrast, or all negative. Goldstein acknowledged missing five Clinton-Gore ads and three Dole-Kemp ads out of a combined 161 ads. Once frequency of airings was calculated, the missing ads were estimated to account for about 2 percent of the total commercial broadcasts in the campaign.

Goldstein's data offer contradictory findings. At the county level, he found demobilizing effects, but at the individual level, he found none. Moreover, the county-level data suggested voter turnout was higher owing to the overall mix of ads than it would have been had no ads appeared. Although Goldstein's data offer a map of advertising exposure, it is a rough one at best. CMR captured the satellite broadcasts of the national networks, but it missed the ads purchased in local buys not in the top seventy-five markets and missed all cable advertising. More critically, Goldstein did not have data on gross rating points (GRPs) and therefore could not fix the level of viewer exposure to the ads, a fact he laments.

For some researchers, the claim that attack advertising demobilizes the electorate is still an open question. Although Finkel and Geer, and subsequently Goldstein, proposed further examination of Ansolabehere and Iyengar's claims, these follow-up studies suffer the critical weakness of being unable to specify how heavily the ads in questions were broadcast. In an attempt to nail down a measure of such exposure, Goldstein introduced CMR data to compensate for the past critical lack of data. His data, however, can offer only rough estimates of exposure, and therefore only tenuous connections between advertising tone and effects on voters.

There are only tentative explanations to account for the hypothesis that attack advertising might demobilize the electorate. It is important to discuss the theory associated with attack advertising in part as a reaction to the post hoc nature of so much of it. Ansolabehere and Iyengar, for instance, offer three post hoc explanations to account for their demobilization effect. One possibility they offer is the asymmetrical effect attack advertising has on partisans: Advertising attacking a candidate might cause his or her supporters to stay home on election day, whereas the intention to vote remains unchanged for those supporting the sponsor of the ad. But as Finkel and Geer and others have pointed out, it is no less probable that supporters of the candidate who sponsors the ad may be energized and consequently turn out in larger numbers.[20]

Ansolabehere and Iyengar offer a second explanation that suggests the overall tone associated with an attack campaign "generates blanket negativity toward both candidates," but they reject this hypothesis because their further research suggests voters do not penalize the sponsors of attack ads.

They settle on a third explanation: "Exposure to campaign attacks makes voters disenchanted with the business of politics as usual," creating a cynical and disengaged electorate.[21] Yet, one could easily imagine the opposite being true. Why, for instance, would cynicism—if it is indeed generated by attack advertising—necessarily be associated with voter demobilization? Could it not also be associated with voter mobilization under the premise that it engages voters to effect some sort of change? Voters who are disenchanted with the business of politics as usual may as a response choose to participate in the political process in order to reform it.

Are we to understand that all questions raised about an opponent's past voting record, for instance, are harmful to the political process and should be considered inappropriate points of discussion? For example, is learning that candidate Smith voted against gun control injurious to the democratic process?

Finkel and Geer propose three reasons to believe attack advertising should enhance voter turnout.[22] They first suggest that attack advertising has been associated with learning effects and the communication of greater policy information. They also note that negative information is given more weight by viewers because it is unexpected and non-normative while also offering greater differentiation of the candidates than does positive advertising. Their third explanation holds that attack advertising may create greater affective responses than positive advertising, resulting in greater enthusiasm to participate in the election. The greater effectiveness of attack advertising may also be accounted for by its enhanced capacity to be recalled.[23] Rather than having debilitating effects, Finkel and Geer posit, attack advertising can have quite salutary ones.

This then becomes a larger question. What, if any, are the effects of ads that attack, contrast, and advocate? If there are effects, where and why do they occur?

Before turning to these questions, we want to indicate why we believe that advertising and fair, accurate attack ads mobilize voters. Political ads contain higher levels of issue information than the public discussion of them would suggest.[24] Indeed, despite the low repute in which they are held, supposedly negative advertisements actually contain more relevant issue content than ads containing no information about the sponsor's opposing candidate.[25] In order to assess issue content, we coded ads produced for presidential campaigns occurring between 1952 and 1996 to determine the percentage of policy content found among the different categories of political advertisements. This analysis also allowed us to determine the percentage of policy content in each candidate's arguments and to combine the percentages into a total for each election year.

Statements were coded as policy if they provided information about the difference between candidates' policy positions that would help a voter make an informed voting decision. References to character, "colorful" or scene-setting statements, summary statements introducing or concluding a list of policy statements, and biographical statements were considered nonpolicy. If a policy was mentioned but was preceded by a negative adjective, and no further detail about the policy was articulated, the statement was considered nonpolicy. For instance, reference to Bob Dole's "risky tax scheme" absent further elaboration would be a nonpolicy statement. Finally, sentences included in order to further emphasize a point—for example, "you know the result," or "make no mistake about it"—were also considered to be nonpolicy statements.

Nine hundred ninety-six individual arguments in general-election ads from the 1952–1996 period were coded for policy content. Only segments running five minutes or fewer in length were included in the database. For the purpose of consistency, longer televised segments were categorized in the database as speeches.

In order to code arguments for policy and nonpolicy content, we used an individual idea unit as the unit of analysis. This analytic scheme resulted in an ability to calculate the amount of policy content as a percent of total-words-in-arguments in the advertisements, thereby correcting for variations in ad length. It is important to note that policy content was not calculated for entire ads but rather was localized inside the arguments found in each ad. Advertisements generally contained only one argument, but some ads had a greater number. Thus, if a spot contained one argument coded as attack and two coded as advocacy, the policy content was calculated for each of these arguments rather than for the ad as a whole. The content analysis was conducted by four coders. Similar to analyses discussed earlier, reliability was greater than the 0.6 level using the stringent Krippendorf's reliability alpha.

Consistent with previous studies, our analysis showed that the attack advertisements did contain a greater percentage of policy words-in-argument than did advocacy or comparison ads. Forty-two percent of attack content was coded as policy, as was 39 percent of contrastive content, but only 32 percent of advocacy content was considered policy. This finding is significant considering that in academic and popular discourse, both attack and comparison ads often fall under the pejorative heading "negative advertising."

Yet both ad types offer more policy information to the electorate than the so-called positive ads. Notably, in none of the three categories did the percent of policy content equal or exceed the percent of nonpolicy content. When words found in arguments coded as attack were calculated as a percentage of total words, it became clear that attack words made up the smallest percent of total words in political ads (16 percent). Advocacy arguments comprised the largest portion of total words (53 percent); considerably less prevalent were contrastive arguments (only 32 percent of total words). Candidates who used advocacy ads were devoting the greatest amount of advertising time to the format yielding the least policy discussion. They were also talking about themselves a lot but devoting less time to discussion of their issue positions.

These findings raise the question, should academics and others continue advocating an increase in "positive advertising" without clearly delineating the type of content these ads contain? In order to contribute to the deliberative process, an ad should be informative. Ideally, candidates should be able both to state their own positions and to criticize those of their opponent without facing accusations of "going negative."

The percent of policy content in each argument of each ad category was also calculated for each major candidate running for president between 1952 and 1996. Only for Bush in 1992 did the advocacy category contain the highest percentage of policy words, although several of the candidates' contrastive arguments did contain the highest percent of policy. Interestingly, in both 1992 and 1996, President Clinton produced contrastive advertisements with levels of policy content exceeding 60 percent. In both campaigns, many of Clinton's ads contained lists of his policy positions and initiatives and the contrasting opinions and initiatives of Bush (1992) and Dole (1996), a format lending itself to heavy use of policy statements. For example, in 1992, the Clinton campaign ran the following ad:

Clinton: We've been under trickle-down economics for twelve years. Just keep taxes low on the wealthy and see what happens. Well, I'll tell you what's happened. Most Americans are working harder for less money. Unemployment is up. Health care costs are exploding. We are not doing what it takes to compete and win. I've worked hard on a different plan. Let's give incentives to invest in new jobs. Let's spend more on education and training. Let's provide basic health care to all Americans—putting our people first—rebuilding this economy—making us competitive. If we do those things we'll compete and win and we'll bring this country back.

The significance of Clinton's tendency to use contrastive advertising is demonstrated in this analysis. Also significant is the 70 percent policy content of Carter's attack arguments in 1976 compared with the 32 percent policy content in his 1980 attack arguments. This disparity may be attributable to the fact that in 1976 Carter was running against an incumbent (Gerald Ford).

These data justify our presupposition that the best format for political advertisements is the one used so successfully by Clinton in the 1992 and 1996 elections: contrastive advertising that many critics have mislabeled as "attack." The content analysis demonstrated that the average contrastive ad contains nearly as a high a percentage of policy content as do attack ads, making contrast a better choice than pure advocacy. This format also requires that candidates express their positions on issues while allowing them to criticize their opponents. Of major significance is that the contrastive format can present voters with a choice between two positions on important issues. Why the media would attempt to relegate all contrastive ads to the category "attack" remains to be understood.

Kathleen Hall Jamieson, Kate Kenski,
Mark Mendoza, Paul Waldman, and Susan Sherr

Chapter Twelve

Does Attack Advertising Affect Turnout?

S OME COMMENTATORS SEE A RELATIONSHIP between plummeting voter participation and the increasing prominence of "negative" political advertising. The more negative ads are, "the lower the turnout is," remarked President Bill Clinton at a press conference in November 1996. Others condemn political spots for "insistently" focusing on "either character assassination or divisive social issues that leave the electorate so angry and dissatisfied."[1] And many pundits and reporters accept as conventional wisdom the notion that attack in campaigns in general and in political advertising in particular minimizes voting. For example, according to nationally syndicated columnist David Broder, "negative campaigning and negative campaign ads have become so lethal and there are so many of them that voters do not want to vote for either candidate if even half of what the politicians are saying about each other is true."[2]

For decades scholars argued that campaigns in general and campaign communication in particular had little effect on ultimate voter preferences or on turnout.[3] As we noted in Chapter 1, in the past decade the minimal-effects assumption—that nothing voters read or see on television is likely to dissuade them from voting according to their established preferences—has been challenged.[4] The issue is whether campaigns are able to do anything beyond activating the existing dispositions of voters.

Here we address the question of whether attack ads mobilized, demobilized, or made no difference in the 1996 general-election campaign. Did attack advertising by Republican nominee Bob Dole and Democratic incumbent Bill Clinton in the 1996 general-election presidential campaign affect turnout?

107

Findings

To determine how advocacy, attack, and contrast may have affected turnout, we regressed turnout in 1996 (as percent of total eligible voters) on turnout in the previous general election (1992), along with visits by both candidates, total issue advertising by the AFL-CIO and Business Coalition, and total advocacy, contrast, and attack by Clinton and Dole. To increase the sensitivity of the distinctions between contrast and the two extremes of the discourse continuum, we restricted our definition of contrast ads to those that contained 30–70 percent attack.

This analysis showed that advocacy was weakly and positively related to turnout, attack was weakly and negatively related to turnout, and contrast was strongly and positively related to turnout.

Aside from the two candidates, the only source we analyzed that was related to turnout was the smaller and more targeted issue advertising directed by the AFL-CIO and generally supportive of Clinton's themes. Visits by the two candidates were positively but not reliably tied to turnout.

A second analysis in which each candidate's advocacy, attack, and contrast ads were entered into the prediction equation (instead of totals for both candidates' ads) showed that the strong relation between contrast and turnout was primarily a result of Dole's advertising and not Clinton's. The weak negative relation between attack and turnout also was primarily attributable to Dole. The weak relation between advocacy and turnout was characteristic of both candidates' advertising.

An important caveat is in order here. Clinton's and Dole's attack advertising weights were highly related to one another. In counties where Clinton spent money on attack ads, the Dole campaign did as well. In fact, the two were closely correlated. Despite this tangle, we believe our data show that the difference in the impact of attack ads on voter turnout between the incumbent and challenger is a real one.

Summary: Voter Turnout

Does advertising cause voter turnout, or are both advertising expenditure and voter turnout caused by some third force? Higher levels of advertising are associated with greater voter turnout. In our study, counties that received more advertising dollars and air time also tended to have a higher percentage of would-be voters who voted. However, in counties where races are heated, both advertising and voting turnout might be elevated in comparison with counties where races are less intense. The causality question cannot be answered with the data we have, but we do see a clear positive relationship between advertising and voter turnout.

Of three types of advertising content we have examined, contrast is the most effective in mobilizing voters. By our definition, this is advertising with only moderate levels of attack. Strong attack advertising can demobilize the electorate—as we see with the challenger's advertising in the 1996 election. The stronger relation between contrast and turnout underscores the importance of this category of advertising and the need for the distinction between contrast and pure attack. In light of the evidence we presented in earlier chapters showing that advertising can contain substantial amounts of policy information, it is unsurprising that it has a mobilizing effect. Advertising is not, in other words, empty rhetoric. At the same time, the fact that the most accountable form of advertising—contrast—is also the most effective at drawing voters to the polls confirms the finding of the survey we reported in Chapter 7. Voters prefer contrast. Contrast mobilizes. In sum, contrast advertising is a win-win form of communication. Voters, candidates, and the process are aided by its use.

Dan Romer, Kathleen Hall Jamieson,
Joseph Cappella.

Chapter Thirteen

Does Attack Advertising Create a Backlash? Mobilize the Other Side? Depress or Increase Support by Those of the Same Party?

HERE IS NO CONSENSUS AMONG SCHOLARS about the effects of attack. The definitions of such concepts as "negativity" are often wildly dissimilar, failing in some cases to distinguish between accurate and inaccurate attack, or between attack that also makes a case for the sponsor and attack that does not.[1] As a result, it is difficult to summarize the literature. In general, some researchers believe that attack is effective,[2] whereas others find that it creates a backlash.[3]

Our analysis of the 1996 data shows that political advertising is associated with voter turnout even though the effects are not as simple as "demobilization" or "mobilization" across the board. Advertising is associated with increased voting, but the specific ad environment is a complicating factor. Advocacy ads from the incumbent spur voters more so than attack and contrastive ads. The challenger's contrastive ads correlate with increased levels of voting as do his or her attack ads. Incumbents are granted the "benefit" of advocacy ads, whereas challengers are expected to offer a reason for change from the status quo, most often found in attack ads. In our study, advocacy from the Dole camp was linked to depressed voting.

All of this discussion ignores a very important question. It is possible that those being motivated to vote are the supporters of one's opponent and that the vote they cast hurts the sponsor of the ad. If so, the sponsor probably would have preferred that the voter stay home. Thus, what kind of voters were turned out by the Clinton and Dole ad campaigns? Did attack and contrastive ads from the Dole campaign produce more Republican or more Democratic voters at the polls? Did Clinton's advocacy ads encourage Republican votes or Democratic votes?

Vote Share As a Function of Dole's and Clinton's Patterns of Attack, Contrast, and Advocacy Advertising

In order to analyze the effects of advertising on vote share in the 1996 presidential race, we employed the same strategy as that used for voter turnout. To do this, we simply replaced voter turnout as a percentage of voters divided by those who are eligible with an equivalent measure using those voting for Clinton divided by the number of "eligibles." A similar measure for Dole was calculated and subtracted from Clinton's vote share to produce a difference score that reflected the difference in share between the candidates in each county. In addition, we controlled for the comparable share point difference in 1992. To assess the effects of advertising content, we calculated comparable difference scores for advocacy, contrast, and attack as defined in the previous chapter.

Our analysis of share point differences in the 1996 presidential general election indicated much clearer and stronger effects of both differential visits by the candidates and advertising content differences. The more either candidate visited each advertising market, the greater his share point gain. But more important for our purposes, content differences in advertising between the candidates produced differential effects on vote share. Advocacy ads were the strongest force for vote share, followed by contrast ads. Attack ads appeared to backfire on the candidate who sponsored them by producing a small but detectable decline in vote share.

Size of Effect of Advertising in the 1996 Election

To determine the overall effect of advertising on vote share in the 1996 election, we calculated the share difference of the total vote between Clinton and Dole (Clinton share minus Dole share) in each county. We then entered the difference in total weighted advertising between Clinton and Dole for each county into a regression analysis to estimate the potential effect of net differences in advertising by each candidate. Also included in the analysis was the total advertising by the AFL-CIO and the Business Coalition, the difference in the number of visits the two candidates made to each media market, and the difference in vote share for the two parties in 1992.[4]

Summary

The strong mobilizing effect that advertising has on voter participation diminishes with increasing advertising weight but is substantial nevertheless. Differential total advertising by the two major candidates in media markets affects their vote share in those markets. The effect is large enough to affect the outcome in the average county in the top media markets.

The relation between advertising content and election outcomes indicates that attack, defined as advertising with more than 90 percent attack content, reduces both turnout and the sponsoring candidate's vote share. Pure advocacy increases vote share but has little effect on turnout. Contrast advertising, defined as advertising with more than 30 percent but less than 70 percent attack, increases both turnout and vote share.

Pure attack advertising does reduce turnout and harm the sponsoring candidate's share. However, contrast advertising, which can contain substantial attack, appears to help the sponsor and increase turnout. This finding suggests that contrast advertising increases the sponsoring candidate's share by recruiting previously inactive voters to the candidate's side. We do not know whether the previously inactive voters were from the same party as the candidate or not. Nevertheless, the effects of contrast advertising are quite different from those of attack and underscore the importance of distinguishing contrast from pure attack advertising. Finally, advocacy advertising, which has the greatest effect on vote share, does not affect turnout. This suggests that advocacy gains its potency by taking share away from the opposition while leaving turnout largely unchanged.

Dan Romer, Kathleen Hall Jamieson,
Joseph Cappella.

Chapter Fourteen

Who Attacked More in Ads in 1996, Clinton or Dole?

I N 1996 THE POLLSTERS FOR BOTH Dole and Clinton found that Dole was perceived as the negative campaigner.[1] Yet, as we will show, Clinton actually used more attack in ads than did the Republican nominee.

The Clinton and Dole campaigns were quite different in the level of attack and advocacy advertising they employed during the 1996 campaign. Shown in Figure 14.1 is the average advertising reach for the Dole and Clinton campaigns in three categories: pure advocacy ads, pure attack ads, and contrastive ads—a mix of attack and advocacy. The Clinton campaign placed heavy emphasis on contrastive and attack ads, with little emphasis on pure advocacy ads. The Dole campaign, by contrast, placed its emphasis on advocacy and contrastive ads. On average, Dole's pure advocacy ads had ten times greater weight than Clinton's. (See definitions and methodology in Appendix I.) Clinton's average attack weight was more than 40 percent higher than Dole's. This evidence runs counter to the widespread perception held by many reporters and pundits in 1996 that Dole's ad campaign was more attack oriented than Clinton's.

Advertising weight is a measure of how likely advertising is to reach an audience in a county because it describes exposure based on audience marketing analyses. But another way to describe the political advertising environment in a county is in terms of percentage of one type of advertising relative to the whole. This breakdown assumes that an audience's psychological portrait of the world of political advertis-

115

FIGURE 14.1 Average distributions of Clinton and Dole attack, contrast, and advocacy advertising reach.

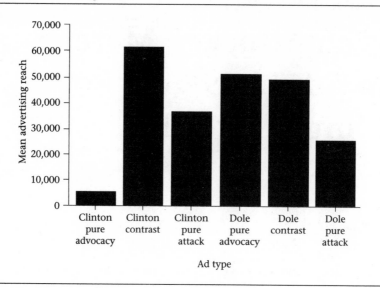

FIGURE 14.2 Average percentage of attack and advocacy advertising for Clinton and Dole campaigns.

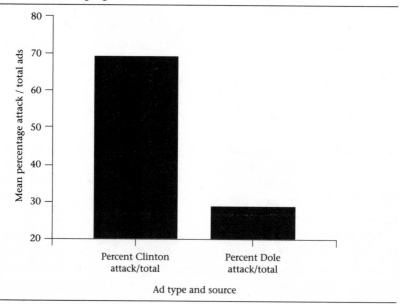

FIGURE 14.3   Average percentage of Clinton and Dole pure attack and pure advocacy advertising.

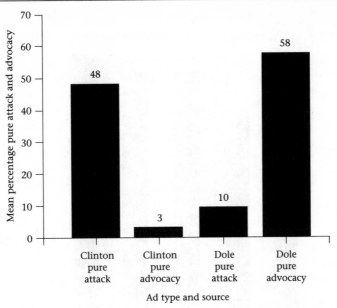

ing is captured by the relative amounts of attack and advocacy advertising.

Figures 14.2 and 14.3 portray Clinton's and Dole's advertising in percentage terms. Figure 14.2 shows Clinton's and Dole's attack advertising as a percentage of their total advertising. Clinton's proportion of attack (69 percent) is more than double that of Dole's (29 percent). Also, the Clinton campaign's proportion of attack in counties in our sample ranged from a low of 44 percent to a high of 100 percent. The Dole campaign, on the other hand, ranged from 0 percent attack to only 76 percent. In effect, the lowest Clinton percentage attack was higher than the average percentage attack for the Dole campaign. The two campaigns literally were in different universes in terms of attack advertising.

The differences are even more pronounced when pure advocacy and pure attack ads are considered. Figure 14.3 shows the average percentage of advertising reach from the Dole and Clinton campaigns for pure attack or pure advocacy ads; in other words, omitted are contrastive ads,

FIGURE 14.4 Advertising weight for Dole campaign's attack, contrast, and advocacy ads by type of county.

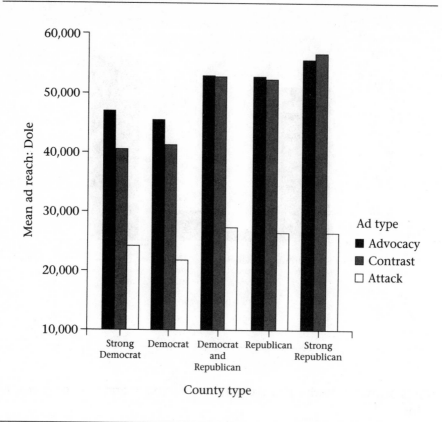

which are a mix of advocacy and attack. On average, 58 percent of Dole's ad reach was carried out through ads that only advocated for his positions or leadership. Only 3 percent of Clinton's ads were pure advocacy. This is a nineteen-fold difference. On pure attack, the reverse occurred. Almost 50 percent of the reach of Clinton's advertising on average employed pure attack, whereas only 10 percent of Dole's did so.

Figure 14.4 (for Dole) and Figure 14.5 (for Clinton) display the ad weight across five types of counties for advocacy, contrastive, and attack ads. The Dole campaign ads aired were primarily contrastive and advocacy with attack ads uncommon and with little reach. Republican counties got a somewhat greater advertising budget. However, the variation across counties in the quantity of each type of ad is very

FIGURE 14.5   Advertising weight for Clinton campaign's attack, contrast, and advocacy ads by type of county.

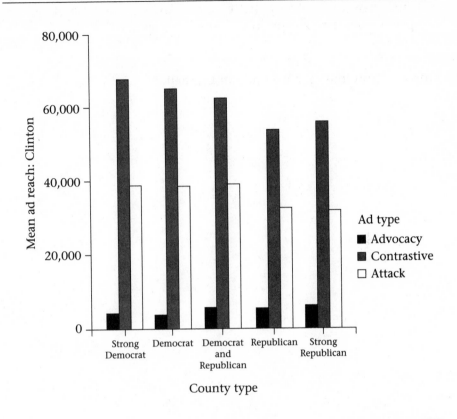

small, accounting for less than 1 percent of the variation in advertising by type of county. This is an important fact when counties are compared. Although they received slightly different amounts of advertising from the Dole campaign, the amounts are just that—slight. The ad environment created by the Dole campaign across types of counties was effectively constant rather than varying substantially by type of county.

The Clinton advertising environment (Figure 14.5) was different from Dole's in one significant aspect. The president's ads were heavily contrastive and attack with pure advocacy spots receiving scant air time. In terms of GRPs, Clinton's weighted advertising attack also exceeded Dole's (63,042 versus 59,110 units of GRPs times ad duration).

Why was Dole perceived to be running the more negative campaign when Clinton's ads contained more attack? As our earlier chapters suggest, the answer is probably that Clinton's use of contrast buffered his campaign from the perception that it was "negative."

Kathleen Hall Jamieson and Joseph Cappella

↦ Chapter Fifteen

Do Adwatches Backfire?

IN RESPONSE TO THE 1988 CAMPAIGN, which many regarded as an election characterized more by mudslinging than meaningful debate, in 1992 the broadcast networks began policing presidential campaign ads. Pioneered by newspapers in 1990, the practice was designed to minimize deception by putting campaigns on notice that the truthfulness of their ads would be scrutinized. It was intended as well to educate viewers, often by expanding the partial truths of ads into a larger story. If an ad was truthful, the adwatch would indicate that fact; if not, it would correct the ad.

A study by Jamieson in 1988 found that when ads were reaired full screen in broadcast news reports, audiences remembered their misleading claims but not the reporter's corrections.[1] Network news coverage, in other words, worked to magnify instead of minimize the effects of the ads the reporter was attempting to debunk. To make this outcome less likely, an Annenberg School research team developed visual means for increasing awareness of the reporter's words. These tactics included placing the ad in a mock television screen, moving the screen into the background, attaching a news logo and a notice that the ad was sponsored by a particular candidate, and superimposing print corrections on the boxed ad. A field experiment by Cappella and Jamieson showed that these techniques blunted the effect of a misleading ad on audiences.[2] In 1992 some version of this structure was adopted by each of the national broadcast news networks.

In 1992 adwatching became standard fare in network news. Whether coincidentally or not, the level of accuracy of the presidential ads was high that year. In election debriefings, consultants for both Bush and Clinton reported that adwatching had increased the attention they gave to the accuracy of their ads. Adwatching appeared to have been a success.

However, the value of adwatching was called into question by a 1995 book titled *Going Negative*[3] and a 1996 article in *Press/Politics*.[4] In these venues, Stephen Ansolabehere and Shanto Iyengar reported the results of experiments evaluating three of CNN's 1992 adwatches. "Journalists should leave advertisements alone," they argued. "[A]dwatch journalism evidently fails to achieve its basic objectives because the candidate who was scrutinized by the media enjoyed increased support among those who watched an adwatch report." If, as Ansolabehere and Iyengar state, the adwatches concluded "by rating the advertisement as either inaccurate or misleading," if they constituted "hostile news," and if "Whenever a false or misleading statement was encountered, the labels FALSE or MISLEADING, in bold, red, [capital] letters, were slapped on the advertisement," then viewers who responded by thinking more highly of the sponsor of the ads were clearly off track and the adwatches backfired. Or, by simply providing additional air time for a candidate's claims, adwatches, in Ansolaberhere and Iyengar's opinion, worked to reinforce the recognizability of the candidate.

Were the ads clearly labeled false, misleading, or inaccurate? Across CNN's three adwatches, the word "false" does not appear at all, and "incomplete" and "misleading" each appear a single time. Four of the superimposed banners label a claim "true," and seven identify claims as "correct but . . . ." In other words, Ansolabehere and Iyengar led readers to believe that the adwatches condemned ads that reporter Brooks Jackson instead found largely true or correct with qualifications. When viewers responded favorably to the sponsor, they were reacting in a way consistent with the adwatch. No boomerang. No backlash. No need to abandon this journalistic form.

With no reason to doubt Ansolabehere and Iyengar's descriptions of the tested adwatches, influential journalists came out against adwatching. "The now routine policing of TV commercials, it turns out, often compounds the damage that those ads inflict on our democracy," wrote Max Frankel in the *New York Times Magazine*.[5] *Washington Post* reporter and columnist David Broder, an early proponent of adwatching, concluded from Ansolabehere and Iyengar's work that adwatches "appear only to reinforce the negative consequences. They 'clearly backfired.'"[6]

For whatever reason, adwatching all but disappeared from network broadcast news in the 1996 general-election season when, coincidentally or not, the proportion of ads that contained at least one misleading claim reached an all-time high in the history of the televised campaign.

Kathleen Hall Jamieson

Part III
Issue-Advocacy Advertising

⇢ Did You Know?

In 1996 the American Federation of Labor and Congress of Industrial Organizations (AFL-CIO), a labor organization consisting of seventy-eight unions with 13.1 million members, engaged in an extensive issue-advocacy campaign spending $25 million to broadcast ads primarily in forty-four congressional districts. An analysis of station logs reveals that in at least fourteen of the districts, the labor group outspent one of the congressional contenders. In ten of the fourteen, the AFL-CIO outspent both congressional candidates combined.

The AFL-CIO is only one of the issue-advocacy groups that sponsored ads in these districts. Where the Democrat in these districts focused ads on the same topics as the AFL-CIO (that is, against corporate tax breaks, for pension protection, support of public education, the minimum wage, and Medicare), the issue advocacy drowned out the voice of the Republican and any independents in the race. Where the Democrat focused on other issues, the AFL-CIO's message drowned out both. In some of the districts in which the Business Coalition responded to the AFL-CIO by buttressing the case for the Republican, the candidates' voices became even less distinct and discernible.

Chapter Sixteen

Do Issue Ads Work?
If So, When?

ADS CAN BOTH INFLUENCE PUBLIC ATTITUDES and, when they traffic in partial truths, mislead. This outcome is particularly likely when the issue is complex, reporting on the issue by the media is deficient, adwatching is minimal or nonexistent, and one side significantly outspends the other. This is as true of issue advocacy as it is of standard candidate advertising.

In political terms, issue advocacy is communication whose principal purpose is to promote a set of ideas or policies. By contrast, express advocacy explicitly advocates the election or the defeat of a candidate. The 1976 Supreme Court decision about campaign finance, *Buckley v. Valeo*,[1] noted that as long as the communication did not "expressly advocate" the election or defeat of a clearly identified federal candidate, the amount of money spent on it could not be limited because it was protected under the First Amendment of the Constitution. Nor could government require that the identity of those funding such ads be disclosed. *Buckley v. Valeo* outlines a series of "magic words" that cannot appear in any form in issue advocacy. They include "vote for," "support," or "oppose."

In recent years, issue advocacy has been a growth industry. In the 1996 election, the Annenberg Public Policy Center of the University of Pennsylvania estimated that more than two dozen organizations sponsored issue ads and spent an estimated $135 million to $150 million. According to the 1996 Annenberg School for Communication general-election survey, 57.6 percent of those polled recalled seeing an issue advertisement. In addition, issue ads utilized more attack statements (41.1 percent) than other forms of political communication, such as candidate ads, debates, free air time, or news coverage.[2] After 1996, expenditures and the number of active groups continued to rise rapidly. In 1997 and

1998, at least seventy-seven groups sponsored broadcast issue ads and spent between $275 million and $340 million.[3]

Issue ads and high-profile policy debates went hand in hand during the 1990s. A great deal of press attention was bestowed on the issue-ad clashes during the 1993 and 1994 health care reform debate. The "Harry and Louise" advertisements sponsored by the Health Insurance Association of America (HIAA) were credited (some argue mistakenly) with building a popular outcry against that reform proposal and contributing to the defeat of President Clinton's Health Security Act. A $14 million media buy powered the issue-advocacy campaign, which received extensive attention from the press and was parodied by the president and first lady.[4]

In 1996, the Democratic National Committee (DNC) used issue-advocacy advertising to demonize the Republican Congress, especially House Speaker Newt Gingrich (R-Georgia). The commercials were credited with influencing public opinion and building support for the Clinton-Gore reelection campaign. The DNC commercials were considered issue advocacy because they did not directly endorse a candidate but rather promoted a set of ideas or policies.

In the 1996 election, issue advocacy exploded as numerous groups followed the Democratic Party's lead and exploited the campaign finance loophole. The number of groups and the size of the expenditures continued to increase in the 1998 elections. The acceptance and legitimacy of issue advertisements increased as a number of interest groups, notably the tobacco companies, devoted significant resources to advocacy campaigns.

As the amount of advertising escalated, assumptions regarding the influence of commercials on public policy and election outcomes have followed suit. Is the influence of issue ads a myth? Or are these commercials a highly persuasive method that shapes the opinions of the electorate and pressures legislators? Analysts, including academics and reporters, do not agree on the success of issue ads. On the one hand, some theorize that issue-advocacy commercials are a powerful lobbying tool that has the ability to fundamentally shape policy debates. On the other, some point to dozens of "failed" campaigns in which the interest group did not affect legislation. The interested parties do agree that these commercials have altered the political environment and changed the dynamic of policy debates. But do issue ads enable wealthy, well-organized interests to overshadow competitors and reframe discussion in their preferred terms?

Between April and August 1998, the five major American tobacco companies sponsored a massive issue-advocacy campaign.[5] This series of advertisements was unprecedented in a number of ways. The $40 million media buy was larger in size and depth than previous efforts. In addition, the issue-advocacy debate over the bill sponsored by Senator John McCain (R-Arizona) was largely one-sided. The antismoking organizations, such as the American Cancer Society and the Campaign for Tobacco-Free Kids, lacked the financial resources to adequately combat the industry's advertising and were outspent 40-to-1.[6]

The tobacco industry's issue ads about the McCain bill were a prime example of saturation advertising. The pro-industry side aired commercials at a high level of frequency and outspent its opponents. Saturation advertising is likely to elicit a level of recall sufficient to make it possible to identify an agenda setting or priming effect if one occurred. Did the advertisements change the way people (legislators and average Americans) viewed the issues surrounding the tobacco legislation sponsored by McCain? Did the advertisements or the surrounding media attention increase awareness of the legislation? Was public opinion recast to reflect the claims of the advertisements? Did the attitudes of those in media markets with more advertising differ from those in markets with little or none?

Even when such ads appear to influence policy and shape public discourse, little academic work has been done on their quantifiable effectiveness. Previous studies of issue advocacy are limited because they are descriptive (campaign-finance driven),[7] narrow (legislative ads toward elites),[8] or experimental (heavy emphasis on inoculation theory and source attribution).[9] Each study highlights important aspects of issue advocacy but fails to address the overall influence of the ads.

Measures of effectiveness have been crude and limited due to the available sources. For example, the success of commercials is often gauged by the number of telephone calls to toll-free numbers included in an advertising campaign. The "Harry and Louise" ads sponsored by HIAA registered 300,000 calls between September 1993 and April 1994. Another common device is counting the amount of "free" air time in news that is devoted to the commercial after it is aired. HIAA's 1993–1994 health care reform advertisements received a total of 324 seconds of network evening news time, compared with 122 seconds for the DNC's commercials.[10]

A better gauge of effectiveness would be to focus on survey data and media-buy information to assess whether issue advertisements shift opinions. Comparing changes in judged accuracy of claims with exposure to advertising will help determine whether issue ads are successful in altering attitudes. Campaigns, not single advertisements, should be analyzed to determine whether attitudes differ in areas exposed and unexposed to the ads.

As the debate over issue-advocacy advertising has grown, so has the confusion over what constitutes an issue commercial. Each author's definition of issue-advocacy advertising reflects the manner in which the subject is tackled. One group of scholars, spurred by the recent campaign-finance debate, describes the problems of issue-advocacy advertising and questions its effect on public discourse.[11] From another point of view, issue advocacy is a legitimate piece of a larger lobbying effort by traditional interest groups.[12] In a third conception, communication theories are applied to issue advocacy to measure effectiveness.[13]

Issue advocacy has a long tradition as a form of corporate image building. In this more traditional conception, "advocacy advertising, although a subset of corporate image advertising, is concerned with the propagation of ideas and the elucidation of controversial issues of public importance. It does so in such a manner that supports the position and interests of the sponsor while expressly or implicitly downgrading the sponsor's opponents and denying the accuracy of their facts."[14]

Corporations have used issue advocacy to address difficult or controversial topics. The majority of these campaigns have focused on elite print outlets, such as the *New York Times* editorial page or the *National Journal*. Since the 1970s, Mobil Oil Corporation has used issue-advocacy advertising to express its point of view, especially when it felt that the media were not portraying the company accurately or fairly. In recent years, industry coalitions, such as the milk producers, the beef coalition, and the cotton growers, have employed issue advocacy to battle competition or to change public behavior and opinion. Because of a lack of financial disclosure, it is difficult to assess whether the corporations involved in this type of issue-advocacy advertising also are involved in its political incarnation. Philip Morris's $1 million campaign supposedly to stop youth smoking would fall under this category of issue ads.

Issue advocacy functions as one component of a larger traditional lobbying effort. Instead of individual corporations sponsoring advertisements, industry or activist groups form coalitions in service of common goals. Advertising is an "outside lobbying technique" used by interest groups to influence legislators and public opinion.[15] Coalitions or individual corporations also utilize campaign contributions, grassroots lobbying, or public relations strategies to lobby Capitol Hill.[16] In Burdett Loomis's conception, ads primarily target Washington elites in hopes of achieving favorable legislation.[17]

Legislative-issue campaigns focus on a particular piece of legislation, such as the national budget or NAFTA. By contrast, election-issue advocacy ads support preferred candidates or oppose those who do not share the sponsoring organizations' political views, without explicitly advocating their election or defeat. In many cases, legislative-issue ads target legislators in the hope of influencing votes. When this occurs, television commercials are concentrated in the Washington, D.C., media market, and print advertisements are run in elite newspapers and journals.

By contrast, election-issue ads influence members of Congress by creating public opinion, or the illusion of it, in their districts. By influencing who is elected, issue advocacy affects legislation. However, these definitions are not rigid; interest groups will employ the targeting strategy that best suits their needs. In the case of the five largest tobacco companies' campaign of 1998, legislative-issue ads were addressed to legislators in the nation's capital but also aired nationwide on cable television to erode support for the bill.

Loomis outlines a series of attributes that are common in issue-advocacy campaigns.[18] The 1998 tobacco campaign embodies each of them. First, when issue ads are present, one side's point of view dominates the public discourse. Second, in order to best control the debate, an interest will broaden or restrict the scope of conflict to achieve a favorable setting and manufacture "the dominant narrative that defined both the problems and potential solutions." In the case of tobacco, the industry expanded the scope of conflict from a negotiation among state attorneys general and federal leaders to a campaign addressing the general public. Finally, only a limited number of interests have the resources or desire to sponsor issue ads. Loomis realizes that the tobacco industry has both of these elements and prior to 1998 had embarked on several campaigns. "Tobacco companies—both individually and in concert—have embarked upon expensive campaigns to counter governmental actions by redefining smoking issues."[19] In other words, the 1998 campaigns are textbook examples of how an interest can shape and dominate a debate.

Political scientist Darrell West expands on Loomis's assumptions by explaining that issue ads allow interests to control the content, the timing, and the delivery of the message.[20] The interest's position is directly transmitted to the public without having to rely on the press. In certain situations, the goal of issue advocacy may not focus on dramatically altering the opinions of the general public but instead focus on influencing elites with a show of force. "Even if citizens themselves are not swayed by grassroots appeals, elites can perceive that there is a groundswell of support or opposition in regard to particular proposals."[21]

Like Loomis, West argues that issue-advocacy ads create problems for representative democracy because the tactic favors powerful, rich, and well-organized interests.[22] Even though issue advocacy is available to all interests, only a few can afford to engage in it. Consumer groups, public interest groups, political parties, and broad-based social movements are limited in their ability to participate because of the cost involved in mounting a campaign.

However, West discounts the effectiveness of issue ads because of their link to known partisan groups and their past failures. He adds, "Interest groups which run ads have clear partisan objectives and therefore are not seen as credible by reporters, legislators, or the public."[23] This conclusion is based on the assumption that a group's identity and interests are clear from the ad. In practice, it is extremely difficult to discern this information from the individual ads, which is one reason the interest groups, especially an organization with a negative or tainted image, will often choose to air issue ads using "stealth" front groups. This tactic divorces the perceived accountability for the advertising campaign from the interest group. In addition, as we noted in Chapter 1, in the 1996 and 1998 elections, political parties were sponsors of issue advocacy. The parties have successfully utilized advertising campaigns to promote their agendas.

Issue Advocacy and Communication Theory

Burgoon, Pfau, and Birk posit that issue ads instill "resistance to potential slippage in the attitudes of supporters rather than [act] as a tool to convert opponents."[24] As a result, they note, issue ads appear in elite newspapers, target elites, and "employ lengthy arguments." In addition, they observe that the target audience is political conservatives who already have favorable opinions of business.

These scholars do not distinguish among types of issue-advocacy advertisements. To test their theories, their experiment relies on Mobil Oil print advertisements. They then apply their hypotheses to both corporate and political-issue advocacy. Within these categories, the researchers fail to divide ads according to the type of sponsor. In the experiment, this creates an uneven match between a nonprofit and a corporate product. If subjects base their assessment of the ad on the legitimacy of the sponsoring organization, the results may be skewed.

In contrast to Burgoon, Pfau, and Birk's framing, Leonard N. Reid, Lawrence C. Soley, and Bruce G. Vanden Bergh conducted an experiment to probe source attribution in issue-advocacy advertisements.[25] They found that when audience members are neutral toward an issue and generally uncommitted, they tend to respond more negatively to a trade organization or commercial sponsor than to a noncommercial sponsor of the same advocacy position. Knowledge about the sponsor influences the impact of the issue ad. When a newspaper reports additional information about the ad or about the sponsoring group, the press alters the environment.

Source credibility is a fundamental concept in understanding how interest groups utilize issue advocacy. By employing a front group to sponsor issue advocacy, a controversial interest group may forestall a backlash. Average viewers may not be able to discern the source of the ads and thus may judge a commercial sponsored by a front group more favorably than an advertisement for an interest identified in its spots. Citizens have difficulty remembering advertising sources. For example, our study of issue-advocacy advertising in the 1996 presidential election found that only half of focus-group participants could correctly identify the advertising sponsors after directly viewing the commercials.

Charles T. Salmon, Leonard N. Reid, James Pokrywczynski, and Robert W. Willett advanced the earlier hypothesis of Reid and colleagues that source credibility influenced the strength of advocacy advertising. This team hypothesized that the format of the advocacy information is related to the effectiveness of the message. The public affairs information presented as a paid advertisement is less effective than a published press release. They found that noncommercial sources are considered less biased than commercial ones. "The implication of the finding is that although advertising in general is perceived as more biased than news stories, a message presented in an advertising format may be perceived as more interesting and more informative, and hence, be more persuasive than a message presented in a news format."[26] These communication studies concentrate on the strength of individual advertisements and the sponsor's credibility and fail to consider the effectiveness of the entire issue-ad campaign. Success of issue advocacy would be better assessed by examining how actual issue ads alter public opinion in a more naturalistic setting.

Issue Advocacy and the Tobacco Debates

In order to understand the effects of the issue advertising in the tobacco debate, it is useful to understand the context in which the deliberation about the McCain bill took place. In the 1990s, the tobacco debate moved to the federal level when the McCain bill sought congressional approval for an agreement between forty state attorneys general and the cigarette companies. In general, the McCain bill (S. 1415) would have increased the power of the Food and Drug Administration to partly restrict tobacco products, regulated tobacco advertising, increased the cost of a pack of cigarettes by $1.10 over five years, penalized the industry if it failed to reduce the number of young smokers, and assessed the industry $516 billion over a twenty-five-year period. In return, a yearly cap of $6.5 billion on awards to aggrieved smokers would be set, the companies would be provided immunity from all class action lawsuits and limited punitive damages from past activities, and tobacco farmers would receive financial help for losses that occurred as a result of the legislation.

The content of the legislation changed as debate over it proceeded. Because the changes affected the accuracy of the content of ads, we are providing a brief catalogue of them: On June 20, 1997, the cigarette makers reached an agreement with forty state attorneys general that broadened the power of the Food and Drug Administration to regulate tobacco products in some respects and restricted it in others, restricted advertising, increased the cost of a pack of cigarettes by about sixty cents over five years, penalized the industry by up to an additional $2 billion a year if the number of young smokers didn't drop below targeted levels, charged the companies $368.5 billion over a twenty-five-year period, and set a yearly cap of $4 billion on awards to individuals. In exchange, this proposed settlement gave the companies immunity from all class action lawsuits and limited punitive damages from past activities. An important provision was that the settlement was subject to congressional approval.

Action was taking place at the state level as well: On July 3, 1997, the tobacco companies settled the Mississippi Medicaid lawsuit for $3.6 billion. On August 25, 1997, the suit brought by the attorney general of Florida was settled for $11.3 billion. On January 16, 1998, Texas settled its Medicaid lawsuit for over $14 billion.

On April 8, 1998, the major tobacco companies declared negotiations dead and announced that they would take their case to the American people. Senate bill 1415, which was supported by President Bill Clinton, was voted out of the Senate Commerce Committee in April 1998 by a nineteen-to-one vote. The bill would have settled the lawsuits brought by the attorneys general with provisions that elicited $516 billion from the industry over twenty-five years; increased the price of a pack of cigarettes at the manufacturing level by $1.10 over a five-year period; increased the regulatory authority of the Food and Drug Administration over the manufacturing, sale, and marketing of tobacco products; imposed up to $3.5 billion in annual financial penalties on the tobacco companies if youth smoking failed to drop at least a specified amount; provided $10 billion over a five-year period to help those such as tobacco growers whose livelihood was negatively affected by the agreement; and placed a $6.5 billion annual cap on the amounts cigarette companies could be assessed in damages. The money raised by the bill would have funded medical research as well as a large-scale campaign to reduce youth smoking. The McCain bill would also have banned billboards advertising tobacco within 1,000 feet of schools and banned human, animal, or cartoon characters in ads for cigarettes. The Commerce Committee bill included financial aid to any tobacco farm owners who experienced a drop in demand as a result of the bill.

In the Senate Finance Committee, Chair William Roth (R-Delaware) tried to change the bill to direct the proposed tax revenue to tax reductions; his proposal was defeated. At the same time, the committee proposed upping the cost of a pack of cigarettes $1.50 over a three-year period. This amendment, which was not binding, was favored by former FDA Commissioner David Kessler and former Surgeon General C. Everett Koop, among others.

Negotiations between the White House and Senator McCain produced a tentative agreement that the yearly cap on liability be raised from $6.5 billion to $8 billion. The same discussions produced agreement that higher penalties be imposed on the tobacco industry if youth smoking didn't drop below the targeted rate.

On May 8, 1998, Minnesota settled for $6.1 billion.

On May 21, the Senate voted to support the Gregg-Leahy amendment to S. 1415. That amendment eliminated legal protections for the tobacco companies, including the annual ceiling on the industry's liability. A Senate vote on the bill was postponed until the members returned from recess in June. "Industry Ad Campaign Helps Stall Tobacco Bill," noted a headline in the *New York Times*.[27]

On June 10, the Senate, backed by President Clinton, "approved a compromise proposal attaching an unrelated marriage tax cut to the pending tobacco measure."[28] The Gramm amendment gave the self-employed a 100 percent deduction for the cost of their health insurance starting in 1999. It also cut the so-called marriage penalty for couples making less than $50,000 a year. The amendment was endorsed by voice vote. This amendment altered the net tax impact of the bill on those most likely to be affected by the increase in the tax on cigarettes.

Other important amendments were made to the bill, as well, opening its sponsors to the charge that the intent of the legislation was funding non-tobacco-related government programs. The Senate adopted amendments providing veterans with $3 billion to cope with smoking-related illness. The Coverdell amendment, funding anti-illegal drug enforcement and interdiction, passed 52-46.

The U.S. Chamber of Commerce was among the groups lobbying for a cap on the fees trial lawyers could claim from the settlement. The Chamber's television ad attacked the transfer of funds from working Americans making under $30,000 to "millionaire" trial lawyers. (Because those with lower incomes are more likely to be smokers, a tax per pack will fall disproportionately on those making under $30,000.) The Gorton amendment, passed 49-48 on June 16, set up a formula capping those fees.

The Durbin-DeWine amendment made the so-called look-back assessments (the penalties paid by the industry if the targeted reductions in youth smoking were not reached by the specified time) more company-specific and set reduction targets at 20 percent in three years, 40 percent in five years, 55 percent in seven years, and 67 percent in ten years. The Reed amendment disallowed tax deductions for advertising, promotional, and marketing expenses relating to tobacco-product use unless certain advertising requirements were met.

The cloture vote that would have moved S. 1415 to a final vote failed 57-42. A 53-46 procedural vote sent S. 1415 back to the Commerce Committee. Proponents of the bill were short of the sixty votes needed to waive the motion.

As all of this activity was going on, the airwaves in some markets were flooded with ads from the tobacco industry. Forming a coalition called the Tobacco Resolution, the five largest American tobacco companies initially joined forces to support a settlement and then, when protection from class action suits was lost, to lobby against passage of the McCain bill.[29] The alliance consisted of Brown & Williamson Tobacco Corporation, Lorillard Tobacco Company, Philip Morris Incorporated, R. J. Reynolds Tobacco Company, and United States Tobacco Company.

The U.S. Tobacco Company was the only one of the five companies not among the sponsors of the first ad that began airing March 12. Its message focused on the benefits of the June 20, 1997, settlement proposal. "There's been bitter conflict about tobacco issues," said the announcer as reinforcing print appeared on the screen. "Isn't it time to move forward? The tobacco companies have agreed to a reasonable settlement." The ad then listed key elements of the agreement: "$500 million a year to reduce youth smoking. Billions of dollars that can be spent on health care. Disclosure to the FDA about the health effects of tobacco products. An end to all outdoor tobacco advertising. No cigarette vending machines. Larger warning labels on cigarettes." The spot then asked, "What do the tobacco companies get? They don't get immunity. Class action lawsuits are settled now and not allowed in the future. Individuals can still sue tobacco companies. No limits on punitive damages for future conduct. A unique opportunity to move forward." The ad closed with the tag line "Get the Facts: Call 1-800-556-9969."

On April 8, the tobacco representatives announced that negotiations had not worked. The new campaign was built on the assumption articulated in one of the television ads. "There was a historic resolution of tobacco issues. This would have changed the tobacco industry. Now politics has taken over."

On April 9, the first full-page print ad appeared in national papers. The same ad was run in regional papers on April 12.

On April 16, the tobacco companies began a $40 million print, radio, and television campaign "to inform the American people about both the proposed national tobacco resolution and proposed legislation before Congress." As a small disclaimer at the beginning of the ad indicated, the first television ad aired by the industry in this series was sponsored by "America's four leading tobacco companies."

When ads ask viewers to do something—buy a product, vote for a candidate, call a number—one measure of their effectiveness is sales, votes, or calls. The tobacco companies' ads closed with a 1-800 number. Those who called were given the option to be patched through to Congress. Alternatively, they could send a telegram. From March 12 through July 28, reported industry spokesman Steve Duchesne, the ads elicited 469,368 calls. Of those, 133,414 were patched through to a congressional office, and 167,748 telegrams were sent. By contrast, after spending $12 million on nine months of advertising, the campaign running the "Harry and Louise" ads had elicited 300,000 calls.

The tobacco ads were also characterized by on-screen documentation of the sources of the companies' claims. The backup documents were offered to stations to clear the ads but were not routinely made available to reporters. "We just haven't seen the critical review of what we were saying in the ads," said Duchesne. "I think that reflects the level of substantiation we have had to live up to. [Because the ads are sponsored by the tobacco companies] we are probably held to a higher standard by those clearing ads for the stations."

On Friday, July 17, the five companies began airing the fourteenth in the series of television ads begun in mid-April to block the bill. Each airing of ads lasted one to two weeks and played in thirty to fifty markets across the country. Some weeks, the group was on the air in fifty markets, in other weeks, thirty, and in some weeks below that level, reported Duchesne.

By and large, local buys were not made in Washington, D.C., or New York City, although the "Christmas tree" ad ran as part of a D.C.-area spot buy. Because the ads aired nationally on CNN, they reached the Washington market that way. The ads were aired coast to coast on both national and spot cable and spot broadcast. Print ads appeared in such elite media as the *Washington Post* and such specialty publications as *Amsterdam News* and *Roll Call*.

The commercials featured the themes of previous tobacco campaigns: smokers' and taxpayers' rights. The advertising focused on how the legislation would increase government bureaucracy, mandate the largest consumer tax increase in history, and create a black market for cigarettes. By tapping into popular antigovernment themes, these claims appealed to smokers but also to the general public. Thus, the advertising increased the scope of discussion from a narrow policy focus to one on civil liberties and the role of government.

The Tobacco Resolution advertising was reinforced by other issue-advocacy campaigns. The U.S. Chamber of Commerce and the National Smokers Alliance both aired commercials advocating the defeat of the McCain legislation. The Tobacco Resolution advertising aired across the nation, but the U.S. Chamber of Commerce sponsored commercials only in the Washington, D.C., media market.[30]

A coalition of anti-tobacco groups attempted to combat the Tobacco Resolution advertising. The Campaign for Tobacco-Free Kids, a nonprofit organization working to reduce youth smoking, was a vocal supporter of the tobacco-control legislation. The campaign sponsored a series of radio commercials calling for eight senators to support the bill.[31] It also produced a commercial in conjunction with the American Cancer Society (ACS), the other leader in lobbying for the bill. The ACS aired advertisements featuring former Surgeon General C. Everett Koop that were shown in Maine, Colorado, Washington, Georgia, and Missouri and on CNN. This May 1998 campaign cost approximately $1 million and was followed in September by a larger $5 million buy.[32] These efforts by the Campaign for Tobacco-Free Kids and American Cancer Society were not able to compete with the larger campaign sponsored by the Tobacco Resolution. The largest buy aired after the McCain bill had been declared dead and the tobacco companies' ads had disappeared. These anti-tobacco commercials chose to take a more direct approach and targeted undecided senators and Beltway elites in hopes of shoring up or increasing support for the legislation.

The tobacco industry's issue ads, a textbook example of the power of saturation advertising, allowed the industry to reshape the debate. The pro-smoking side aired commercials at a high level and outspent the proponents of the McCain bill. The power of the tobacco companies' campaign was magnified by the fact that there was little counterbalancing information in the news.

During the 1996 campaign, the Associated Press offered regular adwatches of presidential general-election ads. During the issue advocacy over the McCain bill, AP produced no adwatches. Neither did the *New York Times* and *Washington Post,* which in 1996 developed alternative forms to evaluate the accuracy of campaign claims. CNN, which did not adwatch the presidential general election of 1996 but did a thorough job in 1992, did not produce adwatches on this exchange either.

The only adwatch by a major media outlet was aired on ABC. In place of adwatching were stories that reinforced the inaccuracies in the ads by running them uncorrected in news. A National Public Radio piece reported: "Although some politicians are wary about making tobacco legislation a campaign issue, it may be out of their hands already. The tobacco industry has been running television ads warning of a Congress gone crazy over anti-tobacco legislation. The latest spot features a self-destructing cuckoo clock."[33] A clip of the ad airs. "These ads are running in fifty markets," continues the reporter.

In a similar move, an ABC *Nightline* report aired a segment of an industry ad that said, "Washington's tobacco legislation, what's in it for you? Half a trillion dollars in new taxes, new federal spending, cigarettes at $5.00 a pack, creating a black market. No wonder it's opposed by millions of hard-working Americans."[34] The reporter then added, "The ads came on top of the millions in campaign contributions the tobacco companies have traditionally given to congressional candidates."

At issue then are questions such as these: Did the advertisements change the way people viewed the tobacco legislation sponsored by Senator McCain? Did the advertisements or the surrounding media attention increase the awareness of the legislation? Were opinions recast to reflect the claims of the advertisements? Did media markets with more advertising differ from those areas with little or no advertising? Did respondents who were heavily exposed to advertising judge the claims of the pro-tobacco side more accurately than those who did not view commercials on the subject? Did the claims of the anti-tobacco forces suffer in areas with heavy exposure? Or were there no discernible effects?

To determine the effect of the ads aired by both sides, Jamieson and Princeton Survey Research Associates created a survey administered to 1,242 adults, age eighteen and older, August 20–30, 1998. The survey sampled individuals exposed to different kinds of media climates. The breakdown was as follows:

- 318 individuals in the twenty-two media markets with heavy Tobacco Resolution campaign advertising—more than 3,500 gross ratings points (GRPs) of advertising on broadcast television outlets between April 1 and July 18;
- 309 individuals in the twenty-one media markets with moderate advertising—between 1,700 and 3,500 GRPs;
- 308 individuals in the twenty-one markets with sparse advertising—less than 1,700 GRPs;

- 307 individuals in twenty randomly selected comparable markets with no Tobacco Resolution campaign advertising on broadcast television.

On average, viewers in heavy advertising areas saw fifty-seven pro-tobacco ads on broadcast television over three and a half months. Viewers in moderate advertising areas saw twenty-five, and viewers in sparse areas saw nine. Because the industry did make national buys on CNN, there was some exposure to the ads in our "no" and "sparse" conditions. Because exposure was uniform across the markets, the relative level of gross ratings points in broadcast would reflect actual levels of difference between markets.

The margin of error for results based on the full sample of 1,242 is ±3 percent. For results based on a subsample, the margin of error is ±6 percent. Following are some findings from the study:

For three of the claims in the ads, individuals in areas with heavy pro-tobacco advertising judged the claims as more accurate than did those in areas with less or no advertising.

- "Under the tobacco plan Congress considered earlier this summer, the price of cigarettes would increase to $5 a pack." In media markets with heavy pro-tobacco advertising, 22 percent of individuals judged this statement very accurate, compared with 15 percent in markets with no advertising.
- "The tobacco plan Congress considered would create a huge black market in cigarettes." Almost half (47 percent) of individuals in areas with heavy advertising said this statement was very accurate, compared with a third (35 percent) in areas with no advertising.
- "The tobacco plan Congress considered would create the largest consumer tax in history." Four in ten individuals (43 percent) in heavy advertising areas said this statement was very accurate, compared with three in ten (31 percent) in areas with no advertising.

These findings hold even after taking into account behavioral, attitudinal, and demographic factors that play a role in determining how people judged the accuracy of these statements.

- Those who smoke or live in a household where someone smokes were more likely than those who do not to think the tobacco plan the Senate considered would have increased cigarettes to $5 a pack (22 percent versus 17 percent), created a black market (54 percent versus 35 percent), and created the largest consumer tax in history (50 percent versus 29 percent).

- Those with an unfavorable opinion of government regulation of business were more likely than those with a favorable opinion to think the plan would have created a black market (46 percent versus 32 percent) and the largest consumer tax in history (41 percent versus 27 percent).

Individuals in areas with heavy advertising judged the two other widely aired claims as no more or less accurate than did those in areas with less or no advertising. The two claims were

- The Senate plan would create seventeen new bureaucracies.
- Under the plan, both smokers' and nonsmokers' taxes would increase.

There was no significant difference among markets on descriptive statements about the bill that were not found in the ads. These statements were that the plan eliminated the marriage tax penalty; the plan would aid tobacco farmers; the plan would reimburse the states and fund campaigns and medical research; the plan made health insurance tax deductible for the self-employed. In addition, there were no differences in perceptions of the accuracy of one claim by the anti-tobacco forces that was backed by a small television and radio buy. The claim made was that 3,000 kids start smoking regularly daily, and as a result one-third die prematurely.

Links between perceptions of the Senate bill and support for the bill underscore the relevance of this study. It is important to understand what shapes people's perceptions because perceptions shape opinion.

Exposure to pro-tobacco ads was unrelated to support for the Senate bill. However, perceptions of what the bill would have done and why the bill was or was not necessary shaped support for the bill:

- Four in ten individuals (39 percent) who thought the Senate tobacco plan would have spawned a black market for cigarettes supported the bill, compared with half (50 percent) who thought a black market was unlikely.
- The belief that the plan would have represented the largest consumer tax in history dampened support for the bill (38 percent versus 54 percent).
- Thinking the plan would have created seventeen new government bureaucracies dampened support (37 percent versus 49 percent),

as did thinking the plan would increase the taxes of both smokers and nonsmokers (38 percent versus 49 percent).

- Knowing the plan would have aided tobacco farmers increased support for the Senate bill (45 percent versus 38 percent), as did knowing the plan would have reimbursed the states for health expenses and funded anti-smoking campaigns and medical research (46 percent versus 32 percent).

Exposure to pro-tobacco advertising played a modest but statistically significant role in shaping people's perceptions of the accuracy of claims at issue in the tobacco debate. Specifically, there were dramatic and statistically significant differences in perception of the accuracy of the claim that "the tobacco plan Congress considered would create a huge black market in cigarettes" (see Table A16.1 in Appendix IV). The differences in perception paralleled differences in exposure to the industry ads' claim.[35]

Overall, even after the study controlled for highly salient behaviors and attitudes and a range of demographic variables, exposure to pro-tobacco ads affected perception of the accuracy of three of the eleven claims tested. This finding is noteworthy because these perceptions shaped opinion about whether the Senate should have passed the tobacco bill.

In the case of the McCain bill, the tobacco industry was able to stall the legislation and then deny it a floor vote. This victory permitted the industry to broker a more favorable settlement between the corporations and the states involved in the class action suit. This case indicates that when the issue is complex, reporting on it deficient, adwatching minimal, and one side substantially outspends the other, ads (in this instance, issue ads) can influence public attitudes.

Deborah Beck and Kathleen Hall Jamieson

Part IV

The Influence
of News

⇥ Did You Know?

Although newspapers overwhelmingly and consistently endorse the Republican presidential nominee, reporters overwhelmingly and consistently identify as Democrats.

Chapter Seventeen

The Test Ban Treaty and the 2000 Campaign

I N THEORY, THE DAY-IN-DAY-OUT news coverage of the political debate over legislation should arm the electorate with a storehouse of knowledge useful in charting the similarities and differences among presidential candidates. To determine whether it does, we analyzed news coverage of the ten days surrounding the Senate vote on the Comprehensive Test Ban Treaty (CTBT).

Since 1996, 154 countries have signed the treaty. In 1996, President Clinton was the first leader to sign. Although fifty-one have ratified it, the treaty must be approved by legislatures in the forty-four countries that have some nuclear capability. By the time the debate occurred in the U.S. Senate, twenty-six of these countries had signed on. The treaty, which required Senate ratification, was defeated in the U.S. Senate on October 13, 1999, by a vote of 51 to 48. Under the Constitution, 67 yes votes are required for ratification.

At the core of the debate over the treaty are two areas of disagreement. Both sides agree that the treaty expands on an earlier ban on atmospheric explosions to include underground nuclear testing. However, those who oppose the treaty doubt that it can be effectively enforced. Proponents and opponents also differ in their confidence that the United States can maintain strategic readiness under the constraints of the proposed treaty.

Beyond those two areas of clash are a number of policy details. An organization would supervise international verification measures. The monitoring system would permit verification of nuclear explosions down to a yield of a few kilotons. Seismological, radionuclide, hydroacoustic, and infrasound monitoring would be included. It is not clear that a citizen needs to know any of these details, however. What is important is that proponents and opponents of Senate ratification disagreed on whether these measures were sufficiently reliable to detect violations.

Because the Republican-controlled Senate rejected a treaty championed by a Democratic president, attentive consumers of news should be able to surmise at least the position of Vice President Al Gore on the question of ratification. An ad that he ran in New Hampshire arguing for ratification adds to the informational menu. If as we argued earlier accurate information about the stands of the parties provides cues that permit voters to function efficiently, then strategic coverage will telegraph that in general Republicans opposed ratification and in general Democrats supported it. That information would be sufficient to position all of the candidates in the Republican and Democratic primary fields. Understanding why the Republicans opposed ratification and the Democrats favored it requires additional information. Presumably, news coverage should have given the public a general sense of that disagreement.

Note that this theory of how the electorate could learn about this important issue presupposes that there is informational value in the party positions included in strategic coverage. This doesn't mean that we wouldn't prefer a higher proportion of coverage that frames policy debates as deliberations over problems and alternative solutions. It does mean that if news about legislative action can guide citizens to rough approximations of the issue stands of candidates, this general understanding can lessen the workload placed on debates, ads, and subsequent news about the campaign. If voters can position the candidates before a candidate debate, they presumably will be better able to learn the reasons for the differences between the contenders in those other arenas.

To test these alternatives, using the key words "nuclear," "test," "ban," and "treaty," we searched Lexis-Nexis from October 8 through October 18, the ten days surrounding the October 13, 1999, Senate vote. This permitted us to analyze the *New York Times*, the *Washington Post*, the *Los Angeles Times*, *USA Today*, and broadcast coverage from NBC, ABC, and CBS on the nightly and morning news.

Our analysis credited a story with descriptive content if it included even a relevant sentence. Very few of the stories that had descriptive detail included more than one sentence of that sort. Many embedded a single descriptive sentence in a broader discussion of tactics. A story on NBC is illustrative.

Meanwhile, another showdown tonight for President Clinton, this one with the United States Senate over the treaty that would ban nuclear tests worldwide. The president has asked the Senate to postpone voting on the treaty, knowing that it will almost certainly go down to defeat. Senate Republicans may go along, but only if the president agrees not to reintroduce it, and he won't make that promise. (*NBC Nightly News,* October 11, 1999)

The next night, however, NBC's Claire Shipman did a good job of indicating why the public should pay attention to this debate.

What would the treaty do? Ban all underground nuclear tests. The U.S. has had a voluntary ban on underground tests since 1992. This would make it binding. Supporters say United States approval of the treaty would lock in superiority, make it difficult for nonnuclear nations to develop the bomb, and compel other nuclear nations, like Russia, China, India, Pakistan, to approve the treaty as well. And backers of the treaty say underground tests are no longer needed to maintain the U.S. nuclear arsenal, because underground tests with smaller amounts of plutonium can still be conducted. And sophisticated computers can also make sure U.S. weapons are ready. But critics warn those systems aren't fully operational yet, and say technology is changing too fast for the U.S. to swear off testing. (*NBC Nightly News,* October 12, 1999)

If policy detail is the standard, Shipman's story was the best of the telecast news we analyzed. Most of the broadcast coverage had no description of the treaty at all. Although coverage was lacking in details, it did cast the disagreement along party lines. Pieces on CBS and ABC are illustrative:

President Clinton suffered a humiliating foreign policy defeat when the Senate rejected the Comprehensive Nuclear Test Ban Treaty. Last night's defeat came after days of negotiations to delay the treaty vote. Mr. Clinton said the treaty was a victim of politics. (*CBS This Morning,* October 14, 1999)

When the Senate rejected the Nuclear Test Ban Treaty this week, it turned a relatively obscure matter into what could become a major campaign issue next year. At his press conference yesterday, President Clinton called some Republican opponents of the treaty "the new isolationists" and said the choice before voters was clear. (ABC, *Good Morning America,* October 15, 1999)

The print reporting fell into four categories: Clinton versus Senate, Republicans versus Democrats, world reaction, and background and analysis. The first two categories defined the political landscape in partisan terms, with Clinton and the Democrats on one side and most of the Republicans on the other. The last two were more likely to include discussions of the substance of the treaty and the international implications of the Senate vote.

- Clinton versus Senate: These stories focused on President Clinton's role in the treaty debate and on his reactions to the defeat. Headlines here included "Senate Rebuffs Clinton, Rejects Treaty to Ban Nuclear Testing" (*Los Angeles Times*, October 14, 1999); "Clinton Fumes at GOP on Test Ban Defeat, Budget" (*Los Angeles Times*, October 15, 1999); "Clinton, GOP Trade Shots over Nuke Treaty" (*USA Today*, October 15, 1999); "Defeat of a Treaty: The Overview; Senate Kills Test Ban Treaty in Crushing Loss for Clinton; Evokes Versailles Pact Defeat" (*New York Times*, October 14, 1999).
- Republicans versus Democrats: These reports focused on the partisan debate surrounding the treaty. The headline "Treaty: Bountiful Blame" prefaced this statement: "Both the Democrats and the Republicans were derelict in their handling of the newly rejected Nuclear Test Ban Treaty" (*Los Angeles Times*, October 17, 1999).
- World reaction: Stories in this category included reactions from leaders of other countries. Headlines included "U.S. Rebuked on Test Ban Vote, Nations Cite 'Dangerous' Message" (*USA Today*, October 15, 1999); "World Condemns U.S. Vote to Reject Test-Ban Treaty; Policy; Governments Express Dismay and Contend That Spread of Nuclear Weapons Will Be More Difficult to Stop" (*Los Angeles Times*, October 15, 1999); "Nations Unite in Assailing Senate Vote on Test Ban Treaty" (*Washington Post*, October 15, 1999).
- Background and analysis: These stories focused on describing the treaty and analyzing its history and significance for the United States and the other possible signatories. Some headlines were "Fumble on the Test Ban Treaty" (*Washington Post*, October 18, 1999); "Defeat of a Treaty: The Arms Experts: A Nuclear Safety Valve Is Shut Off, but US Maintains Other Safeguards" (*New York Times*, October 15, 1999).

What could the public learn from this coverage? We surmised that at the minimum it told readers and viewers that the parties differed, with the Democrats favoring ratification and the Republicans opposed. Because the Comprehensive Test Ban Treaty was discussed briefly in the townhall meetings held in November and early December in the early primary states, it is possible that at least some voters learned about the candidates' positions that way. But because national viewership for these events was small—1.6 million for the first Bradley-Gore exchange, for example—we don't think the media coverage explains all of the learning we found.

As part of our year 2000 survey from November 8 through December 6, Princeton Survey Research Associates (PSRA) interviewed 1,779 American adults age eighteen and older. (The margin of error is ±2 percent for results based on the full sample.) Over one-third of those polled reported accurately that both Bradley and Gore supported the treaty "banning underground testing of nuclear weapons"; another 25 percent believed that Gore supported it but did not know Bradley's position; and 7 percent were sure of Bradley's support but less certain of Gore's. Fifteen percent knew that none of the Republican contenders supported the treaty "banning underground testing of nuclear weapons."

Even though news coverage in general included little descriptive detail, news reports of Clinton's visible support of the treaty and the solid backing of the Democrats in the Senate appear to have prompted a high level of accurate knowledge of Gore's position (62 percent of those surveyed). A respectable 44 percent placed Bradley correctly on the issue as well.

Because some Republicans crossed over to vote with the Democrats for ratification, the cues provided here are more mixed. The 15 percent of those surveyed who said that none of the Republicans supported it did draw the correct inference from the informational environment.

We did not ask whether those surveyed knew why the Republicans opposed ratification or the Democrats favored it, and thus we don't know how well grounded these inferences are. Because our question specified that the treaty banned underground testing, we do know that at least that level of descriptive detail got through to those answering correctly.

Somewhere between the ideal of a fully informed electorate and the fear of an ignorant public resides a level of knowledge required to cast an informed vote. Because Jamieson has argued that strategic coverage plays too dominant a role in political reporting, we want to stress here that when party differences are clear, strategic coverage helpfully reinforces that perception. Telegraphing the stands of parties and hence of their prospective nominees is particularly important to citizens with little time to make sense of policy details. We still believe that a focus on tactics would be more useful if it did not carry the cynical assumption that politicians embrace positions solely for strategic convenience, but that disclaimer does not minimize the importance of the information the strategy frame carries about party differences. Strategic coverage of the campaign process may serve a second function. By identifying the different voting blocs on which the candidates are focused, it may provide rough evidence about how much attention a prospective administration would give to addressing their concerns.

Kathleen Hall Jamieson, Lesley Sillaman,
and Suzanne Morse

~~⇒ Chapter Eighteen

Does Local Television News Inform As Well As Local Newspapers?

BECAUSE AMERICANS REPORT getting most of their news from local television, it is important to ask, What can a voter learn from this news source? For decades, studies have found that, in general, newspaper readers know more about politics than those who rely on other news sources. Is that still true?

To answer the question, we analyzed three surveys. One was a national study (the Annenberg Election Survey) completed shortly after the 1996 presidential election. The second was conducted in the San Francisco Bay Area shortly after the 1998 California gubernatorial race. The third was administered shortly after the 1999 Democratic mayoral primary in Philadelphia. Our analyses indicate that local television news is not very effective in informing voters about national political matters, including local congressional races. Indeed, in some cases, it misinforms voters. However, local television news does seem to do what its label promises—give voters information about the candidates and issues in local and statewide contests. This finding leads us to conclude that one should take the "local" in "local TV news" seriously and rely on newspapers and national broadcast news for information about a presidential campaign.

National Issues: How Knowledge Correlates with Media Use

The Annenberg Election Survey was conducted by telephone with 929 respondents who were identified through random-digit-dialing procedures and who were screened for having voted in the 1996 presidential election.

Respondents were asked to identify the positions of Bill Clinton and Bob Dole on twenty-six issues that had been discussed in the campaign. They were also asked whether either candidate had taken any of four specific actions that had been highlighted in the campaign (for example, cutting the size of the drug czar's office) and whether five economic/social indicators had increased, decreased, or remained the same in the past three years (for example, federal taxes paid by citizens). In addition, they were asked whether they were aware of three people who had been associated with various investigations of campaign financing (Jose Cabrera, John Huang, and Simon Firestone) and for which political party these individuals had raised funds. Finally, they were asked if they knew the names of the candidates running in their local congressional district.

If respondents correctly identified the candidate's position or action (or that both or neither candidate had taken a stand on the issue), they were credited with the correct answer. Knowledge of the five indicators was scored "correct" if the trend was correctly stated. If respondents claimed to know the identity of their congressional district's candidates or the party associated with the three fundraisers, they were scored as knowing the answer. When respondents did not feel confident enough to give an answer, we scored the response as intermediate between right and wrong on the assumption that it is better to recognize lack of knowledge than to have an incorrect impression.

To assess news-media use, the survey contained one of the more thorough batteries of questions regarding media use deployed in a national election. For each of three news sources (national network television news including CNN, local television news, and any daily newspaper), respondents were asked (1) how many days in the past week they had used the news source; (2) how much attention they paid to the source for information about the campaign; and (3) how much they thought they had learned from the source about the campaign.

Answers to all three media-use questions were used to predict the twenty-three issue-knowledge measures. In addition, demographic characteristics of the respondents (age, gender, education, income, race/ethnicity), political ideology (liberal versus conservative), and general following of the election were held constant. This analysis revealed that some type of media use was related to all twenty-three of the knowledge categories. In total, there were forty-two statistically significant relations between media use and knowledge out of 207 possible tests (twenty-three knowledge categories times nine media measures). However, in fourteen of these cases, media use was related to incorrect knowledge, and eight (57 percent) of these occurred for local television news, a proportion that was not likely to have occurred by chance.

FIGURE 18.1   Issue knowledge.

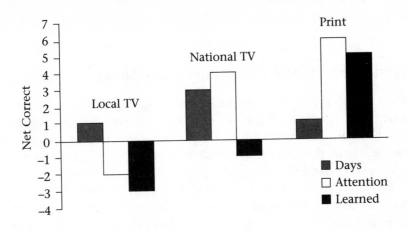

To summarize the findings, we calculated the number of times each measure of media use (days watched, attention paid, and reported learning) predicted correct knowledge and subtracted from this the number of times it predicted incorrect knowledge across all twenty-three issue categories. By this procedure, a net positive score meant that the news source was more often associated with correct knowledge, and a net negative score that the source was more often associated with incorrect knowledge.

As shown in Figure 18.1, use of daily newspapers was positively related to issue knowledge for all three measures of use. In contrast, only number of days of watching local television news was positively related to issue knowledge. Reported attention to local television news for campaign information and reported learning about the campaign were both negatively related to issue knowledge.

National television news fell between newspaper use and local television news viewing. Number of days watching national news and attention to this source were positively related to knowledge, but reported learning from this source was negatively related to knowledge. Those who reported learning a lot were actually less accurate in their knowledge than those who were more modest in their self-assessment.

Although many of the knowledge items referred to national issues, it was still the case that daily newspaper reading, most of which is devoted to the local press, was more related to knowledge of these issues than local television use. Furthermore, although knowledge of the congressional candidates should be relevant to local governance, both newspaper use and national television news were related to greater knowledge of the congressional candidates, whereas local television news viewing was not.

Statewide Elections and Television News

The study of the 1998 California gubernatorial campaign involved interviews with 817 residents of the San Francisco–Oakland Bay Area shortly after the election. The survey included questions about three domains of knowledge about the Democratic and Republican party candidates for governor: (1) recall of the candidates' names (Gray Davis and Dan Lungren), (2) familiarity with previous offices held by each candidate, and (3) identification of the candidates' positions on a range of issues. Our measures of knowledge were the proportions of items in each of the three domains answered correctly. Exposure to mass-media news was assessed as it was in the national study. Respondents were asked how many days in the past week they had used the three major news sources and how much attention they had paid to news about the race for governor in their local newspapers and on local television news programs.

In this election, local television news viewers were more knowledgeable about all three domains. Newspaper readers were more knowledgeable primarily in recalling the candidates' names. None of the media sources was associated with incorrect knowledge about the campaign. There were four significant relations between news exposure and knowledge out of a possible fifteen (three knowledge domains times five media measures), and local television news accounted for three of them. As would be expected, exposure to national television news was not related to any of the knowledge domains.

The findings from this highly contested statewide race suggest that at least in San Francisco in 1998 local television news provided voters with important information about the issues and candidates. At the same time, there was no indication that local television news gave voters incorrect information about the election.

Local Elections and Television News

The survey in Philadelphia was conducted with 340 respondents who said they had voted in the Democratic primary in May 1999. Voters had a choice among five major candidates in this highly contested race. To assess awareness of the candidates, we asked respondents to identify the names of the candidates out of a list of eight names. We scored the total number of correct identifications as well as the total number of incorrect identifications. To assess knowledge of the candidates and their positions, we asked five questions about each of the top three finishers in the election (John Street, John White, Jr., and Martin Weinberg). In addition, we asked for knowledge of nine important endorsements that occurred during the campaign, including three major newspapers, the current mayor (Ed Rendell), and various local organizations (for example, the teachers and police unions).

Use of the three news sources was assessed by asking for days of use in the past week. For newspapers and local television news, we also asked how much the respondent had paid attention to the news source for information about the recently completed campaign. We reduced the number of knowledge items from twenty-six to ten using factor analysis and again conducted regression analyses as we had done in the previous studies.

In this mayoral election, local television news was more comparable to daily newspapers as a source of information about the election. Nevertheless, use of local television news was still associated with incorrect knowledge about the election. In total, there were fifteen significant relations between media use and knowledge across the fifty possible tests (ten knowledge categories times five news sources). Thirteen of these tests involved correct knowledge of the election, with five attributable to local television news and eight to newspapers. Attention to both newspapers and local television news was associated with correct identification of the candidates. In addition, both local news sources were associated with knowledge of endorsements and candidate positions.

Two of the tests indicated that television news was associated with incorrect knowledge. Frequency of local television news use was associated with incorrect knowledge about two endorsements for one candidate, and frequency of national television news use was associated with misidentification of the candidates. As would be expected, users of national television news tended not to differ from nonusers in knowledge about this local election.

In general, these findings confirm that local television news performs relatively better in informing voters at the local level—in this case, in a major city election and a statewide election for governor.

Dan Romer and Kathleen Hall Jamieson

Chapter Nineteen

Do Newspaper Endorsements Matter? Do Politicians Speak for Themselves in Newspapers and on Television?

S TUDIES HAVE FOUND that newspaper endorsements affect voters in presidential elections—with an influence pegged at up to 7 percent of the vote.[1] There is evidence as well that newspaper endorsements can affect votes in local elections,[2] elections with complicated ballot questions,[3] and elections not tied to party.[4] Impact has also been documented on late deciders, low-interest voters, and independents.[5] Some analysts find no effects at the nonpresidential[6] and presidential levels.[7]

Note that these studies were all conducted before the steep drop in newspaper readership that characterized the late 1980s and early 1990s. If the only vehicle of influence is the newspaper, then the decline in readership signals a decline in the influence of the newspaper endorsement. But when the endorsement is also trumpeted in ads, some who were otherwise uninfluenced by the paper's editorial opinion are more likely at least to know it and at best to take it into account in the decision about how to vote. This effect is similar to that of ads—when ads are covered by television news, they enjoy increased effectiveness. To find out whether endorsements mattered in the general-election presidential decisions of 1996 and in the 1999 mayoral primaries in Philadelphia, we included questions about them in our surveys.

1996 Presidential Election

Many Americans in 1996 had no idea which presidential candidate their newspaper supported; many more had the wrong idea. In the Annenberg post–election survey, 79 percent of those registered to vote reported having read a daily newspaper in the past week. Subsequently, readers were asked which paper they "read most often to get information about the presidential campaign" and which presidential candidate that paper had endorsed. Twenty-one percent reported not knowing. Sixty-two percent of those registered to vote, then, had read a paper in the past week and were willing to hazard a guess about their paper's endorsement.

To judge from the responses, many people were guessing. Of the papers read by respondents who reported an endorsement, we were able to identify the actual endorsements made by one-half the papers. Among people who read a paper that had endorsed President Clinton, three-quarters reported that fact; 11 percent reported their paper had endorsed Bob Dole; and 14 percent reported their paper had endorsed no one. Even those figures, however, substantially overestimate knowledge of presidential endorsements in 1996, for there appears to be a considerable bias toward Clinton in these reports—whether due to his incumbency or his victory.

Less than one-half of those who read newspapers that endorsed Dole reported that fact, while one-third reported their paper had endorsed Clinton. And more than one-half of those whose paper had endorsed no presidential candidate reported an endorsement for Clinton. Even assuming that no one who correctly reported a paper's endorsement simply guessed it, our estimate is that no more than 29 percent of registered voters knew whom a newspaper endorsed. If we take the bias in reports as evidence that guessing was common, the true percentage is probably substantially lower.

The low level of accuracy is problematic only if people factored an incorrect piece of information into their voting decision. Of those who indicated that they knew who was endorsed by their newspaper, 1 percent reported that the endorsement played a great deal of a role in the decision on how to vote. Ten percent reported that the endorsement played somewhat of a role, and 89 percent answered "not at all." Of that 11 percent, about a quarter had the endorsement wrong.

1999 Philadelphia Mayoral Primary

Newspaper readership among Philadelphia's registered Democrats in May 1999 was comparable to readership among all registered Americans in 1996: Seventy-eight percent of Democrats reported in the postelection survey that they had read a newspaper in the previous week. Perhaps because a mayoral primary generates considerably less fanfare than a presidential election, a substantially larger fraction of readers of three of the city's major newspapers said they did not know which candidate their paper had endorsed in the Democratic mayoral primary: This included 33 percent of *Inquirer* readers and 42 percent of *Daily News* and *Tribune* readers. Overall, 48 percent of registered Democrats in the city had read a newspaper in the past week and were willing to indicate whom they thought their paper had endorsed.

In the city election, however, a substantially larger percentage of respondents than in the national election were correct—88 percent of *Inquirer* readers, 84 percent of *Daily News* readers, and 81 percent of *Tribune* readers. The difference from the presidential campaign might be attributable to any of several factors—including the higher incidence of "don't knows," which leaves a more knowledgeable subsample responding to the question.

Set against these factors, however, is the fact that Philadelphia Democrats intent upon guessing might have named any of five mayoral candidates; guessing at random thus contributes much less to our estimate of the extent of knowledge in the Philadelphia context than in the national one. Even so, our estimate is that as many as 41 percent of registered Democrats knew which candidate had been endorsed by the paper they read.

With only two races to compare, it is impossible to test the hypotheses that might account for this difference in knowledge of endorsements. All three papers endorsed the eventual winner, John Street; if guesses about endorsements are biased in favor of the winner, that bias is invisible in the Philadelphia case. Other, more substantive hypotheses might be advanced. For example, the increased value of endorsements to voters in a primary, in which partisanship can provide no guidance, might prompt more voters to attend to endorsements. Unlike the presidential case, news of the endorsements in Philadelphia appeared not only in print but also in broadcast ads for the endorsed candidate, John Street, during the final three days of the campaign. This final explanation opens the intriguing possibility that the impact of print endorsements might be felt because of broadcast mediation in ads.

How reliant were Philadelphia voters on the endorsement? And how accurate were those who reported factoring it into their voting decision?

For evidence on the sources of information about endorsements in the mayoral race, we turned to the preelection rolling cross-section survey; its daily interviews with random samples of Philadelphians allowed us to track increases in knowledge over the last three weeks of the campaign. On

FIGURE 19.1 Knowledge of endorsements.

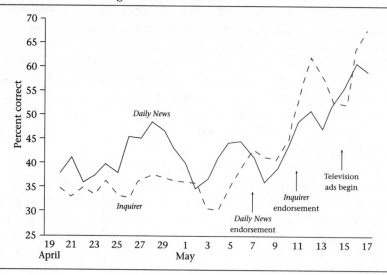

May 7 the *Daily News* endorsed John Street, as roughly 40 percent of registered Democrats in Philadelphia had been predicting (see Figure 19.1). Knowledge of the endorsement spread rapidly after the fact, growing to more than 50 percent a week later. The *Inquirer* endorsed Street on May 11. Accurate predictions of that endorsement were a bit less common than accurate predictions of the *Daily News* endorsement in April and early May, although the percentage predicting that the *Inquirer* would endorse Street grew a bit during the second week of May, perhaps influenced by knowledge of the *Daily News* endorsement. But news of the *Inquirer* endorsement, too, spread quickly, reaching 60 percent the day after publication before falling back to around 55 percent a few days later.

The television ad trumpeting Street's endorsement by the *Daily News* and the *Inquirer*, as well as by the *Philadelphia Tribune*, began airing May 15, three days before the election. The Street campaign purchased a total of 342 gross ratings points for the endorsement ad alone; it was broadcast sixty-four times on six stations over the three days. The ad apparently succeeded in boosting the dissemination of the news: Knowledge of the *Daily News* endorsement climbed another 10 percentage points over those three days, and knowledge of the *Inquirer* endorsement jumped over 15 points. In its broad outline, then, the spread of news about the *Inquirer* endorsement and about the *Daily News* endorsement followed similar patterns: Knowledge grew quickly following publication of the endorsement; the growth of knowledge leveled off (or even fell back) after a few days; and knowledge grew once again as news of the en-

FIGURE 19.2   Opinions about John Street.

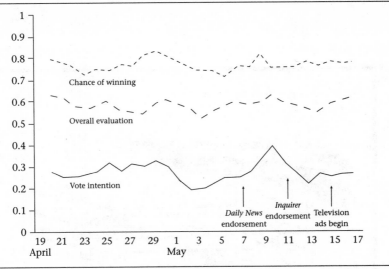

dorsements reached the airwaves. The evidence is strong that a substantial number of Philadelphia's Democrats learned of the endorsements made by the city's principal newspapers.

Knowledge of endorsements, however, apparently exerted no influence on Democrats' impressions of John Street or on their voting intentions. Overall evaluations of Street neither rose nor fell systematically during the last ten days of the campaign following the *Daily News* and then the *Inquirer* endorsements (see Figure 19.2). Judgments about Street's chances of winning the primary, too, remained constant. The proportion of Democrats making that projection jumped a bit two days after publication of the *Daily News* endorsement, but it fell back two days later and stayed constant over the remaining week before the election; if the bump upward represents anything more than random day-to-day variation, it nonetheless cannot be attributable to learning of the endorsement.

In short, more people learn of newspaper endorsements when they carry the "double punch" of television and other media exposure. As the number of daily newspaper readers continues to dwindle, the unmagnified newspaper endorsement alone will be a less important element in determining a candidate's success.

Michael G. Hagen and Kathleen Hall Jamieson

Chapter Twenty

Why Winning a Presidential General-Election Debate Has Little to Do with Performance

WITHIN MINUTES OF THE CLOSE of a presidential debate, network correspondents are on the air announcing the results of a survey indicating who won and lost. How, one might wonder, did the pollsters locate and interview a national random sample of viewers so quickly? The answer is that they knew in advance who would be called because individuals in a random sample weighted to reflect the predebate standings in the polls had been contacted before the debate and asked whether they would be available to be surveyed after it.

The important phrase in the preceding sentence is "weighted to reflect the predebate standings in the polls." These samples are not, in other words, a random selection drawn from the universe of all those who actually watched the debate. As a result, since exposure to extended forms of communication reinforces existing dispositions, those who favored the front-runner are likely to judge that person the winner. Those favoring the person behind in the polls are likely to feel that their candidate has "won" as well. In practice, this means that the process is rigged to favor a supposed "victory" by the person ahead in the polls before the debate even airs.

There are occasional exceptions usually involving lesser-known candidates, which was the case with Ross Perot in 1992. And occasionally a candidate falls so far below expectations that even some of his or her partisans concede that the event was not a "victory," which was the case with Ronald Reagan in the first debate of 1984. But, in general, the way to increase the likelihood of "winning" a presidential general-election debate is to be ahead in the published polls on which the sampling frame for the debate is based.

Kathleen Hall Jamieson

Chapter Twenty-One

Is There Anything New to Learn in Debates? Do Voters Learn from Them?

ALTHOUGH CANDIDATE DEBATES do not usually determine the outcome of a presidential campaign, they are an important source of information for those who watch. One study of the first 1992 general-election debate found that viewers' knowledge improved by 30 percent.[1] Nonviewers did not exhibit the same improvement. Not surprisingly, the topics on which knowledge improved were those discussed in the debate. The reason is simple. Debates contain extended amounts of issue and biographical information delivered in head-to-head fashion that invites comparison and contrast. And all of this occurs in a climate in which the people with whom we come into even casual contact feel comfortable asking what we thought of a debate. This sort of contact—which is in some ways akin to a rise in talk about the Superbowl the Friday before and the Monday after—involves the sort of conversation in which information learned is moved from short- to long-term memory.

In 1996 we found the same result. The second wave of the national Annenberg survey that followed the vice-presidential debate between Al Gore and Jack Kemp asked about twelve of the issues discussed in that event. The survey found that after researchers controlled for education, individuals who watched the debate had learned important issue information. Nonviewers did not exhibit the same improvement. A content

163

analysis of news reports in the five weeks preceding the debate indicated why even highly educated voters gained knowledge from debate viewing. More than half of the twelve positions were either unreported or underreported from September 1 through October 9, 1996.

Kathleen Hall Jamieson and Chris Adasiewicz

Chapter Twenty-Two

Has the Average Length of a Candidate's Statement in News Dropped Since 1968?

MOST AMERICANS NEVER HEAR a full-length stump speech by a candidate for president. Other than in New Hampshire and Iowa—where the size of the state makes retail politics possible and the expectations of the citizenry make personal contact all but mandatory—most voters will not meet a presidential contender outside a school, factory, or shopping mall. Instead, most of us form our impressions of those who aspire to lead us through television ads and news stories and occasionally by viewing a townhall meeting or debate.

However, when the speaking candidate is shown and his or her words heard in news broadcasts, we have an ability to assess credibility denied us when the views are simply paraphrased. Missing in paraphrase is the tone with which the remark was uttered, for example. Thus, in the illustration developed in Chapter 4 about George Bush calling Clinton "bozo" and Gore "Ozone Man," the remark was spoken as a throwaway line, apparently meant to be humorous. In paraphrase, the tone of the broadcast reporter substituted for Bush's. In print, the words looked harsher and crueler than they sounded when spoken by Bush.

A study by Kiku Adatto has been widely interpreted to claim that the average length of a candidate statement in broadcast news has dropped dramatically since 1968.[1] It is true that the amount of time a candidate is shown and heard speaking continuously is down in commercial network broadcast evening news, but that is not the case in two news forms that have emerged since 1968: *NewsHour* with Jim Lehrer (formerly *MacNeil Lehrer*) and the interviews on *Nightline* and the Sunday morning news shows. Beginning in 1988, for example, *NewsHour* aired extended segments of eight to ten minutes of the stump speeches of the presidential contenders. In 1996, these segments averaged eight minutes of the speeches of the three major-party contenders each week of the general-election campaign season. In the primary, the speeches of two of the contenders were featured each week. Many major newspapers, including the *New York Times*, made a similar move by printing boxed segments of candidate speeches.

Although a decrease in the number of seconds or words quoted directly means that we are hearing less of the candidate's voice in nightly news, however, that does not necessarily mean we are learning less about his positions. For example, on October 18, 1999, the *Philadelphia Inquirer* carried a twenty-five-and-a-half-column-inch article by Robert Rankin titled "Health Insurance Emerges as Issue for 2000 Elections." Although it detailed the positions of Democratic candidates Bill Bradley and Al Gore and Republican aspirant George W. Bush, the article did not contain a single direct quotation from any of the three. Instead, the story was rich with paraphrase: Bradley "would require parents to insure all children, and would subsidize premiums for adults with family incomes up to $49,200. . . . Bradley, the former senator from New Jersey, estimated that his plan would insure 95 percent of Americans—and that it might cost up to $65 billion a year. Vice President Gore said that was too expensive. He proposed a more incremental approach by expanding the Child Health Insurance Program to cover all children by 2005. He also proposed new tax credits for health insurance. He has not given a cost estimate for his plan." This fine piece of journalism would go unrecognized if all we were coding was actual candidate speech.

Finally, if 1968 is the point of comparison, it is not correct that "television is giving us less and less direct communication from our leaders and their political campaigns."[2] Unlike the general-elections of 1976–1996, there were no nationally televised presidential debates in the general election of 1968. In years with debates, a sizable national audience hears presidential aspirants speaking at length.

Kathleen Hall Jamieson

Chapter Twenty-Three

Does Local Television News Shape Our Views of Those of Other Races?

A Case Study in Perception and Accuracy in News Media and Their Audience

I N 1988, THE National Security Political Action Committee made political history with an ad featuring the menacing mug shot of William Horton.[1] The ad informed viewers that Horton had killed a young man, raped a woman, and assaulted her fiancé. The spot showed that Horton was black; subsequent news reports filled in the rest of the story, showing that the victims were white.

Those who criticized the ad as racist did so in part because it implied that white audiences had reason to fear that they would fall victim to crimes by black men when, in fact, most violent crime was then and is now intraracial and not interracial.

Why were audiences so susceptible to the ad? Among the possible explanations is a pattern of news portrayal that implies that the atypical is typical; the unlikely, likely. From July 20 to October 22, 1994, under a grant from the Ford Foundation, we coded twenty-seven hours of 11:00 p.m. news broadcasts from Philadelphia's television stations WPVI (Channel 6), WCAU (Channel 10), and KYW (Channel 3). During that time, the more than 600 stories about crime that we captured implied among other things that Philadelphia is an inhospitable place.

But is it? Philadelphia doesn't even fall within the list of the fifty cities with the highest per capita violent crime rate. In 1993, according to the FBI, a person was less likely to fall victim to violence in Philadelphia than in such large cities as Miami, New York, Baltimore, or San Francisco, or such smaller ones as Waco, Texas, or Albany, Georgia. Nonetheless, the motto of Philadelphia local stations appears to be "If it's crime, give it time."

The stories implied as well that Philadelphia is a city with a surfeit of white victims and nonwhite perpetrators. Yet in 1993, only 6 percent of the reported homicides in Philadelphia involved a black perpetrator and a white victim.

The cliché held true: If it bleeds, it leads. But there was a corollary: On all three stations, black and Hispanic persons were twice as likely to appear in crime stories as in other news. And when they appeared, they were much likelier to be identified as alleged perpetrators than victims.

By contrast, white persons not only dominated noncrime stories but also were significantly more likely than African American or Hispanic persons to be shown as the victims of a crime. Only one station (WCAU) was more likely to show nonwhite persons as bystanders or expert commentators in crime stories than to show nonwhite persons in the rest of the news.

This pattern casts African Americans and Hispanics not as experts who explain crime, police who protect us from crime, bystanders who witness crime, or citizens who are working to reduce crime—but as criminals. For example, on WPVI, 87 percent of the perpetrators of violent crime were nonwhite, compared with 57 percent of the victims; on WCAU, 62 percent of the perpetrators were nonwhite, compared with 40 percent of the victims; and on KYW, 67 percent of the perpetrators were nonwhite, compared with 44 percent of the victims.

To help explain these patterns, members of our research team met with representatives of the Philadelphia stations. We came away as puzzled as when we arrived.

The answers they gave us included conjectures such as the following: First, when white people are accused of crimes, they may be more likely to elude the cameras. This might be accomplished by not appearing in court or by refusing to have a photo taken. In other words, the individuals responsible for news believe that Caucasians may be better at outwitting reporters. Thus, even if reporters cover a story about a white perpetrator, they will not have a picture of the person as often as when they cover a story of a black or Hispanic person.

A second explanation, in defiance of the national trends, is that during that fourteen-week period, there may have been more black perpetrators and white victims in the Philadelphia area—and, we would add, during the periods in which other scholars have analyzed local news in other cities. A study by the Rocky Mountain Media Watch in 1995 found the same pattern across fifty local station broadcasts aired on a single day.

For decades scholars have known about Heisenberg's Uncertainty Principle—in the act of studying a phenomenon, the researcher may change its identity or behavior—but we had not before considered the possibility that the act of studying the local news might change the patterns of criminal behavior in local jurisdictions.

A third rationale suggested that because intraracial crime is the norm and blacks are more likely than whites to be the victims of violence, black victims are not newsworthy. News focuses on the unusual—hence on black perpetrators whose victims are white and on white victims regardless of the race of the perpetrator.

To this list of explanations we would add that patterns are often not evident to those assembling stories under the pressure of deadlines.

Whatever the reality, to watch three and a half months of Philadelphia local news was to see a picture of crime that raises serious questions about whether the news at 11:00 p.m. is showing the world as it is or inadvertently and mistakenly constructing a violence-filled city teeming with black and Hispanic perpetrators and white victims.

The way local television news covers crime also raises significant issues about reliance on television for accurate information about the problems of the city. Not only does such coverage raise fears of victimization, but it also explains this fear with hard evidence that the problem has special relevance to white viewers. If it were believed, this coverage could leave viewers with the impression that urban crime primarily represents a threat to the safety of whites and that nonwhite residents are primarily to blame. Hence it is important to ask whether this pattern of reporting gives viewers an accurate representation of criminal behavior in the city or whether it misrepresents the nature of crimes.

In answering this question, we recognized that this pattern of crime reporting was similar to the talk we also observed among residents in the neighborhoods of Philadelphia. When we asked about the problems they saw in their neighborhoods, the answers were often framed in terms of ethnicity with blame assigned along ethnic lines. We called this "ethnic-blame discourse" because it focuses on and condemns the supposed misdeeds of other ethnic groups.[2] What we heard in our interviews often appeared to be a one-sided view of the problems in neighborhoods that cast blame upon the easiest targets and avoided responsibility for much that was arguably not the fault of any single ethnic group. Could television news coverage of crime be just another form of this talk directed to its much larger white (and suburban) audience?

In answering this question, it is important to recognize that ethnic-blame discourse might reflect reality in the lives of those whose neighborhoods have experienced both significant departure of longtime residents and an influx of newcomers. These transitions have often been described as a source of "realistic group conflict," in which the newcomers (often nonwhite) and the established residents (often white) jockey for control of neighborhood resources, such as jobs and schools.[3] According to this view, the tension that results from neighborhood integration represents genuine conflicts of interest. If this theory were correct, the blame that is directed along ethnic lines would be based on those conflicts rather than on talk that deflects criticism from one's ethnic group to another.

In a test of the competing explanations in Philadelphia neighborhoods, Romer, Jamieson, Riegner, Emori, and Rouson found high proportions (approximately 60 percent) of residents who said they had heard ethnic groups were responsible for neighborhood problems such as youth violence, crime, and neighborhood deterioration.[4] Residents exposed to ethnic blame were also more likely to report ethnic tension in their neighborhoods. However, the tension associated with blaming appeared to be less attributable to perceived neighborhood social problems than to actual exposure to blaming itself. Consistent with the discourse explanation, blaming of ethnic groups was associated with friction quite apart from any neighborhood problems that might reflect conflicts of interest among ethnic groups.

Despite evidence that ethnic-blame communication is weakly linked to observable problems, it is always possible to argue that the discourse is fueled by underlying conflicts of interests. Indeed, Levine and Campbell suggest that a neutral assessment of each group's hostile behavior should be used to assess these conflicts.[5] Our examination of television news was designed to test the alternative explanations using police reports of crime as a measure of intergroup conflict and television news reporting of crime as a form of narrative that presumes to give an accurate description of this problem.

Although the police and the criminal justice system are also subject to the persuasive assumptions of the community, the behavior of this system defines a reality that can be measured. Citizens who are victims of crime seek the assistance of the justice system, and alleged perpetrators are apprehended and tried within the system. The news media have the unique responsibility of reporting these events to the community. We asked two related questions about this reporting: (1) whether news reporting emphasizes harmful effects that certain ethnic groups have on other groups and (2) whether this reporting reflects the findings of the justice system or selectively distorts them in a predictable fashion.

Van Dijk is among those who argue that the news media play a major role in perpetuating "ethnocentric" discourse.[6] Because media audiences in the United States and northern Europe tend to be largely non-Latino white in ethnic composition, considerable research in recent years has focused on persons of color as the ethnic grouping most subject to blame. Content analyses of both the U.S. print press and television news confirm the disproportionate presence of persons of color, especially African Americans, in stories about crime and other problems than in the rest of the news.[7] Journalists themselves suggest that they frame behavior differently when selecting stories about persons of color. As one British journalist put it: "[E]verything to do with coloured people takes place against an underlying premise that they are the symbols or the embodiments of a problem. Whether we like it or not, that is the state of public opinion as perceived by news editors; and that is what tends to influence professional news judgment."[8]

By race-tagging crime, local news prompts white viewers who have not been shown a mug shot to report overwhelmingly that the alleged perpetrator is black.[9]

What is less clear from previous research is whether the overrepresentation of persons of color in problem stories is the result of biased, race-based assumptions introduced by news professionals or a function of problem behavior as reported to authorities such as the police. According to the discourse explanation, journalists reporting to largely white audiences frame problem behavior committed by persons of color as intergroup conflict, making such stories more newsworthy than comparable stories about white persons. In the case of crime, stories involving white victims of violence perpetrated by nonwhite actors are especially newsworthy. However, when persons of color assume noncriminal roles related to crime, such as bystanders, experts, or victims, they are less newsworthy than white actors whose reactions and suffering evoke greater identification with the white audience. These reporting practices have the effect of disproportionately showing persons of color perpetrating crime where Caucasians are more likely to be shown engaging in noncriminal behavior.

According to a realistic conflict explanation, persons of color appear frequently in crime and other problem stories because they are disproportionately likely to contribute to such problems. On average, persons of color are poorer and more likely to live in high-poverty, urban neighborhoods than are other groups.[10] To the extent that neighborhood poverty predicts violent crime, a realistic portrayal of violent crime could show persons of color overrepresented in this news category.[11] Nevertheless, this coverage need not imply that persons of color pose a threat to white persons or are to blame for crime. However, realistic conflict theory does predict that to the degree blame characterizes coverage of nonwhite actors in crime stories, the coverage will represent a realistic portrayal of intergroup conflict.

173

To test the competing hypotheses, we closely examined the fourteen weeks of television news we had taped in Philadelphia.[12] The 11:00 p.m. broadcasts we had taped review the most important events of the day with live or recent pictures and interviews of the actors in those stories. In a city such as Philadelphia, the stories cover the central city with its large non-white population (primarily African American) as well as the outlying counties with their larger non-Latino white population, giving residents a unique picture of their home region and the people living in it. Although ethnicity is not typically reported in the verbal text of television news stories, it is clearly evident in the pictures and voices of the featured actors.

We already knew that persons of color were featured to a greater extent in the crime category than in the rest of the news. However, this finding is not sufficient in and of itself to suggest that they were blamed for problems such as crime. Support for this interpretation would come from evidence that they are disproportionately shown contributing to crime rather than preventing it, being victimized by it, or speaking out against it. We reasoned that if persons of color were blamed for crime, their depiction in crime stories would accentuate their role as perpetrators rather than as victims, concerned citizens, or police officers.

To distinguish realistic group conflict from blame discourse as an explanation for the greater coverage of persons of color in crime news, we focused on news of violent crime. Using crime statistics for homicide, we assessed the relation between news reporting of violence and actual records of intergroup violence. There are two major reasons for relying on use of homicide rates. First, most of the reports of violence in local television news concern the dramatic (and unlikely) forms of violence, such as homicide.[13] Second, homicide is the violent crime with the highest recorded rate of perpetrator identification by the police.

One comparison that is particularly useful for determining whether persons of color are disproportionately shown as perpetrators of violence is the rate at which they are also shown as its victims. Homicide tends to involve perpetrators and victims of the same race. Therefore, one would expect aggregate group victimization rates in the news to correspond to perpetration rates. However, previous studies of local television news suggest that this pattern does not occur in news. An extensive study of five local television news programs in Chicago indicated that the majority of perpetrators of violence shown in the news were persons of color, while the majority of victims were white persons. Two more recent studies of a single day of local television news across 50 and 100 stations in the United States found the same pattern across all crime stories whether they involved violence or not.[14]

A simple probability model helps to identify a possible explanation for these divergent rates of perpetration and victimization. This model indicates that the proportion of victims that belongs to one racial group is determined not only by perpetrators of the same group but also by the rate of *intergroup victimization*.[15] To the extent intergroup victimization occurs, a group's victimization rate will be different from its perpetration rate. For example, in 1993 in Philadelphia, FBI data indicated that 10 percent of the homicides attributable to African Americans involved white victims, while the comparable estimate for African American victims of white perpetrators was 18 percent.[16] These estimates indicate that over 80 percent of white perpetrators victimized other whites and that 90 percent of black perpetrators victimized other blacks. Using these estimates in the model leads one to expect that if 20 percent of all perpetrators were white, 24 percent of all victims would be white as well. Although this rate of victimization (24 percent) is greater than the corresponding rate of criminal activity (20 percent), the intergroup victimization rates reported by the police are too low and similar across groups to produce dramatically different proportions of white and nonwhite actors in the victim and perpetrator roles. It would appear, therefore, that local television news covers white victims at a much greater rate than typical intergroup victimization rates would predict.

One explanation of the disparity in coverage of white actors in the victim and perpetrator roles is the rate of intergroup violence directed toward white actors. If this rate were accentuated in the news, as the discourse explanation predicts, the rate of white victimization in the news could be much higher than the comparable rate of white perpetration. Consistent with this analysis, an intensive study of Chicago television news revealed that intergroup victimization of white actors received more coverage than intergroup victimization of persons of color. In this chapter, we examine this prediction to determine whether the rate of intergroup victimization of whites by nonwhites in the news can explain the increased representation of white actors in the victim role.

In summary, by examining the roles of both white and nonwhite actors in crime stories on each of the three major broadcast news programs in Philadelphia, we intended to distinguish two explanations for differential coverage of white and nonwhite actors in the news. To isolate the phenomenon of ethnic blame and to replicate previous findings, we made the following predictions:

1. Persons of color are overrepresented in crime stories in comparison to their appearance in noncrime stories.[17]

2. Within crime stories, persons of color are overrepresented in criminal roles (that is, as perpetrators of both violent and nonviolent crime) but not in noncriminal roles (for example, bystander, expert, and victim).

Using recent official homicide rates for Philadelphia, we were able to determine intergroup victimization of both white and nonwhite (primarily African American) residents. These rates enabled us to test our suspicion that

3. Within violent-crime stories, the proportion of victims who are white is greater than would be predicted by the proportion of perpetrators who are white.

We then tested two predictions drawn from the ethnic-blame discourse explanation for the hypothesized presence of more white victims than the actual statistics would forecast.

4. Intergroup victimization of whites is reported at a higher rate than intergroup victimization of nonwhites.

5. White actors are overrepresented in the victim role because, contrary to official homicide rates, they are disproportionately shown as the victims of intergroup violence.

A final prediction concerned the possible effects of the overrepresentation of white actors in the victim role on the differential representation of white and nonwhite participants in violent-crime news stories.

6. Within violent-crime news stories, those who are white are shown predominantly as victims, and those who are not white are shown predominantly as perpetrators.

Results

As Figure 23.1 indicates, we found dramatic support for the first prediction.[18] Although persons of color were pictured in noncrime stories at about the same rate on each station (about 20 percent of the stories excluding sports and weather), they were shown at more than twice that rate in crime stories on stations WCAU and WPVI. Station KYW exhibited this pattern less than the other two stations with a rate that was only about 60 percent higher in crime stories.

Rates of Presentation Within Crime Stories

To test the second prediction and to determine why persons of color were shown at a greater rate in crime stories, we divided all crime-story

FIGURE 23.1   Percentage appearance of persons of color in crime stories versus in other local news, by Philadelphia television station.

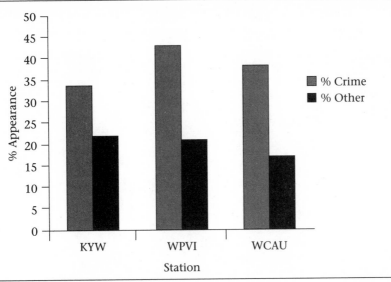

pictures of individuals (up to three per story) into five mutually exclusive roles: (1) bystander or expert commentator, (2) other noncriminal participant in the story, (3) person accused of perpetrating nonviolent crime, (4) person accused of perpetrating violent crime, and (5) victim of violent crime. Noncriminal participants (category 2) included victims of nonviolent crime as well as persons demonstrating about crime, attending meetings about crime, and engaging in other activities related to it.

The results of this analysis are shown in Table 23.1. We compared each station's rate of showing persons of color against the average rate with which persons of color were shown in noncrime stories on the three stations (19.6 percent). All three stations exhibited the same pattern. When persons of color were shown, it was probable that it would be in crime stories as perpetrators of both violent and nonviolent crime. Persons of color were also shown at higher rates as victims of violent crime than they were shown in other stories, but they were shown as victims at a lower rate than they were shown as perpetrators of violent crime.

One of the stations (WCAU) exhibited a somewhat more balanced portrayal of persons of color. On this station, persons of color were also more likely to be shown in crime stories as bystanders or experts (29 percent) and as other noncriminal participants (32 percent). In addition, rates of presentation in these roles were comparable to the rate for perpetrators of nonviolent crime (37 percent). Stations WPVI and KYW did

TABLE 23.1 Proportion of pictures with persons of color according to role in story (percent)

Station	Bystander/ Expert	Noncriminal Participant	Nonviolent Crime Perpetrator	Violent Crime		All Crime-Story Pictures
				Victim	Perpetrator	
SKYW	20	27	46[a]	44[a]	67[a]	34[a]
WPVI	28	25	32	57[a]	87[a]	42[a]
WCAU	29[a]	32[a]	37[a]	40[a]	62[a]	36[a]

[a] $p < .05$ compared to proportion of pictures in noncrime stories (19.6 percent).

not show persons of color at a consistently greater rate as bystanders, experts, or noncriminal participants than in other stories.

Rates of Presentation in Violent-Crime Stories

Images of alleged violent-crime perpetrators and victims accounted for approximately 30 percent of the total picture in the crime category. Figure 23.2 shows the relation between the probability that a victim was white and that a perpetrator was white among those pictured in violent-crime stories (Observed). All three stations showed whites at a greater rate as victims of violence than as its perpetrators. Station WPVI showed white actors at a rate more than three times greater in the victim than perpetrator role. The other stations showed white actors at rates 50 percent and 70 percent greater in the victim than perpetrator role.

The first test of the discourse explanation was based on the rates of intergroup (10 percent) and intragroup (82 percent) homicide of white victims provided by 1993 FBI records for Philadelphia.[19] The predictions that result produced Realistic Rate 1 in Figure 23.2. As the figure indicates, the observed rates of victimization were significantly *higher* than Realistic Rate 1 on each station. A second set of predictions was derived by assuming that the intergroup victimization of white persons was greater than FBI rates but comparable to the rate for intergroup victimization of persons of color (20 percent). This set of assumptions produced the second curve (Realistic Rate 2) with rates that were still significantly smaller than observed for each news station. Thus, predictions based on realistic estimates of intergroup victimization indicate that white actors were shown in the victim role to a greater extent than would be expected from their appearance as alleged perpetrators.

We tested two predictions of the discourse explanation for the over-representation of whites in the victim role using actual rates of intergroup victimization displayed in our news sample. To calculate this rate, we examined stories with pictures of both perpetrators and victims. On average, only about 20 percent of the violent crime stories with pictures featured both victims and perpetrators (N=49); we examined the ethnic identity of these pictures across all three stations. Within these stories, 37 percent featured a white and 63 percent featured a nonwhite perpetrator. For the stories with a white perpetrator, 22 percent showed a person of color as a victim. For the stories with a person of color as the perpetrator, 42 percent showed a white person as victim. Statistical tests confirmed that these differences of victims were unlikely to have occurred by chance alone.

FIGURE 23.2   Portrayal of white perpetrators and white victims on local news.

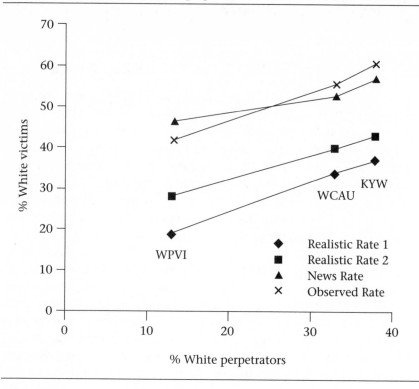

The rate of intergroup victimization we observed in news stories was dramatically higher for nonwhite-on-white violence than FBI data would indicate (42 percent versus 10 percent), but the rate was relatively comparable for white-on-nonwhite violence (22 percent versus 18 percent). Use of these values to predict victimization of whites produced a curve (News Rate) close to the obtained data. The predictions for all three stations were statistically within the range of the obtained rates.

Roles in Violent Crime Within Ethnic Groups

Our analysis of ethnic representation within victim and perpetrator roles controls for the actual rates at which victims and perpetrators were shown. This analysis overlooks the possibility that viewers may be shown relatively few victims despite the unequal rates of presentation within the victim role. As a result, both white and nonwhite actors might still be more likely to be shown as perpetrators than as victims. To assess this possibility, we compared the representation of each ethnic classification in the two roles (Prediction 6).

This analysis revealed the same pattern across all three stations. The majority of white actors were shown as victims on each station (from 60 percent to 65 percent), while the majority of nonwhite actors were shown as perpetrators on each station (from 62 percent to 64 percent). Furthermore, although crime statistics indicate that there are nearly four times as many nonwhite victims of homicide as white victims in Philadelphia, whites were actually shown as victims of violence *more often* than persons of color on two stations (27 percent versus 21 percent on KYW; 29 percent versus 20 percent on WCAU) and were shown about as often on the third (19 percent versus 26 percent on WPVI).

Discussion

Our results confirm what others have found. Persons of color are featured to a greater extent in the crime-news category on local television than in the rest of the local news. We asked two major questions about this phenomenon. The first was whether crime reporting presents persons of color primarily as the source of problems, with white actors serving primarily as bystanders or others affected by crime. Our findings indicated that the high levels of reporting of persons of color within the crime category were primarily the result of stories about them as perpetrators rather than as bystanders, experts, or other participants. Only one of the three stations (WCAU) showed persons of color as bystanders, experts, and other nonperpetrators of crime at a greater rate than in the rest of the news. However, these rates of presentation were still much lower than the rate at which persons of color were shown as alleged criminals.

Although rates of victimization for persons of color within stories about violent crime were also higher than the average rate in noncrime stories, we found greater emphasis on persons of color as perpetrators than as victims, a result found in other studies of local television news as well. However, our analyses went a step further and demonstrated that this disparity could not be explained using typical rates of inter- and intragroup victimization reported by the police. All three stations showed white actors at greater rates as victims of violent crime than news reporting of white actors as perpetrators would predict (Figure 23.2).

181

The findings also indicated that as a result of these story selection patterns, viewers were more likely to see white actors presented as victims and nonwhite actors as alleged perpetrators. This finding is important because even if the rates of presentation of the two groups within the victim and perpetrator roles were different, the overall rate of showing victims or perpetrators could be quite small. For example, perpetrators might dominate the news with the result that both white and nonwhite actors would be shown predominantly as perpetrators in violent-crime stories. However, victim pictures were shown sufficiently often to allow the presentation of white actors predominantly as victims and nonwhite actors predominantly as perpetrators on all three stations. These results indicate more clearly than previous research that persons of color are represented in the crime category primarily for their contribution to crime, while white actors are shown primarily for their reaction to and suffering from crime.

A second question we asked was whether the tendency to focus on the alleged criminal behavior of persons of color was more consistent with ethnic-blame discourse theory than with realistic group conflict theory. Several tests helped to answer this question. First, we compared the intergroup victimization rates for white and nonwhite actors in the news. These rates were significantly higher for white than for nonwhite victims (42 percent versus 22 percent), even though recent homicide rates were actually in the reverse order (10 percent versus 18 percent). If the observed rates of intergroup victimization in the news were realistic, then the rate that persons of color victimize whites would be four times greater than the rate estimated from recent homicide data (42 percent versus 10 percent). At the same time, the victimization rate of persons of color by white actors in the news was quite consistent with recent homicide data (22 percent versus 18 percent). In other words, reporting tended to accentuate the victimization of white persons at the hands of nonwhite perpetrators, a prediction of the communication explanation that is counter to a realistic conflict explanation.

Second, we found that the disparity between rates of perpetration and victimization in the two ethnic groupings was better explained by the overreporting of intergroup victimization of whites than by typical rates of inter- and intragroup victimization. The rate of predicted victimization indicated that the observed rates for white actors were only consistent with their rates of perpetration if the exceedingly high rate of intergroup victimization of whites that was observed in the news was applied to the data. This finding is also more consistent with the discursive explanation than with realistic conflict theory.

Additional results related to the overrepresentation of white actors as victims suggest that these reporting patterns were not representative of the data from the criminal justice system. In the total set of violent-crime participants, white actors were shown as victims about as often as persons of color. On two stations, white actors were actually shown more often as victims of violence than were persons of color. These results stand in contrast to the fact that in Philadelphia in 1993, there were roughly four times as many nonwhite victims of homicide as white victims. Furthermore, one might expect greater reporting of actors in the victim role than in the perpetrator role. Since not all crimes are solved, there tend to be more pictured victims than perpetrators. However, this pattern existed only for white actors. These findings reinforce the conclusion that white victims appear to be more newsworthy than nonwhite victims. A realistic conflict explanation is unable to account for these disparities.

The disproportionately high rate of white victimization by persons of color in the news also provides striking support for the discourse explanation. To journalists selecting stories for a white audience, persons of color attacking white people is consistent with definitions of persons of color as problems for white persons. These stories are more newsworthy than stories showing white people attacking persons of color, even though recent Philadelphia crime statistics indicate that intergroup victimization rates are low and not dramatically different by group.

Other Interpretations of the Results

An alternative explanation for our findings suggested by one of the Philadelphia television news directors was that since intraracial crime is the norm, crime that crosses racial or ethnic boundaries is unusual and hence more newsworthy. However, this explanation would predict that both forms of intergroup victimization would be overrepresented in the news relative to police data. We found only that victimization of whites by nonwhites was overrepresented.

Despite the evidence that the depiction of those in crime stories deviates from typical victimization rates, it is always possible to argue that the news programs we observed happened to report events in which actual rates of crime were responsible for the patterns we obtained. However, the three other studies of local television news that we cited earlier that aggregated results across 5, 50, and 100 stations have found that ethnicity is differentially represented in the victim and perpetrator roles to a degree that our analysis would suggest is unlikely to reflect actual rates of crime. It is unlikely that crime would deviate so markedly from large patterns only when news programs were the subject of study. It is more likely that the decision to feature persons of color more often in the perpetrator role and whites more often in the victim role is a result of the perceived newsworthiness of these actors in these roles. The fact that similar patterns of reporting have been found in crime stories on television news is consistent with the hypothesis that the news engages in a discourse of blame directed against nonwhites. Because non-Latino white persons dominate viewing audiences, stories that blame persons of color would be expected to overshadow blame directed against white persons.

The discourse explanation provides a mechanism to account for the exacerbation of intergroup conflict that is different from theories of in-group favoritism, modern racism, or individually based approaches.[20] Theories of in-group favoritism would predict that white audiences prefer stories showing white victims rather than persons of color, a strong finding in our results. However, these theories would not predict the overrepresentation of intergroup victimization that we found. In-group favoritism does not necessarily imply an interest in intergroup victimization.

Theories of modern racism as well as cognitively based approaches emphasize the influence of individual prejudice and stereotyping. These theories would suggest that increasing the number of journalists of color would eliminate the ethnocentric biases we observed. However, this outcome seems unlikely in view of the dominant market forces that drive television news practices.[21] These forces encourage the adoption of the assumptions of the audience in order to maintain viewer interest and market share. As a result, even nonwhite journalists may be obliged to offer these depictions. In fact, one of the stations in our study had significant nonwhite representation in its journalist and management ranks (WCAU). Although this station showed the greatest interest in nonwhites who were not perpetrators within crime stories, an emphasis on intergroup conflict and white victims was still evident in its reporting.

Effects of Blame Discourse in Crime Coverage

Although we do not have evidence that viewers form their impressions of ethnic groups from television news, laboratory simulations of the effects of receiving information about fictitious groups of people indicate that audiences are sensitive to the proportion of favorable information about a group and form impressions based on it.[22] There is also considerable evidence that television news helps viewers define problems and that these definitions have important implications for intergroup relations.[23] One likely outcome of the reporting practices we observed is the perpetuation of fear of persons of color in urban settings. Experimental studies of exposure to black perpetrators of violent crime indicate that this coverage accentuates fear of crime among white viewers and that it activates unfavorable stereotypes of black men.[24] In the context of heavy exposure to such news coverage, it is not surprising that white residents of cities report more fear of crime the closer they live to black residents.[25]

The form of data we used—homicide rates—is seldom given the attention or disseminated to anywhere near the level television news reports of violence receive. The results suggest that television news reporting disproportionately depicts the harm that persons of color inflict on white victims, but not the reverse. To the extent the audience finds these reports credible, urban residents, whether white or nonwhite, might mistakenly conclude that the blame they frequently hear directed toward persons of color is supported by objective sources of information.

Dan Romer and Kathleen Hall Jamieson

Is the Press Biased? Was the *New York Times* Biased Against Dole in 1996? Is Press Coverage Conservative or Liberal?

T
HE QUESTION OF PRESS BIAS is more complicated than much of the discussion generated by it suggests. With few exceptions, talk of press bias has focused on content analysis of coverage, on comparisons of the ideological dispositions of the press and the public, or on public perceptions of whether press coverage is liberal, conservative, or balanced. Underplayed in these discussions is the fact that the owners of media outlets as well as the editors of most newspapers are Republicans. With 1964 and 1992 as the only exceptions, from 1932 through 1996, the majority of newspaper endorsements supported the Republican nominee for president.[1] During that same period, reporters consistently told surveyors that they were likely to vote for the Democratic nominee. Also underrecognized are a number of studies that suggest that endorsements affect the favorability of coverage of the candidate who receives the paper's nod. In three different studies, it was the ideological disposition of the editors and publishers that predicted bias.[2]

This disparity opens a number of plausible hypotheses about supposed bias and its impact. One might argue that since most people pay more attention to news than to editorial endorsements, the supposed liberal bias of reporters outweighs the supposedly conservative influence of the editorial page. Alternatively, if reporters insinuate a liberal bias into their coverage but the editorial page is controlled by conservatives, one might theorize that the two neutralize each other. One might hypothesize instead that reporters respond to the cues of those who pay their salaries and mask their own ideological dispositions. Another explanation would hold that norms of journalism, including "objectivity" and "balance," blunt whatever biases exist.

Liberal Reporters: How Many Are There?

For the past thirty years, surveys have consistently shown that by large margins reporters are more likely to describe themselves as liberal than are their readers or the population at large. In spring 1996, a Roper Center survey conducted for the Freedom Forum reported that 89 percent of 139 Washington congressional reporters and bureau chiefs had voted for Bill Clinton in 1992, compared with 43 percent of the public at large.[3] Whereas 61 percent described themselves as left of center, only 9 percent characterized themselves as the opposite.

In surveys conducted over the past three decades, national Washington-based reporters have consistently reported that they are more likely to be Democrats than Republicans. A 1976 *Washington Post* survey of elite journalists and news managers (managing editors and news directors) found the Washington correspondents more liberal than conservative by 59 to 18 percent. In 1980 a sample of national media journalists by Lichter and Rothman found 57 percent describing themselves as liberal, 17 percent as conservative.[4] The same survey found that "the media elite" were "lifestyle liberals"—with 80 percent favoring affirmative action and 90 percent pro-choice. In *The Media Elite*, Lichter, Rothman, and Lichter compared the views of journalists with those of scientists in energy fields on such matters as the safety of nuclear power and found journalists more skeptical and more reliant on antinuclear than pronuclear sources for information.[5] When Weaver and Wilhoit updated their 1982 survey for the Freedom Forum in 1992, they found that the ratio of Democrats to Republicans had shifted from 1.5 to 1 in 1971 to almost 3 to 1 in 1992, a change attributed in part to an increase in the ethnic, racial, and sexual diversity of the newsroom.[6]

In 1985 a *Los Angeles Times* survey compared the views of a sample of newspaper readers with those of the journalists writing for those papers.[7] Whereas reporters were more likely to report that they were liberal (55 to 17 percent), readers were more likely to report being conservative (29 to 23 percent). By documenting the dramatic difference in personal ideology of reporters and readers, this study raises two possibilities: First, the ideology of reporters is not reflected in their reporting, or alternatively, if it is reflected, it lacks influence. Although the results vary depending on the content categories analyzed, in general, content analysis has failed to demonstrate a systematic liberal bias in press reports about politics.

Content Analysis Does Not Suggest a Systematic Liberal, Democratic Bias

Do the personal political preferences of reporters translate into a pro-Democratic slant in news? Content analysis of the coverage of presidential campaigns has yielded inconsistent results. One study of the 1980 election found comparable portrayals of Carter and Reagan.[8] But a number of analyses of the 1984 election suggested dramatically more "bad press" for Reagan than for Mondale.[9] To some, the 1988 campaign coverage was evenhanded, with both Dukakis and Bush garnering a high level of negative coverage.[10] But an alternative study of two Washington dailies found bias in that election's coverage.[11] A number of studies suggested that the press tipped against Bush in 1992, with more positive soundbites by noncandidates for Clinton than for the incumbent president and with similar patterns in local media markets.[12] However, Lowry and Shidler found comparability in soundbites by Bush and Clinton in the 1992 coverage. And the authors of a computer-based content analysis of the coverage of 1988, 1992, and 1996 found that "media coverage was not overtly biased for the Democratic candidate in any one election, and there does not appear to be a trend of increasing actual bias for the Democratic candidate over the three elections."[13]

The interesting cases here are not those in which the identified bias favored the eventual winner but rather those that worked the other way around. If the widest disparity in coverage between candidates occurred in 1984 against Reagan, and Reagan won nonetheless, perhaps the bias lacked influence. Alternatively, in the absence of this press bias, Reagan might have won by an even greater margin. In any event, there is ample evidence that major-party candidates receive comparable amounts of coverage.[14]

Perception of the Public

If content analysis does not show a consistent liberal bias, why do observers who see bias overwhelmingly identify it as liberal? First, it is important to note that the majority of voters do not see the press as biased.

Asked to choose among "Democratic bias," "Republican bias," or "no bias," 58 percent told Times Mirror surveyors in 1988 that they saw no bias.[15] In September 1996, 52 percent told Roper pollsters that media coverage of the presidential campaign was evenly balanced.[16] However, of those who saw bias, most identified it as Democratic or liberal.[17]

In a time in which a larger percent of the population identifies itself as conservative than liberal, this result is unsurprising. Scholars have amply documented the human tendency to distort evaluation of social evidence. Hence conservatives are more likely to believe that the press is liberal, and liberals more likely to hold that it is conservative. In a process Vallone, Ross, and Lepper call "The Hostile Media Phenomenon," partisans see identical coverage through their own ideological filters.[18] In practice, this means that the supposed merits of the case and with them a sense of what is fair coverage will differ depending on one's point of view, as will recall of the proportion of the number of references that are unfavorable to one's own side in the news story. We found this phenomenon in our 1996 post-election survey of the electorate, where conservatives reported that the news was liberal and liberals reported the opposite.

Alternatively, one might explain the perception that the press tilts toward a liberal point of view by arguing that conservatives have made the charge more salient to the public than its alternative, a conclusion consistent with data from a Lexis-Nexis search showing that "the liberal press" is a more often reported phrase in mainstream journalism than "the conservative press."[19] Authors of a more systematic analysis found that "For the 1988 election, 79.1% of all coverage of bias that specified an ideological direction characterized the bias as liberal in nature. That percentage dropped for the 1992 election, when 71.8% of coverage of media bias was framed as having a liberal tilt. However, the percentage rises dramatically for the 1996 election, when 91.0% of the bias coverage was framed to suggest a liberal bias."[20]

Press Bias Disadvantages the Person Behind in the Polls: The Case of the *New York Times* in 1996

Those who code news as positively or negatively valenced draw a very different interpretation of the 1988 general election than they would if they focused on which candidate received a higher proportion of strategic coverage. Focus on strategy in the general election disadvantages the candidate behind in the polls—regardless of that person's ideology. Thus, in the general election of 1988, the penalty was felt by Dukakis, in 1992 by Bush, and in 1996 by Dole.[21] In 1984 the strategy frame was not yet sufficiently strong to create this disadvantage for the person who was behind.

Because the Republican nominee made press bias an issue in 1996, we have used his coverage in the *New York Times* as a test case. In the closing days of the 1996 general-election campaign for president, Bob Dole accused the *New York Times* of being "the biggest apologist for Bill Clinton in the world" and "an arm of the Democratic National Committee" (October 28). A postelection poll by the Pew Center for the People and the Press found a differential in the percent of voters who thought the press had been fair to Clinton and Dole. Whereas 73 percent thought the press was fair to Clinton, 65 percent offered the same response about coverage of Dole.

"I can recall *The New York Times* in earlier days, when we had Republicans in the White House," noted Dole in fall 1996, "and they called it Watergate. And oh, they changed. They shift gears pretty rapidly when it's a liberal Democrat, they can overlook a lot of this" (*New York Times,* November 1, 1996, p. A1). "[I]f a Republican did only a fraction of the things the Clinton Administration has done . . . there would be outrage. . . . They'd be putting out special editions of *The New York Times*" (*Times,* October 27).

"[Y]ou probably heard about the drug dealer in Miami who got invited to the White House," mused Republican nominee Bob Dole in Pensacola, Florida, on October 24, 1996. "We will not have drug dealers eating at the White House in a Dole Administration. This is a disgrace! This is a disgrace! I doubt if you even read it in *The New York Times*. They probably put it in the want ads. They don't put any anti-Clinton stories in *The New York Times*. Only anti-Dole stories in *The New York Times*. They should not decide this election." The next day he added, "We are not going to let the media steal this election. . . . The country belongs to the people, not *The New York Times*."

On October 30, the *New York Times* responded to Dole's latest charge in a box under the heading "Dole Repertory Includes *Times*." Dole had noted the day before that he had gotten about twenty-eight words in the *Times* that morning. The *Times* contextualized the comment as "a gag line" and noted: "Reaching into his shirt pocket for an index card, Bob Dole told an audience in Irvine, California, that he wanted to recite the 10th Amendment. It was, he assured them, not too long. 'It's about 28 words,' Mr. Dole said. 'That's about what I got in *The New York Times* today.'" "For the record," maintained the *Times,* in the six days that Dole had been criticizing the paper, it "has published a daily average of 1,476 words of articles and excerpts of Mr. Dole's speeches."

In the course of the campaign, Dole raised five charges against the *Times:* He received less coverage than Clinton; he received less prominent coverage than his Democratic rival (he said his major speeches were treated in section D); polls were interpreted in ways that disadvantaged him; his tax plan was treated unfairly; and scandals involving Clinton were underplayed.

Some of Dole's charges were inaccurate. An account of the "drug dealer in Miami who got invited to the White House" was reported in a story headlined "Democrats Return Drug Trafficker's Twenty-Thousand-Dollar Gift" (October 24, 1996). The report was, in fact, carried on one of the pages devoted to reporting on the campaign.

In other cases, the legitimacy of Dole's claims was a matter of opinion. Although from Dole's perspective, the fundraising "scandals" involving Clinton may have been underreported, they were nonetheless the subject of *Times* accounts.[22] From September 10 to election day, eighteen stories raised questions about James Riady's fundraising for the Clinton campaign, in contrast to two about Republican fundraiser Simon Fireman's violations of the campaign finance laws. In July, Fireman pleaded guilty to laundering contributions illegally through a Hong Kong bank. Sixteen of the eighteen Riady stories appeared in the A section; one of the two Fireman stories did. Two of the articles on Riady appeared on the front page. On November 3 the *Times* produced a half-page summary titled "Ethical Issues Facing the White House."

If there was a bias in the amount and prominence of reporting in the *New York Times*, it was pro-Dole. From September 16 to November 5, 1996, a period of fifty-one days, the *Times* published 346 articles about the presidential candidates, their stands on issues, and the campaign. During this time, there were fifty-nine pictures of Dole and forty-five of Clinton in the paper's first two sections, sixty-one front-page articles about Dole's campaign and fifty-two about Clinton's, and thirty-five "In His Own Words" boxes for Dole and twenty-eight for Clinton. The average front-page Dole story was just over one column inch longer than Clinton's average story. On average, ten more words of Dole's were included in the average "In His Own Words" box than of Clinton's. In the transcript of the first debate, the *Times* highlighted three statements by Clinton and three by Dole. Contrary to two of his charges, Dole received more, not less, front-page coverage than Clinton.

Dole's candidacy was undercut by the *Times* coverage, but not in the ways he described. Instead, the tendency of reporters to see general-election campaigns through the filter of their strategies and not their issue content leads to reporting that subtly disadvantages the person who is behind in the polls. In the general election of 1996, the *Times* front-page stories about Dole were almost twice as likely to focus on the campaign's strategy than were those about Clinton. Thus, Dole was more often the recipient of such headlines as "Changing Tactics, Dole Challenges Clinton's Ethics" (October 9). That headline suggested that Dole's attack was grounded in strategic convenience, not substantive concern.

Press use of the strategy structure reflects a bias not driven by any specific ideology. As Jamieson argues in *Dirty Politics*, when Bush was behind in the polls in 1988, the proportion of his coverage that focused on strategy was higher than Dukakis's; when Bush pulled ahead, that pattern reversed.[23] News coverage that focuses on the tactics and strategy of the projected loser risks creating a self-fulfilling prophecy. "When a candidate is down in the polls," noted a *Times* article on October 25, "it is hard to stir crowds or interest, or inspire local political operatives to help stage a successful campaign stop."

It also seems that it is difficult to secure news coverage focusing on one's plans for the country. Although the proportion of print coverage devoted to strategy dropped slightly from 1992 to 1996, the frame was still clearly in evidence. The captioning categories used by the *Times*, for example, included "Political Memo," "The Strategy," and "The Polls"—categories framed to capture tactics and ploys, not positions.

Among other things, a focus on strategy invites reporters to interpret a lack of movement in the polls as a rejection of message. For example, one set of *Times* headlines read "Dole's Attacks Seem to Be Hurting Him More Than Clinton" (October 22); another was "Aggressive Turn by Dole Appears to Be Backfiring" (October 22).

For the person behind in the polls, losing is cast as all but inevitable. "GOP Leaders Doubtful That Dole Can Close Gap" read a *Times* headline on October 20, 1996. Dole's advisers were described as "Frustrated That Their Candidate Is Still in Second Place" (October 6, 1996). Illustrations abound. From the perspective of the strategy structure, the candidate behind in the polls is unlikely to turn the race around. "Attack on Teacher Unions by Dole Hits a Sour Note" (October 10, 1996); "Dole's Plan: Bet the Ranch on One Shot" (October 16); "G.O.P. Leaders Doubtful That Dole Can Close Gap" (October 20); "Focus Shifts to Contests in the House" (October 20); "Aggressive Turn by Dole Appears to Be Backfiring" (October 22); "Dole's Attacks Seem to Be Hurting Him More Than Clinton" (October 22); "Behind Dole's California Strategy: A Bid to Save His Campaign" (October 31); "For Dole, Movement but No Momentum" (November 1). His campaign was portrayed as in disarray: "Disorders of All Kinds Plague Dole Campaign" (October 25); "After a Long Trip, Election Arithmetic Has Gone Nowhere" (November 4). A retrospective piece recapped the inevitability of Dole's defeat: "Missteps Doomed Dole from Start" (November 8).

The notion that victory was implausible was expressed in such sports language as a "Hail Mary" pass (October 31) and in the report that 1996 probably would be Dole's "final national race" (November 1)—a phrase that did not envision President Dole seeking a second term in 2000.

By contrast, the front-runner's strategy was treated as effective. *Times* headlines for Clinton articles portrayed a campaign heading for victory: "In Spin Wars After the Debate, Clinton Campaign Takes Lead" (October 8); "Clinton, in an Artful Campaign Trip to Georgia, Urges a Tutor Plan for Young Readers" (October 26); "Ohio, Which Picks Winners, Likes Clinton" (November 1).

The relationship between the front-runner and the verb used is direct. Whereas "Clinton Shows Ebullient Side" (September 26), "Dole Appears to Be More at Ease . . . "(September 20); "In the West, Dole Struggles to Resist a Democratic Tide" (October 1)); "Dole Advisers Try to Calibrate Right Amount of Tough" (October 12); "Dole Is Eager and Is Hoping His Feelings Are Catching" (November 4). Occasionally, a juxtaposed set of stories starkly portrays the problems a strategy focus creates for the person behind in the polls. On pages A10–11 of the September 28 *Times,* the left-hand page contained a story on Dole titled "Dole 'Listens to America,' But Is It Listening Back?" while the right-hand page featured an article titled "Clinton Rides Hard in Texas to Lasso Votes."

By determining who is ahead and behind, polls drive strategy coverage. Reliance on polls to determine which issues are resonating can also undercut the power of issues themselves to resonate. For example, on October 28, the *Times* listed endorsements of Clinton and Dole featuring justifications offered by the endorsers. The justifications for endorsing Dole included "Bob Dole has character, Bill Clinton has none. . . . In this election year character is not merely one of several issues demanding our attention. It is the only issue." The same page included an article whose premise undercut this basis for endorsement: "Character Issue Is Dead as an Issue, Voters Say."

Why is the loser behind? One easy explanation is that his message isn't resonating—hence Dole's charge that his tax plan was being treated unfairly. "Dole's Tax Message Heard, Not Heeded in Midwest City" noted one headline (September 18). "Dole's Tax Message Fails to Sway on Shop Floor" explained the headline on the jump page. Other headlines included "By Fits and Starts, Dole Explains His Tax Cut" (September 14); "Dole's Proposal to Trim Taxes Is at Center Stage Again" (October 30). When the focus of the story was the issue and not the strategy, however, the tax plan was shown in a light more favorable to Dole: "Dole's Tax

Plan Adds Up" (September 30); "Dole Tax Plan Would Shelter Some Gains" (October 23). "Good News for Dole in a New Study of His Tax Plan" noted a headline the day of his first attack on the *Times* (October 24). Another explanation questions the leadership capacities of the person behind in the polls: "Staff Turmoil Seems a Staple of Dole's Management Style" (September 14).

Whereas endorsements of Clinton were portrayed as enthusiastic and firm, those of Dole were cast as more tepid: "Fraternal Order of Police Endorse Clinton (September 16); "Oh, and by the Way, Giuliani Is Backing Kemp (and Dole)" (October 27); "Dole Gets Christian Coalition's Trust and Prodding" (September 16).

As president, Clinton had the ability to "sign" legislation, and the headlines reflected the fact that he did that often. But differences between being ahead in the polls and behind were also reflected in the headlines. Whereas Clinton "opens," "stresses," "demonstrates," "urges," "sees," "sows," "reaps," "wins," and "co-opts," Dole "explains," "challenges," "accuses," "struggles," "hopes," "splits," "hints," "is chided," "tries to calibrate," and "[uses a tactic that] appears to be backfiring." Unlike the Clinton campaign, the Dole camp was "plagued" by disorders (October 25) and "haunted" by "searing images" of "debates past" (October 17).

In sum, the *New York Times* was biased against Dole but not in the ways he posited. Instead, his status as the "underdog" in the general election increased the amount of dismissive strategic coverage of his candidacy. This "self-fulfilling prophecy" effect is not unique to the *New York Times*. In fact, it is a large part of the way many candidates are winnowed before the primaries. Nor is the phenomenon apparent only at the presidential level. As we note in Chapter 27, the level of access to local news obtained by the Philadelphia mayoral candidates in the 1999 primary paralleled their supposed standing in the polls, with those in the lead quoted more frequently than were those presumed to be behind.

Kathleen Hall Jamieson and Veronica Davison

LAST ROUND

Chapter Twenty-Five

Who Sets the Print Media Agenda?

A Case Study Focusing on the *New York Times*

T RADITIONALLY, THOSE ADVANCING the notion of agenda setting have examined the relationship between the emphasis placed on specific campaign issues by news reports and those that voters determine to be important. This leaves open the question asked by Gurevitch and Blumler: If the media set the agenda, who sets the agenda for the agenda setters?[1]

Setting the media's agenda is among the preoccupations of campaigns. How well do they succeed? Specifically, did the *New York Times* coverage reflect the issues stressed by the major-party nominees in the general election of 1996? Put differently, did the issue agendas of the *Times* and the candidates align? We expected that the emphasis placed on various issues by the media would generally reflect that of the candidates, with a bias favoring the incumbent, President Clinton, and one favoring those issues that both candidates addressed.

Common sense would suggest that, in general, the *Times* and the candidates would emphasize the same issues. If this hypothesis is correct, when both candidates emphasize an issue, the likelihood that a paper will report it will rise. If one candidate speaks extensively on a topic, the other candidate will respond at some level, creating a debate.

Topics emphasized by one candidate but not by the other should elicit less space than those that both candidates stress. The press tends to favor issues that neatly divide the candidates, as opposed to topics about which the candidates agree or issues on which the differences between them are imprecise. Conflict makes good copy. If only one candidate emphasizes an issue and the other candidate does not, the result should be less coverage.

We also forecast that when the attention given an issue by the candidates differed, the views of the incumbent would be given more coverage than those of the challenger. Our reasoning is straightforward. An incumbent is generally in a better position than a challenger to influence the campaign agenda. Additionally, several commentators have suggested that Dole's campaign failed to present a consistent message. Bob Ward, pollster for the Dole campaign, noted during a campaign debriefing at the Annenberg School that the campaign "had no coherent strategy." Katharine Q. Seelye, a *Times* reporter who followed Dole on the campaign trail, commented during that same debriefing that "Dole never clearly articulated why he wanted to be president." Thus, we hypothesized that issues emphasized primarily by Dole would receive more limited coverage in the *Times*.

Word counts were used to determine how frequently an issue was addressed by the *Times* and the candidates. Speeches were first reviewed to determine which topics were emphasized by the candidates and the language used to address those topics.[2] Using this information, we created a list of over thirty topics with accompanying search terms. For example, any utterance of the word(s) "job(s)," "wage(s)," "employ(s)," or "employ(ment)" was regarded as a reference to the employment issue.

Although word counts are unable to capture qualitative differences—such as *how* a candidate or the press refers to an issue—learning *what* is covered is nonetheless of value. Computerized searches allowed us to examine a large body of material and to draw broad inferences from over 500 articles and 186 speeches.

We used two methods for data tabulation. The first, topic frequency, was based on the percent of speeches or articles in which a particular issue was mentioned at least once. Most of our tables use these figures. We also captured how often a topic was mentioned within a speech. An index was generated by taking the raw frequency of references to a particular topic by a given candidate, divided by that candidate's total number of utterances from all speeches. This figure was multiplied by 1,000 to yield an index of references per 1,000 utterances. This issue-prominence index allows us to ascertain whether emphasizing a topic *within* a speech affects coverage.

Figure 25.1 presents the issues featured most frequently by the candidates and the percentage of *New York Times* stories mentioning them.

The hypothesis that topics emphasized by both candidates would be mentioned by the *Times* more frequently than topics not stressed was generally supported. Table 25.1 presents the ordinal frequency of the top

FIGURE 25.1   Frequency of issue mentions by Dole and Clinton in 1996
campaign and by *New York Times* articles.

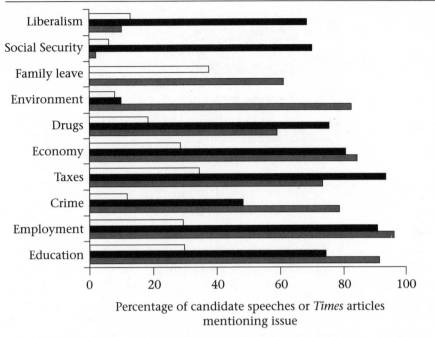

Percentage of candidate speeches or *Times* articles
mentioning issue

TABLE 25.1   Frequency of mention of top five topics by Clinton, Dole, and
New York Times.

	Clinton	Dole	*New York Times*
Employment	1	2	4
Education	2	5	3
Economy	3	3	5
Environment	4		
Crime	5		
Taxes		1	2
Drugs		4	
Family leave			1

NOTE: 1 = most mentioned topic, 2 = second most mentioned topic, and so on.

five topics for the candidates and the *Times*, where 1 = the most mentioned topic, 2 = the second most mentioned topic, and so on. Clinton's
top three topics were among the *Times* top five; Dole's top three topics
and his fifth topic were among the *Times* top five. Two of the issues
among Clinton's top five, and one of Dole's, were not included in the

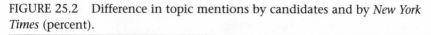

FIGURE 25.2 Difference in topic mentions by candidates and by *New York Times* (percent).

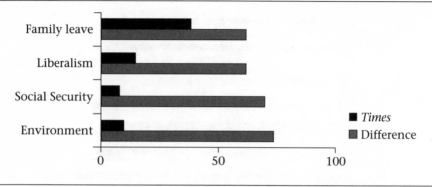

Times list of the five most frequently covered topics; these results are relevant to our second hypothesis.

Our second hypothesis predicted that the *Times* would emphasize those issues focal to one campaign less than those central to both. Figure 25.2 presents those issues for which net difference in mentions was greatest. The *Times* devoted coverage to three of them—liberalism, Social Security, and the environment—in less than 15 percent of its stories. By contrast, those topics that both candidates stressed were covered in 30 percent of all articles.

However, the family-leave issue proved to be at odds with that conclusion. Although Clinton mentioned it in 60.7 percent of his speeches, and Dole did not feature it, the *Times* discussed family leave in 37.3 percent of its articles on the campaign. It may be that Clinton's advertisements that highlighted Dole's objection to the Family and Medical Leave Act attracted the press to this issue. In other words, this finding may actually support the theory that the press favors issues that divide the candidates. In this instance, however, Dole did not stress his objections to the policy in either speeches or ads.

Our third hypothesis posited that where the issue focus of the candidates differed, the *Times* would give more space to topics addressed by Clinton. The results depicted in Figures 25.1 and 25.2 support this prediction. Whereas liberalism, primarily a Dole issue, was covered in 13.1 percent of articles in the *Times*, family leave, Clinton's issue, was mentioned in 37.3 percent of articles. Social Security and the environment, emphasized primarily by Dole and Clinton respectively, both received limited coverage. However, taxes, the issue Dole emphasized the most,

FIGURE 25.3   Issue-prominence index indicating emphasis on topic by Clinton, Dole, and *New York Times*.

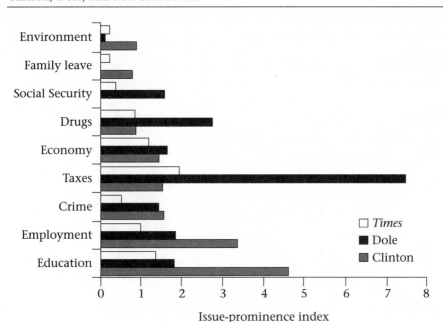

was the second most frequently mentioned topic in the *Times*. Since Clinton mentioned taxes in over 70 percent of his speeches, the press attention devoted to taxes may not have been solely due to Dole's efforts. However, these figures do suggest that Dole was successful in communicating at least part of his issue agenda through the media.

The results of the issue-prominence index we created are summarized in Figure 25.3. This index is a measure of how much emphasis a candidate gave a topic within a speech. Generally, the relationships among topics emphasized by the candidates and the *Times* reflect those presented earlier. The exceptions are taxes and family leave. Dole mentioned taxes in 93.2 percent of his speeches, and Clinton in 73.2 percent of his, but the issue-prominence index for taxes was 7.5 for Dole and 1.5 for Clinton. This finding indicates that not only did Dole mention taxes in more speeches than Clinton, but he also referred to that topic several times within each speech as well. In the index measurement, family leave is no longer the issue mentioned by the candidates who received the most coverage in the *Times*. The effect of Dole's repeated emphasis on taxes may be that it became the top issue.

Our findings suggest that the major-party candidates do exercise some control in setting the media agenda. Their influence is mediated by the concerns of the press. Issues on which the candidates engage and assume opposing positions are more likely to receive coverage. If one candidate emphasizes an issue (such as liberalism or the environment) and the other does not, the topic is less likely to appear in the coverage. At least in 1996, differences in emphasis produced an advantage for the incumbent.

Eric Zimmer, Stacy Benjamin Wood, and
Kathleen Hall Jamieson

➥ Chapter Twenty-Six

Does the Winning Candidate's Agenda Match the Electorate's More Closely Than the Losing Candidate's?

I N 1996, THE AGENDA of the winning candidate (Clinton) tended to match the public agenda to a greater degree than that of the losing candidate (Dole) both in the frequency of topic mentions across speeches and in the prominence given to the topic within speeches. We draw this conclusion by comparing the data reported in the last chapter on candidate focus on issues with answers given by 927 respondents to the Annenberg Election Survey conducted after the 1996 presidential election.

At the outset of the survey, respondents were asked, "What do you think is the most important problem facing this country today?" Up to three answers were recorded and classified into one of forty-six categories. Response frequencies were weighted to match national population data for age, gender, and race/ethnicity.

Figure 26.1 shows the percent of respondents who specified each of ten agenda items mentioned by the candidates; also shown is the proportion of speeches in which the issue was mentioned by each candidate.

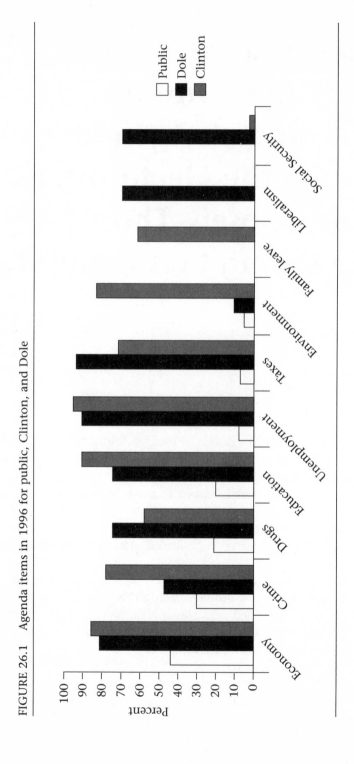

FIGURE 26.1   Agenda items in 1996 for public, Clinton, and Dole

FIGURE 26.2 Candidate and public agendas, 1996.

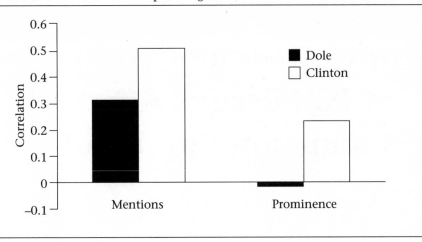

Figure 26.2 shows that both Clinton's speech topics and topic prominence more closely paralleled the public agenda than did Dole's in the 1996 election. We reached the same conclusion in our research of the 1992 election. In each, the winner's agenda was more closely aligned with the electorate's than was the loser's.

Dan Romer and Kathleen Hall Jamieson

Chapter Twenty-Seven

How Does Reporting of Poll Results Affect Campaign Coverage?

I N JANUARY 1999, Philadelphia's mayor, Democrat Ed Rendell, began the last year of his two terms in office. Facing term limits, the popular incumbent endorsed City Council president John Street, who had worked with him to restore the fiscal integrity of the city. Rendell is white, Street, black. About 40 percent of the eligible voters in the city are black; most of them are identified with the Democratic Party. Also seeking the Democratic nomination were Marty Weinberg, a white candidate associated with the mayoral tenure of Frank Rizzo; Happy Fernandez, a white female who had been a member of the council; John White, Jr., an African American candidate who had served as Philadelphia Housing Authority director, and Dwight Evans, also African American and a member of the state House since 1981.

In January, polls reported that Evans had 12 percent of the likely Democratic vote. Press accounts at the end of January, however, showed that he had raised far less money than Street or Weinberg. With money translating into air time in the form of televised ads, Evans supporters took this as a worrisome sign. After the first debate of the Democratic primaries, March 6, a debate in which Evans turned most questions into an answer in favor of gun control, a poll showed Evans's support had dropped.

A *Daily News*, Fox TV, Keystone poll of 350 likely Democratic voters, published April 12, put Street and Weinberg at 23 percent each, Fernandez at 12 percent, White at 12 percent, and Evans at 4 percent. With three black candidates in the race and Weinberg and Street neck and neck for the position of front-runner, on May 1, a group of black clergymen circulated a letter calling for Evans to withdraw from the race. If he stayed in, the letter said, the black vote might be sufficiently split to give the election to Weinberg. "You are intelligent enough to know that your candidacy for mayor cannot succeed and that by remaining in the election campaign you are one of Marty Weinberg's greatest assets," said the letter. "The coalition of persons and organizations that has authorized us to send this letter does not believe that the election of Mr. Weinberg is in the best interest of Philadelphia or the communities we serve. Therefore, we insist that you demonstrate your commitment to the community by withdrawing as a candidate for mayor on or before May 3, 1999." Evans responded that he would stay the course.

On May 4, African American columnist Acel Moore argued in his *Philadelphia Inquirer* column that the ministers had "put the cart before the horse." "To publicly ask one of the black candidates to step aside is purely a racial argument. The real question for those interested in supporting a black candidate is, why don't more black voters participate." Parenthetically, Moore repeated what had become a refrain in press reports: Evans "ranks last in most candidates' polls." On Fox News, a reporter indicated that Evans "placed last in the overall poll" and that some supporters were encouraging him to get out. In its May 10 biographical profile of Evans, the *Inquirer* stated, "Evans says he is all about issues: He can point to many accomplishments but is trailing in the polls." "Dwight Evans is getting just 4 percent," said the WB news report of the Keystone poll. In that report, Weinberg noted that if people didn't have a chance to make themselves known, the well-known candidates would always win, and "no one [else] would have a chance." The reporter added, "And according to the polls, Evans doesn't." A local academic was then quoted: "He [Evans] is so far in the bottom. He is below the margin of error, which means he may not exist at all."

Using data gathered during the 1999 Philadelphia mayoral primary campaign, we examined the relationship between the results of publicized candidate preference polls and newspaper coverage, and the relationship between candidate preference polls and vote intention.[1] Newspapers and broadcast media were content-analyzed for the last month of the campaign. At the same time, we conducted a twenty-nine-day rolling cross-sectional survey of 1,500 Philadelphians, with fifty surveyed daily.

Our content analysis assessed the number of direct quotations of the candidates in the print and broadcast news (see Table 27.1). This measure is a surrogate for the amount of coverage provided for each candidate. Direct quotes give candidates the opportunity to frame the issues and their campaigns. In both print and broadcast news, the number of quotes from each candidate fell almost exactly in line with how each

TABLE 27.1 Frequency of candidate quotes, print and broadcast news

	Print[a]	Broadcast[a]	Final Vote Tally (percent)
Street	22.9	24	36
Weinberg	20.4	28	31
White	16.8	17	22
Fernandez	13.9	14	6
Evans	17.2	14	5
Katz	5.5	4	*unopposed*

[a] Percent of total candidate quotes.

fared in the general election (and how each ranked in the polls conducted during the final month of the campaign). There is one exception. The Republican, Sam Katz, who was running uncontested, received very little coverage in either print or broadcast news, a fact he and his staff complained about often throughout the campaign.

The fact that news coverage paralleled poll results so closely leads to the possibility that reporters index the amount of coverage given to a candidate based on that candidate's relative standing in the polls. This process could create a self-fulfilling prophecy. Polls determine who will get press access; candidates who perform poorly in polls are less likely to garner coverage and have a tougher time increasing their visibility and with it their standing in the polls, which pushes them further out of the media spotlight.

When the press increases its reliance on poll-driven strategy coverage in the closing weeks of an election that has a large number of undecided voters, which was the case in the Philadelphia mayoral primary (see Figure 27.1), the disadvantage inflicted on those behind in the polls is magnified. As we noted earlier, strategy-oriented coverage—which focuses on explaining who is winning and losing—treats candidates trailing in the polls as "on the ropes," whereas leading candidates are discussed in terms of "holding the lead."

These data do not reveal whether the number of quotes by a candidate was dictated by the poll results, or whether poll results were a function, in part, of the degree to which the media covered each candidate. Nevertheless, these two measures were fundamentally related in the 1999 Philadelphia mayoral campaign, a campaign that did not exhibit parity in the media's coverage of each candidate. Strategy coverage increased as poll results drove overall coverage—a deadly combination for trailing candidates.

FIGURE 27.1   Story frames for 1999 Philadelphia mayoral primary, by month, late-night newscasts.

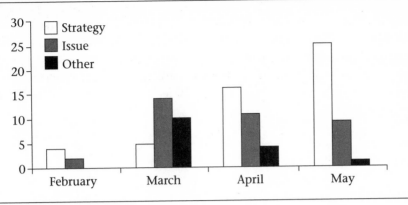

If polls are a reliable indicator of public sentiment and public sentiment is fully formed, indexing the amount of coverage a candidate receives to reflect the candidate's relative poll standing makes some sense. There are two reasons to believe that was not the case in the mayoral primary in Philadelphia. It is important to note that our poll shows that the public was aware of candidate standings in the polls. To have a direct effect, polling results must be known. Presumably the way they become known is through press coverage and resulting talk about it. In our survey, 72 percent of respondents said they had seen or read at least one poll result, and of those, over 80 percent said, accurately, that it reported John Street to be leading the race.

First, about a quarter of the Democratic electorate remained undecided until the final days. Being ahead in the polls takes on different meanings in elections in which 95 percent of voters have made up their minds and in ones in which 75 percent have. In a multicandidate race, there is also likely to be more vote shifting as strategic voters calculate who is most likely to be able to defeat a disliked candidate. In the Philadelphia election, White was the beneficiary of just such a surge in early May, a surge that occurred in the wake of his argument that he was better positioned than Street to beat the Republican nominee, Sam Katz.

We also know that indexing done on the assumption that the polls had accurately pegged Evans's support was misinformed. During the period April 19–30, there was not a statistically significant difference between Evans and White. In short, there was no more reason to assume that one should withdraw from the race than the other. It is also inaccurate to say that during this period Evans was last in the polls. It is even possible that the discussion over whether Evans should have withdrawn actually raised his visibility and increased his support in the time between the Keystone poll and our survey. However, in May, Evans's support collapsed in favor of White. Nonetheless, after being underplayed by press accounts, Evans still received 5 percent of the vote. These data raise the possibility that the press accounts of polls and resulting indexing created a self-fulfilling prophecy—not in eventual outcome but in the order in which the mayoral candidates would finish in the Philadelphia election.

Kathleen Hall Jamieson and Sean Aday

Conclusion

As scholars, we recognize the tendency of other humans to favor negative information over positive. Media analysts routinely report that attack is more readily recalled than advocacy, for example, and offer such explanations as "our potential and distant ancestors who were not alert to the dangers of predators were eaten before they could pass on their genetically based complacency to us."

What we miss in the process, and what my own early writing about politics suggests I ignored as well, is the extent to which media critics themselves are vulnerable to that same tendency. While decrying the disposition of the press to focus on attack rather than advocacy, we focus on instances of bad press behavior rather than the good. While worrying about the effects that an overestimation of the negative has on others, we forget that this very tendency infects us as well.

Those who study such things have identified this tendency as the "third person effect"—a finding that says that others feel the harmful effects of media while we scholars are blessedly immune to them. To rephrase a famous political axiom, "Don't worry about you; don't worry about me; worry about the person behind that tree."

Everything You Think You Know About Politics . . . and Why You're Wrong is largely about the widely held belief that politics in the United States is broken: Soundbites are worthless. Politicians don't keep their promises. Campaigns are increasingly negative. Attack is the dominant form of campaign discourse. The public can't learn from campaigns because they are vapid and vacuous; debates contain no new information. Both advertising and attack drive voters from the polls. Newspapers have lost their impact. In this book, my colleagues and I have argued that these views are mistaken.

Yet it is worth recalling that the potential ancestors who slept smugly next to the campfire, confident that predators would find only others tasty, should have been more vigilant. Somewhere between the view that politics as practiced in the United States is poisonous and simple-minded Pollyannaism resides our message that there are problem areas, the media's reliance on strategic assumptions among them.

For instance, consider the early January Democratic presidential debate between Vice President Al Gore and former Senator Bill Bradley (D–New Jersey) in Iowa—the state holding the first caucuses of the 2000 election season. The moment was a dramatic one. "Let me introduce a friend of mine to you," Gore said. "Chris Peterson is here. Could you stand up, Chris? Chris is a farmer with 400 acres. . . . Back in 1993, 300 of his 400 acres were flooded out. I joined with Tom Harkin to get the extra billion dollars of disaster relief to help Chris and the others who were flooded out." The moderator interrupted to ask for the question.

Turning to Bradley, the vice president asked, "Why did you vote against the disaster relief for Chris Peterson when he and thousands of others of the farmers here in Iowa needed it after those '93 floods?"

Bradley responded, "You know, Al, I think that the premise of your question is wrong." But Bradley did not follow up by rebutting Gore's specific charge. The former New Jersey senator then added, "This is not about the past. This is about the future. This is about what we're going to do to change the agriculture policy we've had the last eight, ten years, during Republicans and Democrats." Rather than rebutting Gore's charge, he proceeded to attack the Freedom to Farm Act and the administration's agriculture policy.

Gore returned to Bradley's alleged lack of concern for the plight of farmers affected by the flood of 1993. "Well, I'm saying like you, I don't want to talk about the past, because in addition to voting against the—you know, those floods, they created a new great lake on the satellite pictures out here. It was a—it was a genuine catastrophe. And most people said, yes, these farmers need help. And there were many other droughts and disasters facing farmers where you were one of a handful who didn't help the farmer."

The next day's headlines focused on the tactical advantage Gore had gained. "Gore Attacks Bradley's Agriculture Record," noted the *Washington Post*. "Vice President's 'Plant' Yields Defensiveness," observed the *New York Times*.[1]

The media seized on what was a supposedly decisive moment. The *Post*, for example, reported: "'Let me introduce a friend to you,' Gore said when the moderator gave him a chance to question Bradley, his rival for the Democratic nomination. 'Chris Peterson is here. Could you stand up, Chris?' Turning to Bradley, Gore asked, 'Why did you vote against the disaster relief for Chris Peterson when he and thousands of other farmers here in Iowa needed it after those '93 floods?'"

"Bradley appeared taken aback and sought to recover throughout the rest of the hour-long debate, which was broadcast statewide on public television and nationally on several cable networks. 'You know, Al, I think the premise of your question is wrong,' Bradley said. 'This is not about the past. This is about the future. . . . You can talk about the past, but I prefer to talk about the future.' Gore chuckled and said, 'Well, I can understand why you don't want to talk about the past. . . . Those floods, they created a great lake on the satellite pictures out here. It was a genuine catastrophe.' Gore then pointed to 'many other droughts and disasters facing farmers where you were one of a handful who didn't help the farmers.'"

The frame in Iowa was the same. The *Des Moines Register* reported that "Vice President Al Gore and former U.S. Sen. Bill Bradley clashed sharply over farm policy during their first presidential debate in Iowa Saturday. Gore demanded Bradley answer why he opposed disaster aid while a senator, pointing to a farmer sitting in the audience whose land was flooded in 1993. Bradley countered by asking farmers if they were better off than when Gore took office seven years ago."[2]

What some articles only implied by not correcting Gore's statement, others made explicit. "Perhaps most dramatically," noted an article in the *New York Times*, "Mr. Gore highlighted Mr. Bradley's vote against federal disaster relief for farmers by singling out Chris Peterson, a farmer in the audience, and describing the 1993 flooding of 300 of his 400 acres."[3]

Only on February 17, more than a month after the Iowa farm debate, and long after both Iowans and residents of New Hampshire had balloted, the *New York Times* reported, "Mr. Gore's accusation was false and unfair. Mr. Bradley supported the 1993 legislation that provided $4.8 billion in emergency flood relief for farmers like Mr. Peterson. What Mr. Bradley and 31 other senators opposed was an amendment that would have provided an additional $900 million in disaster compensation. The Clinton administration also opposed the amendment until literally minutes before floor debate ended."[4]

Long before this, within a week of the Iowa farm debate, the Gore campaign laid the groundwork to emphasize the message that Bradley had failed to support flood relief. On January 13, it began airing radio and TV ads. In the TV ad, as pictures of flood victims and flooded farmland rolled across the screen, Senator Tom Harkin (D–Iowa) noted: "The 1993 floods in Iowa were something that we'll tell our grandchildren about. The floods devastated Iowa, and Al Gore came through for us as he's done so many times when I've called on him to help Iowa."

But what of Bradley? Harkin continued: "In fact, Al Gore was the only Democratic candidate for president who helped make sure that Iowa got the help we desperately needed after those floods. I'm Tom Harkin. I'm here to say that Al Gore has stood up for Iowa."

The ad says nothing directly about his opponent, but it implies that Gore was a more determined advocate than Bradley. As vice president in 1993, Gore could not compile a Senate voting record, but he could work inside the administration as an advocate for the Iowa farmer. Did the Clinton-Gore administration in fact aggressively champion the extra 900 million for Iowa? On August 4, 1993, on the floor of the Senate, the same Tom Harkin, whose ads in January 2000 were now praising Gore's commitment, had said, "The administration has written a letter saying they will not oppose the amendment. I must say, in all candor, Mr. President, I thought the administration would support the amendment (S10300)." Senator Kit Bond (R–Missouri) made even clearer the same implications of the administration's position: "The administration initially set up a proposal saying for you farmers, we are going to cut you in half. We are going to give you half of what is authorized. But for small businesses, small communities, airports, railroads, transportation infrastructure, the unemployed, everybody else, we are going to give you 100 percent of what is authorized (S10300)." Under threat that Senator Harkin and Senator Paul Wellstone (D–Minnesota) would go to the floor and condemn the actions of the administration, the White House signaled that it supported the amendment.

In sum, the Gore attack was misleading on two counts: It said Bradley failed to help the farmers when, in fact, he voted for nearly $5 billion in aid for them, and it suggested that unlike Bradley, the Clinton-Gore administration championed additional funds when it merely acquiesced to demands for them.

Did the exchange over Chris Peterson's plight and the subsequent Harkin ad make a difference in the campaign? The answer seems to be yes. Local polls showed Bradley trailing on the eve of the debate, and this is confirmed by the analysis done by Richard Johnston and Michael Hagen of the Annenberg Year 2000 Iowa "Rolling Cross Section" survey. But our poll, like others, shows that Bradley was very much in the game on January 8, with vote-intention shares among likely Democratic voters around, possibly over, 40 percent. Shortly after the debate, Bradley's share dropped to around 30 percent and never recovered. The drop was steepest among respondents claiming to have seen at least some of the debate. Even if these respondents saw the debate only as news, most news reports covering the debate emphasized the key moment with Chris Peterson. Bradley's share may have dropped even further, although only temporarily, after the Harkin ads began airing on January 13. In reinterviews after the Iowa caucuses, we asked which of the candidates "did more for the American farmer." The fact that the vast majority said Gore is not surprising. He had just won this quintessential farm state, after all. But respondents who actually saw some of the debate were much more likely to say this than respondents who had not—even though Bradley supporters were more likely to watch the debate in the first place.

There are two lessons here. The first is the one learned by Michael Dukakis in 1988. Failure to rebut a high-profile attack is hazardous to one's campaign. Second, when inaccurate information is reinforced— not corrected—by news coverage and underscored in ads, it can influence votes. Our data suggest the possibility that Gore built his victory in the Iowa caucuses in part on a partial truth unchallenged in the debate or in ads by Bradley and uncorrected by the press.

As luck would have it, the early primaries of 2000 provided other tests of some of the key claims in *Everything You Think You Know About Politics . . . and Why You're Wrong*, as well. Is attack an indispensable part of successful campaigning? Are voters receptive to contrast that is low key and accurate? Do they penalize attack that is hyperbolic, personal, and untrue? Does campaigning that makes a case against an opponent and for the sponsor on consequential issues attract voters to the polls? Do messages matter? At least so far in 2000, the answer to all of these appears to be yes.

As I argued earlier, the demise of the Bradley campaign in Iowa can be attributed at least in part to his failure to rebut an inaccurate charge in the Iowa farm debate. Learning a lesson from the defeat in Iowa, Bradley began not only to respond to attack but also to launch contrastive arguments of his own in New Hampshire. As the effects of this change took hold, he began to close in the polls. Bradley's shift raises this question: Had he moved more aggressively sooner to begin contrasting his record and proposals with Gore's, would he have been able to win Iowa or New Hampshire?

There is no way to know the answer to that question, but what intrigues us about Bradley's campaign and Senator John McCain's (R–Arizona) experience when he swore off contrast ads in South Carolina is that in each instance the candidate who held to the supposed "high road" lost ground. We suspect that happened because each failed to appreciate the distinction between legitimate attack that is fair and accurate, and the sleazy illegitimate kind. Swearing off all attack simply makes no sense in an electoral process in which voters must make choices. And, as Democratic nominee Michael Dukakis learned in 1988, an unrebutted attack, whether true or false, is likely to be believed by enough voters to matter.

We take other lessons from the early primaries of 2000 as well. After Senator McCain unexpectedly trounced Texas Governor George W. Bush in the New Hampshire primary of 2000, the importance of the South Carolina primary increased dramatically. A second win by McCain perhaps could have shaken the confidence of the large number of governors, senators, and House members whose support of Bush and sizable war chest had made his nomination seem all but inevitable. Bush's win in the South Carolina primary of February 19 was as decisive as McCain's had been in New Hampshire. And turnout was double what it had been in the South Carolina primary of 1996.[5]

This outcome provided support for three of the central findings we reported in this book. First, contrast mobilizes. Second, what voters reject, and regard as negative, is untrue, personal, overstated attack that provides no justification for supporting the sponsor. The candidate who succeeds in casting his opponent's ads in this light gains a strategic advantage. Finally, media coverage helps shape public perceptions.

Recall our conclusion that attack that argues against an opponent and for the sponsor will draw citizens to the voting booth. In South Carolina, the level of contrast was high and turnout was up. The Bush ad that made an issue of McCain's claim about trust-twisting was a contrast ad that said, "Politics is tough. But when John McCain compared me to Bill Clinton and said I was untrustworthy, that's over the line. Disagree with me, fine. But do not challenge my integrity. I'm a leader and reformer who gets results. I fought the education establishment for high standards and local control, and won. While Washington politicians deadlocked, I delivered a patients' bill of rights. . . . I fight for what I believe in, and I get results."

Although Bush actually opposed key parts of the patients' bill of rights in Texas, no ad watches appeared in South Carolina pointing that out. This ad serves as a reminder of a point we made in the chapters on "negativity." Reporters are quicker to evaluate the accuracy of attack even though claims about a candidate's own record are more likely to be the misleading ones. In any event, this ad, titled "Integrity," was a contrast ad. So, too, was a radio ad called "Charity" that noted: "John McCain has attacked Governor Bush's tax cut plan as too big, yet the McCain plan would not cut taxes for 71 percent of Americans who file tax returns."

Bush's final ad of the South Carolina primary was a contrast ad as well. "It's disappointing," said the announcer in the ad. "Friday John McCain promised to stop running a negative campaign. Then Sunday, he attacked Governor Bush on national television with false charges on campaign finance . . . Governor Bush supports comprehensive reform that would outlaw foreign, corporate and union money to political parties." Having indicated Bush's position, the ad again veered to attack McCain who, according to the spot, "five times voted to use your taxes to pay for political campaigns." It concluded, "That's not real reform." Note that each of these ads justified Bush's charges by positioning it as a response to an unfair attack by McCain.

By every measure, including number of attack spots and percent of each spot devoted to attack, more attack was aired against McCain in South Carolina than vice versa. Yet the Voter News Service (VNS) survey found that "more voters said Mr. McCain, not Mr. Bush, was the author of unfair attacks and nearly half said they thought Mr. McCain was capable of political duplicity."[6] If amount of attack is synonymous with level of illegitimate campaigning, as some pundits suggest, Bush should have been penalized. Instead, the person who had run the most attack was perceived as having conducted the fairer campaign. Voters, in other words, did not dismiss all attack as "negative" and equate "negative" with "dirty or unfair."

Our analysis of the impact of the various types of ads in 1996 and 1998 led us to believe that voters disapprove of attack that is personal, hyperbolic, and untrue. In an ad and on the stump, Bush indicted McCain's ad containing the Clinton analogy as "over the line."[7] In the South Carolina debate, Bush framed the issue directly. "[H]e ran an ad that equated me to Bill Clinton—he questioned my trustworthiness . . . [Y]ou can disagree on issues, we'll debate issues, but whatever you do, don't equate my integrity and trustworthiness to Bill Clinton. That's about as low a blow as you can give in a Republican primary." By casting McCain's attack as a personal assault on his integrity and trustworthiness, Bush suggested to voters that his opponent had engaged in inappropriate attack. In the South Carolina debate and in stump speeches, Bush also charged that a flier distributed by the McCain campaign was untrue.

After launching the ad analogizing a Bush ad to Clinton's "twisting of the truth" on February 7, McCain withdrew it February 11, declaring that he would run only positive ads for the remainder of the primary. In the debate, the Arizona senator reiterated that pledge, saying "we're running nothing but a positive campaign." When Bush responded by pulling an attack flier of McCain's from his coat pocket, he effectively called into question the credibility of McCain's disavowal of attack.

More important is the fact that, in keeping with his pledge, McCain stopped broadcasting responses to Bush's contrastive ads. As a result, Bush reaped the advantage of being able to tag his opponent with hypocrisy for promising one thing and doing another and as a sponsor of personal and untrue attacks. Meanwhile, Bush benefited from the perception that his ads were merely defending his record in a truthful and nonpersonal way. This is another explanation for the perception that the person whose ads attacked the most was running ads that were fairer and that McCain, too, was capable of duplicity.

The dynamics changed between the South Carolina and Michigan primaries. In the two days between the South Carolina vote and the balloting in Michigan, press accounts replayed and recounted telephone messages to prospective voters. Armed with tapes provided by the McCain campaign, reporters cast the pro-Bush forces, specifically Christian Coalition founder Pat Robertson, as the purveyors of personal attack. In a telephone message, Robertson called McCain's campaign chairman, Warren Rudman, a "vicious bigot." As the press pointed out, Robertson's calls distorted Rudman's actual views. "Rudman never 'wrote that conservative Christians in politics are anti-abortion zealots, homophobes and would-be censors [as the Robertson call alleges],'" noted an essay in Salon.com on the day of the Michigan vote. "He wrote that there are some 'conservative Christians in politics' who fit that description, but he certainly never said that all of them do." As an article in the *New York Times* noted, "[F]rom television pundits to New York pedestrians, he [Rudman] has found many rallying to his defense."[8]

Bush, too had made an attack on Rudman. In the CNN South Carolina debate, the Texas governor declared, "Warren Rudman, the man who you had as your campaign man in New Hampshire, said about the Christian Coalition that they're bigots." Rudman had not called members of the Christian Coalition, which Robertson heads, "bigots." Instead, he had condemned a number of Christian conservatives in November 1995 for denouncing General Colin Powell as a prospective Republican presidential contender in 1996. "Not only did these political pipsqueaks question Powell's views on such issues as abortion and gun control," wrote Rudman, "but they challenged his character and his military record. This from people who not only have never heard a shot fired in anger, but have never even dropped by a PX for an ice cream cone. It was an amazing display not only of arrogance but of fear, because these people know that Colin Powell embodies the very opposite of the ignorance and bigotry that they represent."[9] Had McCain corrected the record, the correction would have filtered into news accounts before Robertson's calls propelled it there. Instead McCain said, "George [is] entitled to his opinion on that issue."

But once the Robertson call became news and Rudman's statements had been retrieved, it was not difficult for editors to recall Bush's earlier indictment. To make matters worse, Robertson's message inaccurately described McCain's campaign finance proposal as taking "First Amendment freedoms from citizens groups while he gives unrestricted power to labor unions." Before the polls closed in Michigan, David Gergen and I used part of our time on *NewsHour* with Jim Lehrer to condemn the calls. And just after the Michigan results were in, CNN's Jeff Greenfield elicited one concession after another from Robertson about the inaccuracy of his phoned message.

The McCain forces also worked mightily to associate George Bush with the shrill anti-Catholic rhetoric of the founder of a school at which the Texan had spoken. In a phone message that the McCain campaign initially denied but later confirmed was from the McCain camp, a voice reminded Catholic voters that in South Carolina Bush had spoken at Bob Jones University, a school whose founder had called the pope the anti-Christ and the Catholic Church a satanic cult.

Bush's appearance at Bob Jones University had been the subject of press speculation during the South Carolina primary, but the discussion focused largely on his failure to repudiate the school's policy against interracial dating. In Michigan the focus shifted to whether Bush should have used his platform at Bob Jones to speak out against anti-Catholic bigotry. "This is a Catholic Voter Alert," said the McCain phone call. "Governor George Bush has campaigned against Senator John McCain by seeking the support of Southern fundamentalists who have expressed anti-Catholic views. Several weeks ago, Governor Bush spoke at Bob Jones University in South Carolina. Bob Jones has made strong anti-Catholic statements, including calling the pope the anti-Christ, the Catholic Church a satanic cult!"

The frame adopted by the press is clear in an article in the *Philadelphia Inquirer*. "Clearly," noted the reporter, "the Bush strategy is to turn the tables and claim that McCain has falsely smeared him as a bigot. But the McCain phone transcript—as released by the Bush campaign—did not call Bush a bigot; instead, it recites the basic facts of the case, notably that 'Governor Bush has stayed silent' rather than criticize the Bob Jones school's 'anti-Catholic bigotry.'"[10]

The claim that Bush had failed to repudiate the anti-Catholic views of a presumed supporter put to the test the argument we advanced in the first chapter. If messages matter in a campaign, such a message, if considered true, should shift Catholic voters from Bush to McCain. That does seem to be the case. Whereas McCain defeated Bush in Michigan 51 percent to 43 percent among all voters, Catholics favored McCain by a wider margin, 51 percent to 35 percent.[11]

The early primaries contained a second test of the power of messages. On the practical policy decisions about abortion rights, Bush and McCain took identical positions. Each would ban abortion except in cases involving incest, rape, or a threat to the life of the mother. Neither would use position on abortion as a litmus test in selecting a vice-presidential running mate or in nominating a justice to the Supreme Court. In the Senate, McCain has a strong pro-life voting record.

There are symbolic differences between the two, however. Bush would not change the Republican platform of 1996 that declares "the unborn child has a fundamental individual right to life which cannot be infringed." McCain would instead specify the exceptions that both he and Bush favor. And in the South Carolina debate, McCain responded to a question predicated on the assumption that his daughter "needed an abortion" by saying, in part, "It's a family decision." Finally, McCain would permit the use of fetal tissue for medical experiments.

During the run-up to the South Carolina primary, National Right to Life endorsed George Bush. Some speculated that the reason was not a difference between Bush and McCain on abortion rights but rather their disagreement over campaign finance reform. In any event, radio ads in South Carolina and Michigan by the national and state-based Right to Life political action committees argued that "the Republican Pro-Choice Coalition called other remarks by McCain in New Hampshire, quote: 'pro-choice.' This pro-abortion group reported that in the New Hampshire primary, quote 'Pro-choice Republicans overwhelmingly preferred McCain above all other candidates.'" The ad concluded its appeal by saying, "George Bush has been endorsed by South Carolina citizens and National Right to Life, and by congressional pro-life leaders like Henry Hyde. So, if you want a strong pro-life president, don't vote for John McCain. Vote for George Bush." The controversial phone message by Pat Robertson reinforced the message. In it Robertson declared, "Protect unborn babies and restore religious freedom once again in America."

Whether McCain is in fact more pro-choice than Bush doesn't matter for purposes of analysis here. If messages matter, the endorsement of Bush by National Right to Life should provide pro-choice voters with a clue that McCain is closer to their point of view and should guide pro-life voters toward Bush. In fact, that is what happened. In both South Carolina[12] and Michigan,[13] those who want abortion to be legal in all or most cases were more likely to favor McCain; those who think abortion should be illegal in most or all cases were more likely to vote for Bush.

In sum, campaigns matter, as does the discourse of candidates and the coverage provided by the press. Rebuttal is part of a robust politics, as is accurate, fair attack that speaks to issues of importance to voters. Some forms of candidate communication are more likely to draw voters to the polls than others.

In some important ways, ours is a story of a system that is self-correcting. Although there is nothing wrong with accurate, fair attack, contrast is a form of communication more helpful to voters. They prefer it to attack. It is more effective at relaying information. We are seeing increasing amounts of it. And it mobilizes voters.

None of this means that we should not aspire to improve the quality of campaigns and their discourse or the quality of deliberation in our institutions and among the citizenry. But the move to correct should be based on realism, not pessimism. Indeed, one might even conclude in the tentative manner conventionalized in this cynical age that the evidence we have marshaled justifies optimism.

Kathleen Hall Jamieson

Methods for Analysis
of Ad Impact

Definitions of Terms in Our Analysis of Advertising Impact

A **rating point** is a measure of audience viewership on a scale of 0 to 1400.[1] One rating point is equal to 1 percent of the potential viewing universe. The viewing universe is defined as those households with televisions capable of receiving a given broadcast signal. Consequently, an individual commercial broadcast that achieved a rating of 4.2 indicates that 4.2 percent of the potential viewing universe tuned into the commercial.

Gross rating points (GRPs) are the sum of rating points over a given time and include duplicated audiences. For example, a commercial that aired only twice and achieved a rating of 4.2 each time would record GRPs of 8.4, regardless of any overlap of audiences between the two airings. Likewise, if we were interested in determining the GRPs achieved by a specific political commercial from September 1 through November 3, we would simply sum the rating points achieved by each broadcast of the commercial during that time period. Because they measure duplicated audiences, GRPs have no upward bound.

For earlier years of broadcast television and for cable television in general, GRPs are not available. To establish viewership levels in these cases, we turn to dollars spent as the best available surrogate.

GRPs are reported by **designated market areas** (DMAs), "a Nielsen Media Research term for a group of counties in which a TV station obtains the greatest portion of its audience."[2] Each county belongs to only one DMA.

Because voting data are gathered and reported by county but advertising time is bought and reported by DMA, we assigned the same GRPs to each county within each media market. This procedure allowed us to determine the sizes of audiences within and across markets.

Since cable buys are reported in dollars, not GRPs, we created a cable GRP measure by dividing dollars spent on cable within a market by the number of GRPs purchased by one dollar of broadcast in the market. Information on cable buys was obtained from the campaigns. We assembled information on local media market buys in the top fifty markets in the United States by checking station logs

223

secured from Nielsen. To verify the accuracy of the Nielsen logs, we compared the Philadelphia, Cleveland, and Minneapolis Nielsen logs to the ones we copied in those markets.

To track national buys, we used data from the Dole and Clinton campaigns as well as reports from competitive media reports (CMRs). These sources were also used to confirm the accuracy of the station logs. When the records conflicted, as they did in twenty-seven cases, we queried the campaigns for assistance. When that failed to resolve the conflict, we accepted the accuracy of the station logs over the reports of the campaigns and CMRs.

Coding Attack Versus Advocacy

Content analysis of ads is performed at the level of the **idea unit**. We use idea unit, not sentence, as our unit of analysis because the verbal content of ads is often expressed in phrases rather than sentences. A single sentence may include idea units that advocate and others that attack (for example, "Clinton favors family medical leave but Dole opposes it"). Each idea unit is coded as either advocacy or attack, based on the assumption that that which does not attack, advocates. In the example above, we judge the idea unit "but Dole opposes it" as attack, and "Clinton favors family medical leave" as advocacy.

To determine what percent of an ad falls into each category, we count the words in idea units that attack and those that advocate as a percent of the total number of words in each ad. In this coding scheme, an ad in which 61 percent of the words occurred in idea units that focused on unfavorable characteristics of the opponent or his record would be assigned a value of 0.61 attack.

We assume that anything not coded as attack is advocacy. An ad that both attacks and advocates would be considered contrastive. For example, the words in capital letters in the following ad would be coded as attack, those in regular type as advocacy:

TO FIGHT DRUGS, ALL BOB DOLE OFFERS ARE SLOGANS, "JUST DON'T DO IT" AND LOOK WHAT HE'S DONE. VOTED TO CUT THE PRESIDENT'S SCHOOL ANTI-DRUG EFFORTS BY 50 PERCENT. AGAINST CREATING A DRUG CZAR. AGAINST CREATING STUDENT LOANS. AGAINST THE PRESIDENT'S PLAN TO LIMIT CIGARETTE ADS TO TARGET OUR KIDS. JOINED WITH NEWT GINGRICH TO CUT VACCINES FOR CHILDREN. THAT'S THE REAL BOB DOLE RECORD. "JUST DON'T DO IT." ONE SLOGANS CAN'T HIDE. President Clinton: Protecting our values."

In this seventy-seven-word ad, five words are advocacy and seventy-two attack, for 94 percent attack and 6 percent advocacy.

We establish an ad's attack score using the following formula: The number of words that occur in idea units that attack is divided by the total number of words occurring in the ad. If the example above constituted the entire ad, it would receive an advocacy score of 5/77, or 0.06. Its attack score would be 0.94.

To determine the **weight** of an ad, we multiplied an ad's duration in seconds by the gross rating points it achieved in the market. To further differentiate attack advertising from advocacy, we calculated the proportion of the ad's weight that was devoted to attack:

Attack weight = ad duration in seconds x gross rating points x attack score.

Attack and advocacy weight add up to the total weight for each ad.

Each of the political advertisements aired by the Dole and Clinton campaigns was coded in terms of the amount of attack and the amount of advocacy (in GRP-seconds). A similar procedure was followed for the ads aired by the AFL-CIO and the Business Coalition.

To verify that the ad tapes secured from the campaigns were complete, we compared their contents to the station logs, to media reports, and to our record of ads taped off the air during the campaign in ten media markets.

Determining Voter Turnout

In our analysis of the effects of political advertising, we expressed voter turnout as a proportion: votes cast for president divided by voting-age population. Both sets of figures are available at the county level, our unit of analysis. Thus, there are three variables in this formula: votes cast, voting-age population, and county.

Votes cast for president (and other offices) are certified and disseminated by each state's Office of the Secretary of State. States provide vote totals for listed candidates on a county-by-county basis. Official state figures, however, are subject to revision. This is not an infrequent occurrence, although it is in most cases a trivial one. If one runs across different vote totals at either the county, state, or federal level, it is most likely due to the influence of official state revisions. Finally, one cannot assume that official state vote tallies reflect all votes cast, as some states may opt not to count absentee ballots in races so heavily decided that the absentee ballots could not possibly change the outcome.

Voting-age population data are based on the U.S. Census Bureau's county-level population estimates. The Bureau's estimate of a county's voting-age population includes the entire resident population age eighteen and older. Thus, those ineligible to vote for reasons of alien status, felony conviction, or mental incapacity are included in the voting-age population. Further, transient populations (such as students and military personnel) will be included in a county's voting-age population even though some may vote by absentee ballot in another county or state. Census Bureau figures are *estimates*, which the Bureau continuously revises. Consequently, they are fluid figures and apt to change.

Counties, our unit of analysis, are also subject to geographic and population change. The Census Bureau defines a county as "a type of governmental unit that is the primary legal subdivision of every State except Alaska and Louisiana." (The county equivalent in Louisiana is the parish, and in Alaska the borough.) Although relatively fixed, county boundaries sometimes do change. As part of its county population estimates, the Census Bureau publishes "Geographic Change Notes," which report boundary "annexations and de-annexations, formation of new counties (or equivalents), incorporated places, or minor civil divisions, disincorporation or disorganization of governmental units, and governmental unit mergers or consolidations." The significance of boundary changes arises from the shifting population figures likely to occur when a county's boundaries expand or contract.

The counties included in the sample are those in the top fifty media markets in the United States as of the 1996 presidential election. Of the 3,112 counties across the states, 1,101 fall into the top fifty media markets. Three of these counties were dropped from analysis because the official number of votes tallied in the 1996 or 1992 presidential races was greater than the number of reported eligible voters, according to the Census. Thus, the sample of counties is 1,098 for all of our analyses.

Measuring Total Advertising Weight

For each county in the sample, the "weight" of each ad was calculated by multiplying the ad's GRPs by its duration. The total weight for each county was the sum of the weights across all ads aired. The "attack weight" was also calculated by multiplying each ad by the percentage of its content that was geared toward attack. "Advocacy weight" was calculated with an analogous formula. Thus, for each county, eight values described the advertising environment: "attack weight" and "advocacy weight" for the Clinton and Dole campaigns and for ads aired by the AFL-CIO and the Business Coalition.

By analyzing the association between attack and advocacy weight and voter turnout, we can assess the degree to which counties that receive more attack advertising have more or less turnout and whether Democrats or Republicans are advantaged by attack and advocacy ads.

We picked September 1 as the starting date for analysis on the assumption that voters think of the general-election period when answering questions about negativity in presidential campaign ads and because it seemed implausible to conclude that ads aired as early as June 1995, the start date of Clinton-Gore-DNC advertising, would have a measurable effect on general-election turnout and attitudes.

Describing Counties

This sample was divided into five groups as a function of how "Republican" the county was in the presidential elections of 1984, 1988, and 1992. The elections of 1984 and 1988 represented definitive victories for the Republican candidates, Ronald Reagan and George Bush. The 1992 election was a victory for Democrat Bill Clinton, but the margin of victory was narrow with Clinton earning only a plurality of the popular vote. Because of the strong bias toward Republican victories in this set of elections, we chose a measure that weighed the Republican margin of vote percentage in the three presidential elections leading up to 1996.

A second index was also calculated that counted the number of times the county voted more for the Republican candidate than the Democratic candidate. This number varied from 0 to 3. All analyses reported in the text were carried out on both indexes with no substantial differences in conclusions.

A Nontechnical Technical Appendix

Surveys

This book draws on a large number of public opinion surveys. All the surveys analyzed here consist of interviews with people chosen at random from a particular population—whether residents of Philadelphia, registered voters in the San Francisco–Oakland Bay Area, the voting-age population of the nation, or of some other group. Random selection is the foundation of modern polling; paradoxical though it may seem at first blush, random selection ensures a sample of respondents that is representative of the population from which the respondents are chosen. Random selection permits generalizations about a population to be made on the basis of a sample and permits calculations about the precision of the generalizations.

The surveys employed here were conducted in several different ways. The most familiar is the ***cross-section***, which involves interviewing all the individuals in a sample once, in a relatively short span of time. A cross-sectional survey is sometimes described as a "snapshot" of a population: It furnishes a picture of a population and of the differences among individuals at a single point in time. It cannot reveal changes in a population or within individuals over time.

Changes in a population are best studied in a ***rolling cross-section***, in which the sampled individuals are interviewed only once, but a new random sample is interviewed every day or every week over a period of months or years. When such a survey is conducted carefully, the day-to-day or week-to-week differences among the samples can illuminate the causes of changes in a population.

Changes in individuals are the focus of a ***panel*** study, in which the people in a sample are interviewed repeatedly. The interval between interviews is sometimes weeks, sometimes months, sometimes years. Whatever the time span, the purpose of a panel is to identify how and why individual respondents have changed.

Content Analysis

At several points, the book relies upon content analysis to support claims about the nature of texts—television news, newspapers, candidates' speeches, and so on. Content analysis is a set of systematic procedures for characterizing a text, in large measure by counting and classifying elements of the text. The main advantage of content analysis, in comparison with less quantitative methods, is that it is reproducible: Making explicit the rules for classifying words or phrases makes it easier for different analysts to reach the same conclusions about a given text.

Statistical Analysis

The book takes advantage of statistical techniques beyond simple averages and percentages to analyze claims about politics rigorously. Technical material has been kept to a minimum, but some references to the methods employed are unavoidable. A sentence or two here about the most common may help make the analysis clearer.

Ordinary least-squares (OLS) regression makes it possible to isolate the effects of each of a large number of related factors simultaneously and efficiently. If the goal is to identify the relative importance of several potential explanations for something we observe, regression is frequently the technique of choice.

Logistic regression is a variant of ordinary least-squares regression used in the special case when what we wish to explain has only two possible outcomes—for example, whether an individual did or did not vote. The fundamental purpose of logistic regression is the same as that of OLS regression.

Factor analysis is a method for identifying patterns in a large collection of data—for example, in the responses individuals gave to a long list of questions about their knowledge of politics. In such a case, factor analysis might be used to find groups of questions that people tended to answer in the same way.

Statistical significance is used here (as in most social science) to identify quantitative results strong enough that we can be confident that they are not due to chance, to the fluctuations inherent in the process of sampling at random.

Survey Descriptions

The National Election Survey is a nationally representative survey conducted every presidential election year by the Institute for Survey Research at the University of Michigan to assess perceptions of the presidential candidates, the major issues in the election, and vote choice.

The 1996 Annenberg Presidential Election Survey was a nationally representative survey conducted four times during the fall election season (three times before the election and again immediately after). At each wave, approximately 900 adults were interviewed. A separate sample of respondents constituted a panel that was reinterviewed at all four waves (N = 309).

The 1998 Annenberg Gubernatorial Election Survey was conducted in Illinois and California for six weeks prior to the fall election (November 2, 1998). Interviewing was restricted to the Chicago and San Francisco media markets. Interviews with adult residents of the two states were scheduled on a daily basis (N = 2,902) so that trends in citizen reaction to the campaigns could be detected.

The Philadelphia Mayoral Election Screener Survey was conducted by the Annenberg Public Policy Center in December 1998 to identify potential participants for an upcoming deliberative forum that was scheduled to continue throughout the mayoral primary and general elections. Over 2,300 Philadelphia residents representative of the city were interviewed and screened for interest in the program. They were also asked to indicate the three most important problems facing the city.

The Philadelphia Pre-Primary Survey of Philadelphia Residents was conducted by the Annenberg Public Policy Center for twenty-nine days prior to the mayoral primary (May 18, 1999). Approximately fifty interviews representative of the city's adult residents were scheduled daily (N = 1,500) so that trends in citizen reaction to campaign events could be detected.

Appendix IV

Tables and Figures from Selected Chapters

Chapter 1. Do Campaigns Matter?

Paul Waldman and Kathleen Hall Jamieson

FIGURE A1.1   Sponsorship of Issue Advertising (1997–1998).

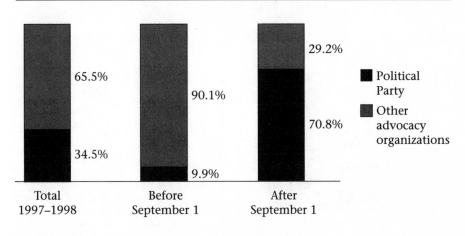

Chapter 2. The Morning After: Do Politicians Keep Their Promises?

Mark Mendoza and Kathleen Hall Jamieson

FIGURE A2.1   Percentage of voters who thought Clinton would keep promises

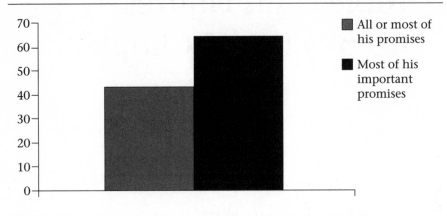

SOURCES: CBS News/*New York Times* poll, January 12–14, 1993; ABC News/*Washington Post* poll, January 14–17, 1993.

FIGURE A2.2   Perceived promisekeeping by president (percent).

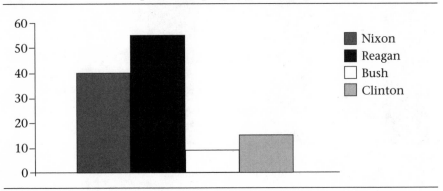

SOURCES: Louis Harris and Associates, April 1–7, 1972; ABC News poll, January 12–16, 1989; CBS News/*New York Times* polls, June 17–20, 1992 and August 16–18, 1996. 1996.

Chapter 4. What Is Happening Now?
The Quality of Campaign Discourse

Susan Sherr, Paul Waldman, David Dutwin, and Kathleen Hall Jamieson

FIGURE A4.1   Attack content of campaign discourse in 1952–1996 elections (percent).

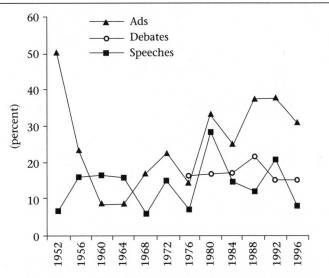

FIGURE A4.2   Contrast content of candidate discourse in 1952–1996 elections (percent).

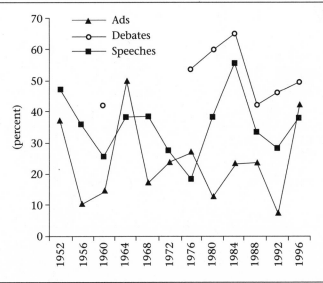

FIGURE A4.3   Advocacy content of campaign discourse in 1952–1996 elections (percent).

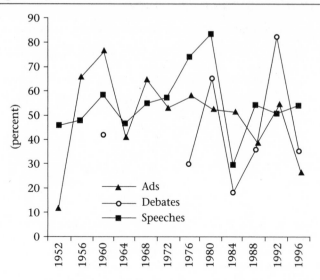

FIGURE A4.4   Comparison of attack, contrast, and advocacy content of all campaign discourse in 1952–1996 elections (percent).

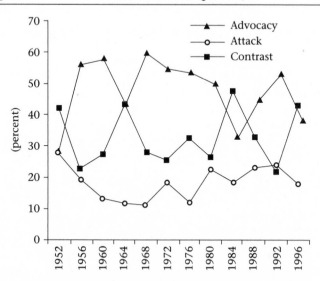

Chapter 7. Are Voters Smarter Than Pundits, the Press, and Scholars About Attack in Politics?

Kathleen Hall Jamieson, Chris Adasiewicz, and Mary McIntosh

FIGURE A7.1 Contrast ads judged more responsible, more useful than one-sided attacks.

Attack vs. Contrast: Social Security	Responsible	Useful		Attack vs. Contrast: Crime	Responsible	Useful
Attack: Social Security is in trouble, but my opponent's plan for saving it will not work. My opponent wants to allow people to invest their Social Security contributions in the stock market.	37%	40%		**Attack:** Crime threatens our neighborhoods, but my opponent's crime plan misses the mark. My opponent thinks the death penalty is wrong, even for violent criminals.	37%	40%
Contrast: Social Security is in trouble, and here is what I promise to do about it. We should use the federal budget surplus to make the program financially sound. But my opponent disagrees. My opponent wants to allow people to invest their Social Security contributions in the stock market.	65%	75%		**Contrast:** Crime threatens our neighborhoods, and here is what I promise to do about it. We need to give more violent criminals the death penalty. But my opponent disagrees. My opponent thinks the death penalty is wrong, even for violent criminals.	65%	75%

FIGURE A7.2 Contrast ads judged as higher quality, attack ads as lower quality.
High-quality ad = responsible + useful + not negative + does not turn voters off

Attack vs. Contrast: Social Security	High Quality	Low Quality		Attack vs. Contrast: Crime	High Quality	Low Quality
Attack	35%	65%		**Attack**	44%	56%
Contrast	76%	24%		**Contrast**	71%	29%

FIGURE A7.3 Evaluation of contrast, attack largely reflect feelings about ad format, not content.

Attack vs. Contrast: Social Security	Favor Investing in Stock Market	Oppose
Attack	37%	34%
Contrast	79%	72%

AD JUDGED
AS HIGH QUALITY

Attack vs. Contrast: Crime	Against Death Penalty	Favor
Attack	45%	45%
Contrast	64%	73%

AD JUDGED
AS HIGH QUALITY

FIGURE A7.4 Inflammatory attack less responsible, more negative, more of a turnoff.

Inflammatory vs. Civil Attack: Social Security	Responsible	Negative	Turns Off
Inflammatory Attack: My opponent does not care that Social Security is in trouble. My opponent wants to allow people to invest their Social Security contributions in the stock market. My opponent is wrong and dangerous for our future.	29%	80%	79%
Civil Attack: Social Security is in trouble, but my opponent's plan for saving it will not work. My opponent wants to allow people to invest their Social Security contributions in the stock market.	37%	67%	68%

Inflammatory vs. Civil Attack: Crime			
Inflammatory Attack: My opponent does not care that crime threatens our neighborhoods. My opponent thinks the death penalty is wrong, even for violent criminals. My opponent is wrong and dangerous for our children.	33%	78%	71%
Civil Attack: Crime threatens our neighborhoods, but my opponent's crime plan misses the mark. My opponent thinks the death penalty is wrong, even for violent criminals.	44%	68%	66%

FIGURE A7.5 Attack on personal life less responsible, less useful, more negative.

Personal Life vs. Policy Attack	Responsible	Negative	Turns Off
Personal Life Attack, Drug Experimentation: My opponent admits trying marijuana in college. These are not the values America needs.	27%	33%	78%
Personal Life Attack, Extramarital Affair: My opponent admits having an affair while married. These are not the values America needs.	31%	37%	75%
Policy Attack, Social Security	37%	40%	67%
Policy Attack, Crime	44%	45%	68%

FIGURE A7.6 Misleading criticism judged least favorably of all ad formats tested.

Misleading Criticism: Social Security	High Quality	Low Quality
Misleading Criticism: Candidate A has criticized the opponent for wanting to allow people to invest Social Security contributions in the stock market. But this is misleading because in fact Candidate A has come out in favor of this plan as well.	37%	40%
Attack on Personal Life (drug experimentation)	27%	73%
Inflammatory Attack	28%	72%
Attack (presumed accurate, about policy, civil)	35%	65%

Misleading Criticism: Crime	High Quality	Low Quality
Misleading Criticism: Candidate A has criticized the opponent for thinking the death penalty is wrong. But this is misleading because the opponent in fact supports the death penalty in some cases.	29%	71%
Attack on Personal Life (extramarital affair)	30%	70%
Inflammatory Attack	34%	66%
Attack (presumed accurate, about policy, civil)	44%	56%

FIGURE A7.7 Evaluations of inflammatory, misleading attack largely reflect feelings about format.

Inflammatory and Misleading Criticism: Social Security	Favor Investing in Stock Market	Oppose
Inflammatory Attack	74%	70%
Misleading Criticism	76%	80%

AD JUDGED
AS LOW QUALITY

Inflammatory and Misleading Criticism: Crime	Against Death Penalty	Favor
Inflammatory Attack	66%	66%
Misleading Criticism	70%	71%

AD JUDGED
AS LOW QUALITY

Chapter 9. The Gender Gap in Political Knowledge: Are Women Less Knowledgeable Than Men About Politics?

Kate Kenski and Kathleen Hall Jamieson

FIGURE A9.1   Average residuals, 1996 vote.

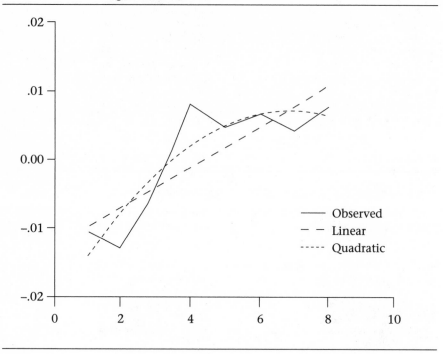

TABLE A9.1 Regression models predicting correct, incorrect, and don't-know answers based on 29 political-knowledge items

	Correct answers		Incorrect answers		Don't know answers	
	Model 1	Model 2	Model 1	Model 2	Model1	Model 2
Sex (male'1, female'0)	2.082**	2.130**	-.370		-1.712**	-1.703**
	(.297)	(.287)	(.293)		(.363)	(.349)
Age	.020*	-.030**	-.030**	-.025**	.009	
	(.010)	(.010)	(.010)	(.009)	(.013)	
Education	.647**	.647**	-.299**	-.350**	-.348**	-.337**
	(.099)	(.092)	(.098)	(.091)	(.121)	(.112)
Income	.073		-.131		.057	
	(.102)		(.101)		(.125)	
Media use	.119**	.126**	.019		-.139**	-.124**
	(.038)	(.038)	(.038)		(.047)	(.043)
Political interest	1.082**	1.089**	-.212		-.870**	-.875**
	(.196)	(.195)	(.194)		(.240)	(.238)
Political talk	.978**	.996**	-.487**	-.554**	-.491**	-.488**
	(.126)	(.125)	(.125)	(.118)	(.154)	(.153)
Race (white'1, other'0)	.251		-1.169**	-1.413**	.918	1.049*
	(.446)		(.441)	(.424)	(.546)	(.523)
Party						
Republican or not (Republican'1, else'0)	.182		-.383		.201	
	(.360)		(.356)		(.440)	
Party other than Democrat or Republican (Other party'1, else'0)	-.202		.095		.107	
	(.353)		(.350)		(.433)	
Constant	4.435**	.478**	16.745**	16.015**	7.819**	8.394**
	(.840)	(.709)	(.831)	(.728)	(1.029)	(.761)
R-square	.30	.30	.08	.07	.11	.11

NOTE: OLS regression used for each model. The second models were based on the step-wise procedure. * $p < .05$. ** $p < .01$.

239

TABLE A9.2 Models predicting correct answers if study participants who answered "don't know" had guessed

	Guessing randomly		Guessing after successfully eliminating 1 wrong answer		Guessing after successfully eliminating 2 wrong answers	
	Model 1	Model 2	Model 1	Model 2	Model1	Model 2
Sex (male'1, female'0)	1.654** (.251)	1.728** (.243)	1.517** (.241)	1.599** (.234)	1.248** (.232)	1.339** (.225)
Age	.023** (.009)	.024** (.008)	.024** (.008)	.024** (.008)	.026** (.008)	.030** (.007)
Education	.560** (.084)	.593** (.078)	.532** (.080)	.567** (.075)	.476** (.077)	.532** (.072)
Income	.088 (.086)		.092 (.083)		.100 (.080)	
Media use	.085** (.032)	.093** (.032)	.074** (.031)	.083** (.031)	.050 (.030)	
Political interest	.864** (.165)	.873** (.165)	.795** (.159)	.804** (.159)	.655** (.153)	.691** (.152)
Political talk	.855** (.106)	.879** (.106)	.816** (.103)	.842** (.102)	.742** (.099)	.778** (.098)
Race (white'1, else'0)	.481 (.376)		.554 (.362)		.697* (.349)	.863* (.337)
Party						
Republican or not (Republican'1, else'0)	.232 (.304)		.248 (.292)		2.86 (.281)	
Party other than Republican or Democrat (Other party'1, else'0)	-.176 (.298)		-.167 (.287)		-.140 (.276)	
Constant	6.390** (.710)	6.948** (.600)	7.016** (.683)	7.642** (.578)	8.241** (.657)	8.396** (.596)
R-square	.30	.30	.29	.29	.26	.25

NOTE: OLS regression used for each model. The second models were based on the step-wise procedure. * $p < .05$. ** $p < .01$.

TABLE A9.3   Gender differences found in political-knowledge answers when controlling for age, education, media use, political interest, and political talk using logit regression. Participants were asked who favored the following positions (Clinton, Dole, both, or neither)

Political-knowledge items	Significant gender differences found
Making it harder for women to obtain abortions	
The deepest cuts in federal government spending on domestic social programs	
The greatest increase in defense spending	X
The greatest reduction in future Medicare spending	X
Government vouchers to allow parents the choice of sending their children to public, private, or parochial schools	X
A constitutional amendment to balance the federal budget	X
A constitutional amendment to allow voluntary prayer in public schools	X
The elimination of the U.S. Department of Energy	
The immediate development of an antimissile defense system	X
Guaranteeing that the children of legal immigrants have access to public schools	
Increasing federal funding for job-training programs	
Expanding family leave	X
Opposed creation of the office of the drug czar	
Cut the size of the drug czar's office	
Supports forming a bipartisan commission to address the future of Medicare	
Shifting the greatest amount of control of federal programs to the states	X
Fifteen percent across-the-board tax cut	X
The ban on cigarette advertising to children	
The elimination of the Department of Education	X
Permitting late-term abortions using the so-called partial birth abortion procedure when the life of the mother is at stake	X
Legalizing same-sex marriages	
NAFTA	X
Opposing the death penalty	X
Ending the IRS as we know it	X
Cleaning up two-thirds of the toxic waste dumps in the next four years	X
Every child being able to read on his or her own by age eight	
Target tax cuts	X
A bill in Congress call McCain-Feingold to reform the way campaigns are financed	
Permitting campaign contributions only from citizens	

Chapter 10. Does Political Advertising Affect Turnout? If So, How, When, and for Whom?

Joseph Cappella, Kathleen Hall Jamieson, Dan Romer, and Ned Nurick

TABLE A10.1   Regression of 1996 vote percent (voters/eligibles) on 1992 vote, appearances, advertising weight (Business Coalition, AFL-CIO candidates) (N = 1,098)

	B	Standard Error	Beta	T
(Constant)	1.77E-02	.006		2.747
(Constant)	1.77E-02	.006		2.747
Percent Voters/Eligibles, 1992	.844	.010	.930***	81.6
Percent Voters/Eligibles, 1992	.844	.010	.930***	81.6
Clinton and Dole appearances	5.11E-04	.000	.018	1.634
Clinton and Dole appearances	5.11E-04	.000	.018	1.634
AFL-CIO ad weight	7.35E-08	.000	.049***	4.26
AFL-CIO ad weight	7.35E-08	.000	.049***	4.26
Business Coalition ad weight	1.97E-07	.000	.018	1.540
Candidates' total ad weight	2.58E-08	.000	.060***	5.21

NOTE: ***p < .001.

Chapter 12. Does Attack Advertising Affect Turnout?

Dan Romer, Kathleen Hall Jamieson, Joseph Cappella.

TABLE A12.1   Regression of 1996 voter turnout (voters/eligibles)

	B	Standard Error	Beta	t
Constant	1.80E-00	.007		2.63***
Percent voters/eligibles	0.84E-00	.011	.923	79.17***
Clinton and Dole appearances	4.97E-02	.000	.018	1.57
Business Coalition total	1.62E-05	.000	.015	1.26
AFL-CIO total	7.73E-06	.000	.052	4.47***
Advocacy total (Clinton and Dole)	5.53E-06	.000	.023	1.27
Contrast total (Clinton and Dole)	2.41E-05	.000	.083	3.35***
Attack total (Clinton and Dole)	−5.81E-06	.000	−.042	−1.85*

NOTE: * p < .10; ** p < .05; ***p < .01.

TABLE A12.2   Regression of 1996 voter turnout (voters/eligibles)

	B	Standard Error	Beta	t
Constant	1.50E-00	.007		2.18**
Percent voters/eligibles	0.85E-00	.011	.931	77.04***
Clinton and Dole appearances	6.34E-02	.000	.023	1.97*
Business Coalition total	1.86E-05	.000	.017	1.45
AFL-CIO total	8.42E-06	.000	.057	4.82***
Clinton advocacy	2.44E-05	.000	.023	1.21
Clinton contrast	3.97E-06	.000	.012	.45
Clinton attack	6.29E-07	.000	.003	.12
Dole advocacy	2.00E-06	.000	.007	.42
Dole contrast	9.60E-05	.000	.069	4.02***
Dole attack	−8.16E-06	.000	−.027	−.95

NOTE: * p < .10; ** p < .05; ***p < .01.

Chapter 13. Does Attack Advertising Create a Backlash? Mobilize the Other Side? Depress or Increase Support by Those of the Same Party?

Joseph Cappella, Kathleen Hall Jamieson, and Dan Romer

TABLE A13.1   Regression for share point difference (Clinton-Dole) in 1996 election

	B	Standard Error	Beta	t
Constant	1.81E-00	.002		8.33***
Share Point Difference, 1992	0.91E-00	.010	.921	88.18***
Clinton-Dole appearances	2.20E-02	.001	.030	2.77***
Business Coalition total	−5.99E-06	.000	−.004	−.42
AFL-CIO total	−6.31E-07	.000	−.003	−.33

NOTE: * p < .10; ** p < .05; ***p < .01.

Chapter 16. Do Issue Ads Work? If So, When?

Deborah Beck and Kathleen Hall Jamieson

TABLE A16.1   "The tobacco plan Congress considered would create a huge black market in cigarettes"

	0	1	2	3
Very accurate	110	126	145	143
	21%	42.4%	48%	47.8%
Somewhat accurate	113	101	89	88
	36.6%	34%	29.5%	29.4%
Not too accurate	39	46	39	35
	12.6%	15.5%	12.9%	11.7%
Not at all accurate	47	24	29	33
	15.2%	8.1%	9.6%	11%

NOTE: 0–3 represents level of advertising in respondents' media market from none to very high.

TABLE A16.2   Model 1: Ordinary least-squared regression with index of judged accuracy as the dependent measure

Model 1	B	Standard Error	Significance
Constant	9.842	.776	.000
Gender	−.236	.234	.313
Party	.206	.140	.142
Age	.019	.008	.016
Education	.118	.045	.009
Race	.291	.127	.023
Income	−.018	.084	.825
GRP	−.0000831	.000	.098
National news	−.046	.055	.403
Newspaper	−.022	.046	.634
Local news	−.058	.056	.300
Internet	.001	.056	.982
Talk radio	−.076	.047	.107

$R^2 = .037$

Notes

Chapter One

1. T. Holbrook (1996), *Do Campaigns Matter?* (Thousand Oaks, CA: Sage).

2. J. Klapper (1960), *The Effects of Mass Communication* (Glencoe, IL: Free Press).

3. P. Lazarsfeld, B. Berelson, and H. Gaudet (1948), *The People's Choice* (New York: Columbia University Press); B. Berelson, P. Lazarsfeld, and W. McPhee (1954), *Voting* (Chicago: University of Chicago Press).

4. S. Finkel (1993), "Reexamining the 'Minimal Effects' Model in Recent Presidential Campaigns," *Journal of Politics* 55(1), pp. 1–21.

5. T. Patterson and R. McClure (1976), *The Unseeing Eye* (New York: Putnam).

6. E. Tufte (1978), *Political Control of the Economy* (Princeton: Princeton University Press); S. Rosenstone (1983), *Forecasting Presidential Elections* (New Haven: Yale University Press); M. Lewis-Beck and T. Rice (1992), *Forecasting Elections* (Washington, DC: Congressional Quarterly Press).

7. T. Holbrook (1996), *Do Campaigns Matter?* (Thousand Oaks, CA: Sage).

8. Larry M. Bartels (1997), "How Campaigns Matter," unpublished manuscript.

9. S. Iyengar and D. Kinder (1987), *News That Matters* (Chicago: University of Chicago Press).

10. D. Kinder and D. R. Kiewiet (1981), "Sociotropic Politics: The American Case," *British Journal of Political Science* 11, pp. 129–161.

11. S. Rosenstone (1983), *Forecasting Presidential Elections* (New Haven: Yale University Press); G. Markus (1988), "The Impact of Personal and National Economic Conditions on the Presidential Vote," *American Journal of Political Science* 32, 137–154; M. Lewis-Beck and T. Rice (1992), *Forecasting Elections* (Washington, DC: Congressional Quarterly Press).

12. M. Hetherington (1996), "The Media's Role in Forming Voters' National Economic Evaluations in 1992," *American Journal of Political Science* 40, pp. 372–395.

13. S. Popkin (1991), *The Reasoning Voter* (Chicago: University of Chicago Press).

14. A. Gelman and G. King (1993), "Why Are American Presidential Election Campaign Polls So Variable When Votes Are So Predictable?" *British Journal of Political Science* 23, p. 449.

15. V. O. Key (1966), *The Responsible Electorate* (Cambridge: Harvard University Press).

16. S. Popkin (1991), *The Reasoning Voter* (Chicago: University of Chicago Press).

17. M. Delli Carpini and S. Keeter (1996), *What Americans Know About Politics and Why It Matters* (New Haven, CT: Yale University Press).

18. K. H. Jamieson and D. Birdsell (1988), *Presidential Debates: The Challenge of Creating an Informed Electorate* (Oxford: Oxford University Press).

19. W. McGuire (1986), "The Myth of Massive Media Impact: Savagings and Salvagings," *Public Communication and Behavior* 1, pp. 173–257.

245

20. W. Miller and J. M. Shanks (1996), *The New American Voter* (Cambridge: Harvard University Press).

21. J. Zaller (1996), "The Myth of Massive Media Impact Revived," in D. Mutz, P. Sniderman, and R. Brody, *Political Persuasion and Attitude Change* (Ann Arbor: University of Michigan Press).

22. L. Bartels (1992), "The Impact of Electioneering in the United States," in D. Butler and A. Ranney (eds.), *Electioneering: A Comparative Study of Continuity and Change* (Oxford: Clarendon Press), p. 267.

23. D. Matthews (1978), "Winnowing," in J. D. Barber, *The Race for the Presidency* (Englewood Cliffs, NJ: Prentice-Hall).

24. D. Broder (1987, April 13), *Washington Post National Weekly Edition*, p. 7.

25. B. Cohen (1963), *The Press and Foreign Policy* (Princeton: Princeton University Press).

26. M. McCombs and D. Shaw (1972), "The Agenda-Setting Function of the Mass Media," *Public Opinion Quarterly* 36, pp. 176–187.

27. M. Roberts and M. McCombs (1994), "Agenda Setting and Political Advertising: Origins of the News Agenda," *Political Communication* 11, pp. 249–263.

28. Richard R. Johnston, André Blais, Henry E. Brady, and Jean Crête (1992), *Letting the People Decide* (Palo Alto: Stanford University Press); B. Berelson, P. Lazarsfeld, and W. McPhee (1954), *Voting* (Chicago: University of Chicago Press), p. 263.

29. S. Iyengar and D. Kinder (1987), *News That Matters* (Chicago: University of Chicago Press).

30. Z. Pan and G. Kosicki (1993), "Framing Analysis: An Approach to News Discourse," *Political Communication* 10, pp. 55–75.

31. S. Iyengar (1991), *Is Anyone Responsible?* (Chicago: University of Chicago Press).

32. T. Patterson (1993), *Out of Order* (New York: Knopf); K. H. Jamieson (1992), *Dirty Politics* (New York: Oxford University Press).

33. J. Kleinnijehuis and J. de Ridder (1997), "Effects of Strategy News Framing on Party Preferences," Paper presented at the meeting of the American Political Science Association, Washington, DC, August.

34. T. Patterson and R. McClure (1976), *The Unseeing Eye* (New York: Putnam).

35. J. Cappella and K. H. Jamieson (1997), *Spiral of Cynicism: The Press and the Public Good* (Oxford: Oxford University Press).

36. W. D. Burnham (1970), *Critical Elections and the Mainsprings of American Politics* (New York: W. W. Norton); E. Ladd (1978), *Where Have All the Voters Gone?* (New York: W. W. Norton).

37. S. Kirkpatrick, W. Lyons, and M. Fitzgerald (1975), "Candidates, Parties, and Issues in the American Electorate," *American Politics Quarterly* 3, pp. 247–283.

38. Norman H. Nie, Sidney Verba, and John R. Petrocik (1979), *The Changing American Voter* (Cambridge, MA: Harvard University Press), p. 47.

39. Arguing for the continued influence of partisanship are Bruce Keith, David Magleby, and Candice Nelson (1992), *The Myth of the Independent Voter* (Berkeley: University of California Press); a contrary view is offered by M. Wattenberg (1996), *The Decline of American Political Parties, 1952–1994* (Cambridge: Harvard University Press).

40. M. Wattenberg (1991), *The Rise of Candidate-Centered Politics* (Cambridge: Harvard University Press), p. 34.

41. Ithiel de Sola Pool (1971), "What Will Be New in the New Politics?" In Ray E. Hiebert, Robert Jones, John Lorenz, and Ernest Lotito, *The Political Image Merchants* (Washington, DC: Acropolis), p. 256.

42. M. Mendelsohn (1996), "The Media and Interpersonal Communications: The Priming of Issues, Leaders, and Party Identification," *Journal of Politics* 58, pp. 112–125.

43. C. Hovland (1959), "Reconciling Conflicting Results Derived from Experimental and Survey Studies of Attitude Change," *American Psychologist* 14, pp. 8–17.

44. S. Ansolabehere, R. Behr, and S. Iyengar (1991), "Mass Media and Elections: An Overview," *American Politics Quarterly* 19, pp. 109–139.

45. L. B. Becker, M. A. McCombs, and J. M. McLeod (1975), "The Development of Political Cognitions," in S. Chaffee (ed.), *Political Communication* (London: Sage).

Chapter Two

1. H. Fineman (1991, October 14), "The No Bull Campaign," *Newsweek*, pp. 22–23.

2. K. Walsh (1992, October 5),"Warning to Voters: The Worst Is Yet to Be," *U.S. News & World Report*, p. 16.

3. J. Perry (1994, January 10), "Young Guns," *Wall Street Journal*, p. A1.

4. P. Magnusson (1996, June 10), "It's the Issues, Stupid," *Business Week*, p. 35.

5. M. Lerner (1996, July-August), "Clinton's Moral Backbone Problem and the Fate of the Democrats," *Tikkun*, p. 5.

6. M. Carlson (1996, November 11), "The Rules from 1996," *Time*, p. 4.

7. Dick Gregory (1972), *Dick Gregory's Political Primer*, ed. by James R. McGraw (New York: Harper & Row).

8. Abraham Lincoln, January 11, 1837.

9. Benjamin Page (1978), *Choices and Echoes in Presidential Elections: Rational Man and Electoral Democracy* (Chicago: University of Chicago Press), pp. 153–160; Page notes (pp. 166–167) that "Dewey in 1948 was either silent or very general."

10. R. Joslyn (1991), "Candidate Appeals and the Meaning of Elections," in Benjamin Ginsberg and Alan Stone (eds.), *Do Elections Matter?* (Armonk, NY: M. E. Sharpe), pp. 8, 28.

11. M. Hershey (1989), "The Campaign and the Media," in Gerald M. Pomper (ed.), *The Election of 1988* (Chatham, NJ: Chatham House), p. 99.

12. The Annenberg Public Policy Center survey asked: "Which of the following is closer to your beliefs: A. Clinton and Dole talked about issues I care about *or* B. Clinton and Dole ducked the important issues facing the country." National telephone survey of 1,026 registered voters conducted November 6–12, 1996, Chilton Research, Political Knowledge Survey Report, November 27, 1996.

13. John R. Petrocik (1996, August), "Issue Ownership in Presidential Elections, with a 1980 Case Study," *American Journal of Political Science*, 40(3), p. 825.

14. G. Pomper (1980), *Elections in America* (New York: Longman), p. 142.

15. N. Polsby and A. Wildavsky (1996), *Presidential Elections* (Chatham, NJ: Chatham House Publishers), pp. 299–300.

16. J. Fishel (1985), *Presidents and Promises* (Washington, DC: Congressional Quarterly Press), pp. 37–38.

17. D. Truman (1981), *The Governmental Process: Political Interests and Public Opinion* (Westport, CT: Greenwood Press), pp. 282–283.

18. G. Pomper (1980), *Elections in America* (New York: Longman), p. 161.

19. James Bryce (1888; 1995), *The American Commonwealth* (London: Macmillan), Vol. II, p. 208.

20. B. Berelson, P. Lazarsfeld, and W. McPhee (1954), *Voting* (Chicago: University of Chicago Press), p. 236.

21. "Tax-Cut Tortoise and Hare?" (1996, June 6), *Investor's Business Daily*.

22. "Promises, Promises, Promises" (1996, October 29), *Investor's Business Daily*.

23. M. Duffy (1993, January 25), "Ready or Not," *Time*.

24. N. Gibbs (1996, May 13), "It's All in the Timing," *Time*.

25. S. Jones (1996, December 7), "Media Panelist Critiques Clinton, Dole," *Editor and Publisher*.

26. "Here's the Man, So Where's the Plan?" (1993, January 23), *The Economist*.

27. J. Schmalz (1993, January 18), "An Impatient Public; Letting Go of Hope as Clinton Softens Pledges," *New York Times*.

28. T. Friedman with Elaine Sciolino (1993, March 22), "Clinton and Foreign Issues: Spasms of Attention," *New York Times*.

29. "A Threat to Abortion Rights" (1993, September 21), *New York Times*.

30. D. Rosenbaum (1993, August 3), "A Fading Call to Arms; Clinton Wins a Crucial Fight on the Deficit, But Some of the Sense of Mission Is Lost," *New York Times*.

31. M. Wines (1994, December 18), "The Talk Is Tax Cuts: Look Who's Talking Too," *New York Times*.

32. "No More Nice Guy" (1993, June 28), *The Nation*.

33. B. Hume (1993, August 23), "Campaign Mode; Bill Clinton's Travels and Campaign-Style Tactics Geared to Protect His Problems with the Press," *National Review*.

34. "Bent Promises" (1993, November 11), *Time*.

35. M. Ruby (1997, June 21), "And Pigs May Sing," *U.S. News & World Report*.

36. A. Wilson-Smith, (1996, September 2), "Promises and Pain," *Macleans*.

37. C. Becker (1993, April 19), "Budget Serves Up Mixed Bag for Cities; Fiscal Reality Sets In," *Nation's Cities Weekly*.

38. L. Klein (1994, March-April), "A Retrospective Look at Putting People First," *Challenge*.

39. M. Kelly (1997, February 10), "Rope-a-Hope," *New Republic*.

40. "How many of his campaign promises do you think Bill Clinton will try to keep—all of them, most of them, some of them or hardly any of them?" National telephone survey of 1,179 adults conducted January 12–14, 1993, CBS News/*New York Times*, January 18, 1993.

41. "Do you believe (Bill) Clinton will try to keep most of his important campaign promises during his term as president, or not?" National telephone survey of 1,510 adults conducted January 14–17, 1993, ABC News/*Washington Post*, January 18, 1993.

42. National telephone survey of 1,507 adults conducted January 20–23, 1994, ABC News/*Washington Post*.

43. National telephone survey of 1,138 adults conducted August 16–18, 1996, CBS News/*New York Times*, August 19, 1996.

44. "Do you think Bush will try to keep most of his important campaign promises during his term as president, or not? (If 'Yes,' ask:) Do you think Bush will be able to keep most of his campaign promises, or won't he be able to keep most of them?" National telephone survey of 1,503 participants conducted January 12–16, 1989, ABC News.

45. "Do you think Reagan will keep most of his important campaign promises during his second term, or not?" Survey started on January 11, 1985, Roper Center.

46. "How many of his 1988 campaign promises do you think George Bush has been able to keep—all of them, most of them, some of them, or hardly any of them?" National telephone survey conducted June 17–20, 1992, CBS News/*New York Times*, June 24, 1992.

47. Douglas Harbrecht, Richard Dunham, and Lee Walczak (1992, October 5), "This Wasn't in the Playbook," *Business Week*, p. 40.

48. "Do you think Reagan kept most of his campaign promises during his eight years as president or not?" National telephone survey conducted January 12–16, 1989, ABC News, January 1989.

49. "Let me read you some statements about President Nixon. For each, tell me if you tend to agree or disagree. . . . He has kept most of the promises he made in 1968." National personal survey of 2,973 adults conducted April 1–7, 1972, Harris Survey.

50. S. Craig (1993), *The Malevolent Leaders: Popular Discontent in America* (Boulder, CO: Westview Press), p. 13.

51. P. Quirk and S. Matheson (1997), "The Presidency: Elections and Presidential Governance," in Michael Nelson (ed.), *The Elections of 1996* (Washington, DC: Congressional Quarterly Press), p. 121.

52. "Do you agree or disagree with the following statements: . . . 'Clinton's word is no good'?" National telephone survey of 1,026 registered voters conducted November 6–12, 1996, Chilton Research, Political Knowledge Survey Report, November 27, 1996.

53. C. Shaw (1996, August), "Has President Clinton Fulfilled His 1992 Campaign Promises?" Department of Government, University of Texas, paper presented at the 1996 Annual Meeting of the American Political Science Association, San Francisco, CA, pp. 19, 22.

54. K. Crockett (1996, August 29), "Promises; Clinton's Deeds Follow His Words," *Phoenix Gazette*.

55. R. Rankin and A. Cannon (1996, August 25), "Focus on Politics: The Clinton Campaign; Promises Kept?" *Orange County Register*, p. A25.

56. "Clinton's Promises" (1996, August 25), *St. Petersburg Times*.

57. Bruce Buchanan (1996), *Renewing Presidential Politics: Campaigns, Media, and the Public Interest* (Lanham, MD: Rowman and Littlefield), p. 105.

58. "Regardless of which presidential candidate you preferred (in the 1988 election), do you think the Bush administration will or will not be able to avoid raising taxes?" National telephone survey of 1,008 adults started on November 14, 1988, Gallup.

59. "Do you think it is highly likely, somewhat likely, somewhat unlikely, or highly unlikely that federal taxes will be raised to help balance the budget during Bush's term in office (as president)?" National telephone survey of 1,251 adults conducted November 11–14, 1988, Harris Poll.

60. "Do you think George Bush will ask Congress to increase taxes in the next four years?" National telephone survey of 1,627 adults conducted November 10–16, 1988, CBS News/*New York Times* poll, November 20, 1988.

61. J. Weisberg (1994, September 5), "Why Bill Clinton Is a Great President: No, Really," *New York Times*, p. 18.

62. T. Koppel (1997, October 30), "Truth and Consequences," *Nightline*.

63. M. Means (1996, November 15), "Next Two Months Set Pace of Next Four Years," *Times Union* (Albany, NY).

64. Joan Beck (1996, November 4), "What Could Happen if Clinton Re-Elected," *The Post and Courier* (Charleston, SC).

65. C. Rowan (1997, January 21), "Wounded Politicians Spell Bad Government," *Buffalo News*.

66. C. Crawford (1997, January 5), "Political Probes, Predictions," *Orlando Sentinel*.

67. "Opportunity Squandered" (1996, November 6), *Las Vegas Review-Journal*.

68. C. Rowan (1996, December 14), "Clinton Reneging on 'Fixing' Welfare Reform," *Buffalo News*.

69. A. Reed, Jr. (1997, January 21), "A Slave to Finance: Clinton's Adherence to a Corporate Agenda Undermines Hard-Won Social Protections," *Village Voice*.

70. R. Pear (1997, July 30), "Legal Immigrants Would Benefit Under New Budget Agreement," *New York Times*, p. A17.

71. M. Kelly (1997, September 1), "A Promise Kept," *New Republic*, p. 41.

72. J. Alter (1997, August 11), "Hostage to the Winds," *Newsweek*.

Chapter Three

1. An earlier version of this chapter appeared in *Media, Culture, and Society* in Spring 1998.

2. Lawrence McGill, Andras Szanto, and Marianne Johnston (1997), in John W. Mashek with Lawrence McGill and Adam Clayton Powell III, *Lethargy '96: How the Media Covered a Listless Campaign* (New York: Freedom Forum), p. 100.

3. Joseph Cappella and K. H. Jamieson (1996), "News Frames, Political Cynicism, and Media Cynicism," *Annals of the American Academy of Political and Social Science,* 546:71–84.

4. Kathleen Hall Jamieson (1992), *Dirty Politics* (New York: Oxford University Press); Thomas Patterson (1993), *Out of Order* (New York: Alfred A. Knopf).

5. *ABC World News Tonight,* October 7, 1996.

6. For more on the press's emphasis on the negative, see Doris Graber (1989), *Mass Media and American Politics,* 3d ed. (Washington, DC: Congressional Quarterly Press); Kathleen Hall Jamieson (1992), *Dirty Politics* (New York: Oxford University Press); Thomas Patterson (1993), *Out of Order* (New York: Alfred A. Knopf); Michael Robinson and Margaret Sheehan (1983), *Over the Wire and on TV: CBS and UPI in Campaign '80* (New York: Russell Sage Foundation).

7. The Pew Research Center for the People and the Press (1996, November), *Fewer Happy with Clinton Victory Than with GOP Congressional Win* (Washington, DC).

8. "Managing the Costs of Entitlements" (1997, Spring), *Congressional Quarterly,* p. 97.

9. "The Voters Sober Up" (1996, October 20), *New York Times,* p. E15.

Chapter Four

1. Funding from the Ford Foundation, the Carnegie Corporation, and the Pew Charitable Trusts made it possible for us to examine these presidential campaigns.

2. October 29, 1992, McComb County, Michigan.

3. *NBC Nightly News,* October 29, 1992.

4. *CBS Evening News,* October 29, 1992.

5. *ABC World News Tonight,* October 29, 1992.

Chapter Five

1. This chapter draws on material included in Kathleen Hall Jamieson (1992), *Dirty Politics* (New York: Oxford University Press); and Jamieson, *Eloquence in an Electronic Age* (New York: Oxford University Press).

2. Karl Wallace (1955, January), "An Ethical Basis of Communication," *Speech Teacher* 4, pp. 1–9.

3. Thomas R. Nilsen (1958, October), "Free Speech, Persuasion, and the Democratic Process," *Quarterly Journal of Speech,* p. 243.

4. Henry David Thoreau, *Life Without Principle,* Number 37, as reflected in the 1906 Houghton Mifflin edition. Found on Web site http://www.walden.org/thoreau/writings/essays/reform/Life-without-Principle.htm.

5. Francis Bacon (1620), *The New Organon* [Novum Organum], *Aphorisms Concerning the Interpretation of Nature and the Kingdom of Man,* XLIII.

6. Walt Whitman, "Origins of Attempted Secession," in *Prose Works* (n.d.) (Philadelphia: David McKay).

7. James E. Watson (1936), *As I Knew Them* (Indianapolis: Bobbs-Merrill), pp. 13–14.

8. John Jay, "An Address to the People of the State of New York on the Subject of the Constitution," in P. L. Ford (ed.) (1888), *Pamphlets on the Constitution of the United States*, Brooklyn.

9. M. M. Miller (ed.) (1913), *Great Debates in American History* (New York: Current Literature), pp. 219–220.

10. Ibid., p. 335.

11. Ibid., pp. 332–333.

12. Ibid., pp. 333–334.

13. M. M. Miller (1916), *American Debate* (New York: G.P. Putnam's and Sons).

14. B. Franklin (n.d.), *The Complete Works in Philosophy, Politics, and Morals of the Late Dr. Benjamin Franklin*, Vol. I (London).

15. Charles Arthur Willard (1989), *A Theory of Argumentation* (Tuscaloosa and London: University of Alabama Press), p. 2.

16. D. J. O'Keefe (1977), "Two Concepts of Argument," *Journal of the American Forensic Association* 13, pp. 121–128.

17. J. B. Stiff (1986), "Cognitive Processing of Persuasive Message Cues: A Meta-Analytic Review of the Effects of Supporting Information on Attitudes," *Communication Monographs*, 53, pp. 75–89.

18. E. Abernathy (1964), *The Advocate: A Manual of Persuasion* (New York: Mckay), p. 230.

19. R. E. Petty, J. T. Cacioppo, and R. Goldman (1981), "Personal Involvement as a Determinant of Argument Based Persuasion," *Journal of Personality and Social Psychology*, 41, pp. 847–855; D. Hample (1985), "Refinements on the Cognitive Model of Argument: Concreteness, Involvement, and Group Scores," *Western Journal of Speech Communication*, 49, pp. 267–285; and D. D. Morley (1987), "Subjective Message Constructs: A Theory of Persuasion," *Communication Monographs*, 54, pp. 183–203.

20. R. E. Petty and J. T. Cacioppo (1984), "The Effects of Involvement on Responses to Argument Quantity and Quality: Central and Peripheral Routes to Persuasion," *Journal of Personality and Social Psychology*, 46, pp. 69–81.

21. R. A. Reynolds and M. Burgoon (1983), "Belief Processing, Reasoning, and Evidence," in R. N. Bostrom (ed.), *Communication Yearbook 7* (Beverly Hills, CA: Sage), pp. 83–104.

22. M. W. Cronin (1973), "An Experimental Study of the Effects of Authoritative Testimony of Small Group Problem-Solving Discussions," *Dissertation Abstracts International*, 33, 6485A.

23. R. S. Cathcart (1955), "An Experimental Study of the Relative Effectiveness of Four Methods of Presenting Evidence," *Speech Monographs*, 22, pp. 227–233; H. Fleshler, J. Ilardo, and J. Demoretcky (1974), "The Influence of Field Dependence, Speaker Credibility Set, and Message Documentation on Evaluations of Speaker and Message Credibility," *Southern Speech Communication Journal*, 39, pp. 389–402.

24. See M. W. Cronin (1973), "An Experimental Study of the Effects of Authoritative Testimony of Small Group Problem-Solving Discussions," *Dissertation Abstracts International*, 33, 6485A; P. H. Bradley (1981), "The Folk-Linguistics of Women's Speech: An Empirical Examination," *Communication Monographs*, 48, pp. 73–90.

25. David Berlo, James Lemert, and Robert Mertz (1969), "Dimensions for Evaluating the Acceptability of Message Sources," *Public Opinion Quarterly*, 33(4):563–576.

26. R. Hamill, T. D. Wilson, and R. E. Nesbett (1980), "Insensitivity to Sample Bias: Generalizing from Atypical Cases," *Journal of Personality and Social Psychology*, 39, pp. 578–589.

27. F. S. Murray (1968), "Judgment of Evidence," *American Journal of Psychology*, 81, pp. 319–333; F. M. Andrews (1982), "The Influence of Evidenciary [*sic*] and Extraevi-

denciary [sic] Factors on Decisions in a Simulated Rape Trial," *Dissertation Abstracts International*, 43, 516B–517B.

28. J. T. Cacioppo, R. E. Petty, and K. J. Morris (1983), "Effects of Need for Cognition on Message Evaluation, Recall, and Persuasion," *Journal of Personality and Social Psychology*, 45, pp. 805–818; R. E. Petty and J. T. Cacioppo (1984), "The Effects of Involvement on Responses to Argument Quantity and Quality," *Journal of Personality and Social Psychology*, 46, pp. 69–81; R. E. Petty, S. E. Harkins, and K. D. Williams (1980), "The Effects of Group Diffusion or Cognitive Effort on Attitudes," *Journal of Personality and Social Psychology*, 38, pp. 81–92.

29. Hannah Arendt (1968), *Between Past and Future, Eight Exercises in Political Thought* (New York: Viking Press), p. 238.

30. S. E. Toulmin, R. Rieke, and A. Janik (1979), *An Introduction to Reasoning* (New York: Macmillan), p. 158.

31. Immanuel Kant, 11 "Of Aesthetic Judgment," Section 53.

32. Stephen Toulmin (1990), *The Uses of Argument* (Cambridge: Cambridge University Press), p. 97.

33. Aristotle, *Nicomachean Ethics*, 1141b

34. *Philadelphia Inquirer*, December 9, 1998, p. A20.

35. *New York Times*, December 9, 1998, p. A27.

36. *New York Times*, December 9, 1998, p. A25

37. *New York Times*, December 9, 1998, p. A26.

38. *New York Times*, December 11, 1998, p. A33.

39. Walter Lippmann (1955), *Essays in the Public Philosophy* (Boston: Little, Brown).

40. Jill Lawrence (1999, December 7), "Gore Takes over the Attack Role," *USA Today*, p. 13A.

41. Katharine Q. Seelye (1999, December 10), "Newly Aggressive Gore Follows Clinton Model," *New York Times*, p. A32.

42. This information is available in an excellent article by Jane Fritsch (1996, October 15), "Two Approaches to Repairing Cities," *New York Times*, p. A23.

43. *Roll Call*, May 18, 1995.

44. Anthony DePalma (1996, October 11), "Both Kemp and Gore Erred in Debate Over Policy on Mexico," *New York Times*, p. A25.

45. Hilda Betterman and H. Todd Van Dellen (1996, March 3), *Minneapolis Star*.

46. Thomas Jefferson to William Johnson (1823), ME 15:44/. From University of Virginia Web site http://etext.lib.virginia.edu/jefferson.

Chapter Seven

1. The demographic analyses in this report are based on multiple regression analysis and combine the Social Security and crime ads. Media exposure is a scale of how many times in the previous week respondents reported watching national network TV news, local TV news, or C-SPAN, listening to talk radio, reading a daily newspaper, or going online for information about current events or politics. Political involvement is a scale of interest in politics, attention paid to state campaigns this year, number of political advertisements seen this year, and frequency of voting.

Chapter Nine

1. Michael X. Delli Carpini and Ester Fuchs (1993), "The Year of the Woman? Candidates, Voters, and the 1992 Election," *Political Science Quarterly*, 108(1), 29–36;

Daniel Wirl (1986), "Reinterpreting the Gender Gap," *Public Opinion Quarterly*, 50, 316–330.

2. Linda L. M. Bennett and Stephen Earl Bennett (1989), "Enduring Gender Differences in Political Interest: The Impact of Socialization and Political Dispositions," *American Politics Quarterly*, 17(1), 105–122; Steven H. Chaffee, Xinshu Zhao, and Glenn Leshner (1994), "Political Knowledge and the Campaign Media of 1992," *Communication Research*, 21(3), 305–324; Michael X. Delli Carpini and Scott Keeter (1991), "Stability and Change in the U.S. Public's Knowledge of Politics," *Public Opinion Quarterly*, 55, 583–612; Michael X. Delli Carpini and Scott Keeter (1993), "Measuring Political Knowledge: Putting First Things First," *American Journal of Political Science*, 37(4), 1179–1206; Michael X. Delli Carpini and Scott Keeter (1996), *What Americans Know About Politics and Why It Matters* (New Haven: Yale University Press); Doris Graber (1988), *Processing the News: How People Tame the Information Tide* (New York: Longman); M. Kent Jennings (1996), "Political Knowledge over Time and Across Generations," *Public Opinion Quarterly*, 60, 228–252; Robert E. Lane and David O. Sears (1964), *Public Opinion* (Englewood Cliffs, NJ: Prentice-Hall).

3. Linda L. M. Bennett and Stephen Earl Bennett (1989), "Enduring Gender Differences in Political Interest: The Impact of Socialization and Political Dispositions," *American Politics Quarterly*, 17(1), 105–122.

4. Michael X. Delli Carpini and Scott Keeter (1991), "Stability and Change in the U.S. Public's Knowledge of Politics," *Public Opinion Quarterly*, 55, 583–612.

5. Joe D. Francis and Lawrence Busch (1975), "What We Now Know About 'I Don't Knows,'" *Public Opinion Quarterly*, 39(2), 207–218; Ronald B. Rapoport (1981), "The Sex Gap in Political Persuading: Where the 'Structuring Principle' Works," *American Journal of Political Science*, 25(1), 32–48; Robert Y. Shapiro and Harpreet Mahajan (1986), "Gender Differences in Policy Preferences: A Summary of Trends from the 1960s to the 1980s," *Public Opinion Quarterly*, 50, 42–61.

6. See page 455 in Maria Elena Sanchez and Giovanna Morchio (1992), "Probing 'Don't Know' Answers: Effects on Survey Estimates and Variable Relationships," *Public Opinion Quarterly*, 56, 454–474.

7. Joe D. Francis and Lawrence Busch (1975), "What We Now Know About 'I Don't Knows,'" *Public Opinion Quarterly*, 39(2), 207–218.

8. Ibid., p. 211.

9. Ibid., p. 211.

10. Maria Elena Sanchez and Giovanna Morchio (1992), "Probing 'Don't Know' Answers: Effects on Survey Estimates and Variable Relationships," *Public Opinion Quarterly*, 56, p. 465.

11. Participants' responses had a standard deviation of 4.83 for correct answers, a standard deviation of 4.17 for incorrect answers, and a standard deviation of 5.33 for "don't know" responses.

12. Ordinary least-squares regression was used.

13. Richard Nadeau and Richard G. Niemi (1995), "Educated Guesses: The Process of Answering Factual Knowledge Questions in Surveys," *Public Opinion Quarterly*, 59, 323–346.

14. See page 110 in Doris A. Graber (1988), *Processing the News: How People Tame the Information Tide* (New York: Longman).

Chapter Eleven

1. Sara Rimer (1996, November 6), "Costly Race Keeps Kerry in Senate," *New York Times*, p. 2.

2. James Bennet (1996, November 6), "The 1996 Elections: The Presidency—the Exit Polls," *New York Times*, p. 1.

3. "Excerpts from President Clinton's Press Conference," November 9, 1996, p. A16.

4. Edwin Chen and Maria L. La Ganga (1996, September 13), "Some in GOP Don't Like What They Hear When Dole Listens," *Los Angeles Times*, p. 18.

5. Michael J. Sandel (1996, December 29), "Making Nice Is Not the Same as Doing Good," *New York Times*, 1996, p. 9.

6. Stephen Ansolabehere and Shanto Iyengar (1995), *Going Negative* (New York: Free Press).

7. Eleanor Randolph (1996, October 31), "Campaign 2000," *Los Angeles Times*, p. 3.

8. Larry M. Bartels et al. (1998), "Campaign Reform: Insights and Evidence," Report of the Task Force on Campaign Reform sponsored by the Pew Charitable Trusts, Princeton University, Woodrow Wilson School of Public and International Affairs, pp. 12–13.

9. Stephen Budiansky (1996), "Tune In, Turn Off, Drop Out," *U.S. News & World Report* 120(7):30.

10. Jack Germond and J. Witcover (1996), "Why Americans Don't Go to the Polls," *National Journal* 28:2562; Nexis-Lexis, Congressional Universe.

11. Gina Garramone (1984), "Voter Responses to Negative Political Ads," *Journalism Quarterly* 61:250–259.

12. In Erica Austin and Bruce Pinkleton (1995), "Positive and Negative Effects of Political Disaffection on the Less Experienced Voter," *Journal of Broadcasting and Electronic Media* 39:215–235.

13. William Christ, Esther Thorson, and Clarke Caywood (1994), "Do Attitudes Toward Political Advertising Affect Information Processing of Televised Political Commercials?" *Journal of Broadcasting and Electronic Media* 38:251–270.

14. Ronald Faber, Albert Tims, and Kay Schmitt (1993), "Negative Political Advertising and Voting Intent: The Role of Involvement And Alternative Information Sources," *Journal of Advertising* 22(4):67–76.

15. Bruce Pinkelton (1997), "The Effects of Negative Comparative Political Advertising on Candidate Evaluations and Advertising Evaluations: An Exploration," *Journal of Advertising* 26:19–29.

16. Stephen Ansolabehere, Shanto Iyengar, Adam Simon, and Nicholas Valentino (1994), "Does Attack Advertising Demobilize the Electorate?" *American Political Science Review* 88:829–838; Stephen Ansolabehere and Shanto Iyengar (1995), *Going Negative: How Political Advertisements Shrink and Polarize the Electorate* (New York: Free Press).

17. S. Finkel and J. Geer (1998), "A Spot Check: Casting Doubt on the Demobilizing Effect of Attack Advertising," *American Journal of Political Science* 42:573–595.

18. Kathleen Hall Jamieson, Paul Waldman, and Susan Sherr (2000), "Eliminate the Negative? Categories of Analysis for Political Advertising," in James A. Thurber, Candice Nelson, and David Dulio (eds.), *Crowded Airwaves: Campaign Advertising in Modern Elections* (Washington, DC: Brookings).

19. Kenneth Goldstein (1997), "Political Advertising and Political Persuasion in the 1996 Presidential Campaign," paper submitted to the American Political Science Association, August 28–31, p. 17.

20. S. Finkel and J. Geer (1998), "A Spot Check: Casting Doubt on the Demobilizing Effect of Attack Advertising," *American Journal of Political Science* 42:573–595.

21. Stephen Ansolabehere and Shanto Iyengar (1995), *Going Negative: How Political Advertisements Shrink and Polarize the Electorate* (New York: Free Press), pp. 834–835.

22. S. Finkel and J. Geer (1998), "A Spot Check: Casting Doubt on the Demobilizing Effect of Attack Advertising," *American Journal of Political Science* 42:573–595.

23. A. Lang (1991), "Emotion, Formal Features, and Memory for Televised Political Advertisements," in F. Biocca (ed.), *Television and Political Advertising*, Vol. 1, Psychological Processes, pp. 221–243 (Hillsdale, NJ: Erlbaum).

24. Richard A. Joslyn (1986), "Political Advertising and the Meaning of Elections," in Lynda Kaid, Dan Nimmo, and K. R. Sanders (eds.), *New Perspectives of Political Advertising* (Carbondale: Southern Illinois University Press); Thomas Patterson and Robert McClure (1976), *The Unseeing Eye: The Myth of Television Power in National Elections* (New York: Putnam's).

25. Lynda Lee Kaid and Anne Johnston (1991), "Negative Versus Positive Television Advertising in U.S. Presidential Campaigns, 1960–1988," *Journal of Communication* 41 (Summer), p. 53; Darrell M. West (1997), *Air Wars*, 2d ed. (Washington, DC: Congressional Quarterly Press).

Chapter Twelve

1. E. J. Dionne, Jr. (1991), *Why Americans Hate Politics* (New York: Simon & Schuster), p. 16.

2. David Broder (1997, Spring), "Interview," *Miller Center Journal*, p. 3.

3. B. Berelson, P. Lazarsfeld, and W. McPhee (1954), *Voting* (Chicago: University of Chicago Press); Angus Campbell, Philip E. Converse, Warren E. Miller, and Donald Stokes (1960), *The American Voter* (New York: Wiley).

4. Larry M. Bartels (1993, June), "Messages Received: The Political Impact of Media Exposure," *American Political Science Review*, 87(2):267; Stephen Ansolabehere and Shanto Iyengar (1995), *Going Negative: How Political Advertisements Shrink and Polarize the Electorate* (New York: Free Press); T. Holbrook (1996), *Do Campaigns Matter?* (Thousand Oaks, CA: Sage); J. Zaller (1996), "The Myth of Massive Media Impact Revived," in D. Mutz, P. Sniderman, and R. Brody, *Political Persuasion and Attitude Change* (Ann Arbor: University of Michigan Press).

Chapter Thirteen

1. Kathleen Hall Jamieson, Paul Waldman, and Susan Sherr (2000), "Eliminate the Negative? Categories of Analysis for Political Advertising," in James A. Thurber, Candice Nelson, and David Dulio (eds.), *Crowded Airwaves: Campaign Advertising in Modern Elections* (Washington, DC: Brookings).

2. Lynda Lee Kaid and John Boydston (1987), "An Experimental Study of the Effectiveness of Negative Political Advertisements," *Communication Quarterly* 35:193–201; R. R. Lau (1982), "Negativity in Political Perception," *Political Behavior* 4:353–377; Karen Johnson-Cartee and Gary Copeland (1991), *Negative Political Advertising: Coming of Age* (Hillsdale, NJ: Lawrence Erlbaum Associates); J. F. Pentony (1995), "The Effect of Nega-

tive Campaigning on Voting, Semantic Differential and Thought Listing," *Journal of Social Behavior and Personality* 10:631–644; J. Klein (1991), "Negativity Effects in Impression Formation: A Test in the Political Arena," *Personality and Social Psychology Bulletin* 17:412–418.

3. R. P. Abelson, D. R. Kinder, S. T. Fiske, and M. D. Peters (1982), "Affective and Semantic Components in Political Person Perception," *JPSP* 42:619–630; Gina Garramone (1984), "Voter Responses to Negative Ads," *Journalism Quarterly* 61:250–259; Gina Garramone (1985) "Effects of Negative Political Advertising," *Journal of Broadcasting and Electronic Media* 29:147–159; Sharyne Merritt (1984), "Negative Political Advertising: Some Empirical Findings," *Journal of Advertising* 13:27–38; Brian Roddy and Gina Garramone (1988), "Appeals and Strategies of Negative Political Advertising," *Journal of Broadcasting and Electronic Media* 32:415–427; W. J. Roese and G. N. Sande (1993), "Backlash Effects in Attack Politics," *Journal of Applied Social Psychology* 23:632–653.

4. The coefficient for total advertising by the two candidates was 1.83 E–05, t = 8.56, p < .001. This coefficient translates into a share increase of .27 for each additional increase of 500 GRPs (weighted by 30 seconds or 15,000 weighted units of advertising). Although our estimate is lower than the 2.2 share points found by Shaw (1999) for a comparable level of advertising gain, we do not include interactions between advertising and other jurisdiction differences in voter characteristics in the same equation. As Shaw noted, his estimates of advertising impact were heavily conditional on the other variables he included in his analysis. Although our estimate is lower, it is interesting that it corresponds closely to the average share difference across the counties and therefore represents a plausible winning margin at least as far as the 1996 election indicated.

Chapter Fourteen

1. "Going Negative," *The NewsHour,* February 22, 2000, with Jim Lehrer, PBS.

Chapter Fifteen

1. Kathleen Hall Jamieson (1992), *Dirty Politics* (New York: Oxford University Press), pp. 146–147 and Appendix II.

2. Joseph N. Cappella and Kathleen Hall Jamieson (1994), "Broadcast Adwatch Effects: A Field Experiment," *Communication Research* 21(3):342–365.

3. Stephen Ansolabehere and Shanto Iyengar (1995), *Going Negative* (New York: Free Press).

4. Stephen Ansolabehere and Shanto Iyengar (1996), "Can the Press Monitor Campaign Advertising?" *Press/Politics* 1(1):72–86.

5. Max Frankel (1996, January 14), "Word and Image: Let Lying Dogs Sleep?" *New York Times Magazine*, p. 18.

6. David Broder (1996, January 12), "Negative Ads Translate into Apathy," *Washington Post.*

Chapter Sixteen

1. *Buckley v. Valeo*, 424 U.S. 1 (1976).

2. D. Beck, P. Taylor, J. Stanger, and D. Rivlin (1997), *Issue Advocacy Advertising During the 1996 Campaign* (The Annenberg Public Policy Center of the University of Pennsylvania).

3. J. Stanger and D. Rivlin (1998), *Issue Advocacy Advertising During the 1997–1998 Election Cycle* (The Annenberg Public Policy Center of the University of Pennsylvania).

4. For more on the "Harry and Louise" ads, see J. Cappella and K. H. Jamieson (1997), *Spiral of Cynicism: The Press and the Public Good* (New York: Oxford University Press).

5. J. Eilperin and S. Torry (1998, August 8), "Tobacco Bill Written Off in House; Industry Continues Advertising Campaign Against Legislation," *Washington Post*, p. A6.

6. K. H. Jamieson (1998), *Annenberg Public Policy Center Survey Shows Influence of Ads by Tobacco Industry* (The Annenberg Public Policy Center of the University of Pennsylvania).

7. A. Corrado, T. Mann, D. Ortiz, T. Potter, and F. Sorauf (1997), *Campaign Finance Reform: A Sourcebook* (Washington, DC: Brookings Institution Press); D. Beck, P. Taylor, J. Stanger, and D. Rivlin (1997), *Issue Advocacy Advertising During the 1996 Campaign* (The Annenberg Public Policy Center of the University of Pennsylvania); K. H. Jamieson (1994), *The Role of Advertising in the Health Care Debate*, Parts 1–3, University of Pennsylvania releases; and M. Hamburger (1998, April 17), "Political Advertising, Issue Advocacy, and Our Grim Future," paper presented at the Conference on Political Advertising in Election Campaigns, American University, Washington, DC.

8. A. J. Cigler and B. A. Loomis (1995), "Contemporary Interest Group Politics: More Than 'More of the Same,'" in A. J. Cigler and B. A. Loomis (eds.), *Interest Group Politics*, 4th ed. (Washington, DC: CQ Press), 393–406; B. Loomis (1995, April 6–8), "Organized Interests, Paid Advocacy and the Scope of Conflict," paper presented at the Midwest Political Science Association Meeting, Chicago; D. M. West (1998, April 17), "How Issue Ads Have Reshaped American Politics," paper presented at the Conference on Political Advertising in Election Campaigns, American University, Washington, DC.

9. M. Burgoon, M. Pfau, and T. S. Birk (1995, August), "An Inoculation Theory Explanation of the Effects of Corporate Issue Advocacy Advertising Campaigns," *Communication Research* 22(4):485–505; L. N. Reid, L. C. Soley, and B. G. Vanden Bergh (1981), "Does Source Affect Response to Direct Advocacy Print Advertisements?" *Journal of Business Research*, 9:309–319; C. T. Salmon, L. N. Reid, J. Pokrywczynski, and R. W. Willett (1985, October), "The Effectiveness of Advocacy Advertising Relative to News Coverage," *Communication Research* 12(4):546–567.

10. K. H. Jamieson (1994), *The Role of Advertising in the Health Care Debate*, Part 1, 18, University of Pennsylvania releases.

11. A. Corrado, T. Mann, D. Ortiz, T. Potter, and F. Sorauf (1997), *Campaign Finance Reform: A Sourcebook* (Washington, DC: Brookings Institution Press); D. Beck, P. Taylor, J. Stanger, and D. Rivlin (1997), *Issue Advocacy Advertising During the 1996 Campaign* (The Annenberg Public Policy Center of the University of Pennsylvania); K. H. Jamieson (1994), *The Role of Advertising in the Health Care Debate,* Parts 1–3, University of Pennsylvania releases; M. Hamburger (1998, April 17), "Political Advertising, Issue Advocacy, and Our Grim Future," paper presented at the Conference on Political Advertising in Election Campaigns, American University, Washington, DC.

12. A. J. Cigler and B. A. Loomis (1995), "Contemporary Interest Group Politics: More Than 'More of the Same,'" in A. J. Cigler and B. A. Loomis (eds.), *Interest Group Politics*, 4th ed. (Washington, DC: CQ Press), 393–406; B. Loomis (1995, April 6–8), "Organized Interests, Paid Advocacy, and the Scope of Conflict," paper presented at the Midwest Political Science Association Meeting, Chicago; D. M. West (1998, April 17), "How Issue Ads Have Reshaped American Politics," paper presented at the Conference on Political Advertising in Election Campaigns, American University, Washington, DC.

13. M. Burgoon, M. Pfau, and T. S. Birk (1995, August), "An Inoculation Theory Explanation of the Effects of Corporate Issue Advocacy Advertising Campaigns," *Com-*

munication Research 22(4):485–505; L. N. Reid, L. C. Soley, and B. G. Vanden Bergh (1981), "Does Source Affect Response to Direct Advocacy Print Advertisements?" *Journal of Business Research*, 9:309–319; C. T. Salmon, L. N. Reid, J. Pokrywczynski, and R. W. Willett (1985, October), "The Effectiveness of Advocacy Advertising Relative to News Coverage," *Communication Research* 12(4):546–567.

14. C. T. Salmon, L. N. Reid, J. Pokrywczynski, and R. W. Willett (1985, October), "The Effectiveness of Advocacy Advertising Relative to News Coverage," *Communication Research* 12(4): 547.

15. A. J. Cigler and B. A. Loomis (1995), "Contemporary Interest Group Politics: More Than 'More of the Same,'" in A. J. Cigler and B. A. Loomis (eds.), *Interest Group Politics*, 4th ed. (Washington. DC: CQ Press), 393–406.

16. See B. Loomis (1995, April 6–8), "Organized Interests, Paid Advocacy and the Scope of Conflict," paper presented at the Midwest Political Science Association Meeting, Chicago.

17. Ibid.; B. Loomis (1996, April 18–20), "Narratives and Networks: Telecommunications Lobbying, 1992–1996," paper presented at the Midwest Political Science Association Meeting, Chicago; B. Loomis (1996, August 29–September 1), "Interests, Narratives, and Deliberation: 'Saving Medicare' and Passing Kennedy-Kassebaum," paper presented at the American Political Science Association Meeting, San Francisco; B. A. Loomis and E. Sexton (1995), "Choosing to Advertise: How Interests Decide," in A. J. Cigler and B. A. Loomis (eds.), *Interest Group Politics*, 4th ed. (Washington, DC: CQ Press), 193–213.

18. B. Loomis (1996, April 18–20), "Narratives and Networks: Telecommunications Lobbying, 1992–1996," paper presented at the Midwest Political Science Association Meeting, Chicago; B. Loomis (1996, August 29–September 1), "Interests, Narratives, and Deliberation: 'Saving Medicare' and Passing Kennedy-Kassebaum," paper presented at the American Political Science Association Meeting, San Francisco; B. A. Loomis and E. Sexton (1995), "Choosing to Advertise: How Interests Decide," in A. J. Cigler and B. A. Loomis (eds.), *Interest Group Politics*, 4th ed. (Washington, DC: CQ Press), 193–213.

19. B. Loomis (1995, April 6–8), "Organized Interests, Paid Advocacy and the Scope of Conflict," paper presented at the Midwest Political Science Association Meeting, Chicago, p. 2.

20. D. M. West and Richard Francis (1996, March), "Electronic Advocacy: Interest Groups and Public Policy Making," *PS: Political Science and Politics*, 29(1):25–32; D. M. West (1998, April 17), "How Issue Ads Have Reshaped American Politics," paper presented at the Conference on Political Advertising in Election Campaigns, American University, Washington, DC.

21. D. M. West (1998, April 17), "How Issue Ads Have Reshaped American Politics," paper presented at the Conference on Political Advertising in Election Campaigns, American University, Washington, DC, p. 7.

22. D. M. West and Richard Francis (1996, March), "Electronic Advocacy: Interest Groups and Public Policy Making," *PS: Political Science and Politics*, 29(1):25–32; D. M. West (1998, April 17), "How Issue Ads Have Reshaped American Politics," paper presented at the Conference on Political Advertising in Election Campaigns, American University, Washington, DC.

23. D. M. West (1998, April 17), "How Issue Ads Have Reshaped American Politics," paper presented at the Conference on Political Advertising in Election Campaigns, American University, Washington, DC, p. 8.

24. M. Burgoon, M. Pfau, and T. S. Birk (1995, August), "An Inoculation Theory Explanation of the Effects of Corporate Issue Advocacy Advertising Campaigns," *Communication Research* 22(4):485–505.

25. L. N. Reid, L. C. Soley, and B. G. Vanden Bergh (1981), "Does Source Affect Response to Direct Advocacy Print Advertisements?" *Journal of Business Research*, 9, pp. 14–15.

26. C. T. Salmon, L. N. Reid, J. Pokrywczynski, and R. W. Willett (1985, October), "The Effectiveness of Advocacy Advertising Relative to News Coverage," *Communication Research* 12(4):546–567.

27. "Industry Ad Campaign Helps Stall Tobacco Bill," *New York Times*, May 22, 1998, p. 1.

28. *Wall Street Journal*, June 11, 1998, p. A24.

29. For more on the Tobacco Resolution's campaign, see K. H. Jamieson (1998), *Tax and Spend vs. Little Kids: Advocacy and Accuracy in the Tobacco Settlement Ads of 1997–98* (Annenberg Public Policy Center).

30. J. Stanger and D. Rivlin (1998), *Issue Advocacy Advertising During the 1997–1998 Election Cycle* (The Annenberg Public Policy Center of the University of Pennsylvania).

31. Senators Brownback (R-Kansas), Roberts (R-Kansas), Snowe (R-Maine), Collins (R-Maine), Kerrey (D-Nebraska), Torricelli (D-New Jersey), and Reid (D-Nevada).

32. J. Stanger and D. Rivlin (1998), *Issue Advocacy Advertising During the 1997–1998 Election Cycle* (The Annenberg Public Policy Center of the University of Pennsylvania).

33. National Public Radio, May 13, 1998.

34. *Nightline,* June 17, 1998.

35. A factor analysis was conducted to determine if the eleven claims regarding the tobacco legislation were measuring similar dimensions. Three components were extracted. One centered on the five tobacco companies' central arguments. This grouping contained questions regarding a possible increase in cigarettes to $5 a pack, the creation of a black market, the formulation of seventeen government new bureaucracies, increasing taxes for both smokers and nonsmokers, and the creation of the largest consumer tax in history. This factor was marginally reliable (alpha $\cdot$ = .608) and was formed into an index of pro-tobacco accuracy.

In a regression (see Table A16.2 in Appendix IV) controlling for gender, party, age, education, race, income, and several variables measuring media consumption, the level of exposure was statistically significant ($p < .10$). For every one-unit increase in GRP, judged accuracy increased slightly by –0.0083. The unstandardized coefficient was negative because the highest level of accuracy was coded one and the lowest level was coded four. Thus, as the level of exposure increased or approached one, the level of accuracy also rose. Even though the GRP coefficient was small, the effect signaled that issue-advocacy commercials have the power to alter levels of judged accuracy and make the sponsor's claims more acceptable. For Model 1, the R^2 equals 0.037 and the analysis of variance is significant ($F = 2.389$, $p < .005$). Age, education, and race were also statistically significant in Model 1.

Chapter Nineteen

1. John P. Robinson (1972, Summer), "Perceived Media Bias and the 1968 Vote: Can the Media Affect Behavior After All?" *Journalism Quarterly*, 49:239–246; John P. Robinson (1976, Summer), "The Press and the Voter," *Annals of the American Academy of Political and Social Science*, 427:95–103; John P. Robinson (1974, Winter), "The Press as King-Maker: What Surveys from Last Five Campaigns Show," *Journalism Quarterly*, 51:587–594; Robert S. Erikson (1976, May), "The Influence of Newspaper Endorsements in Presidential Elections: The Case of 1964," *American Journal of Political Science*, 20:207–233; Dale Vinyard and Roberta S. Sigel (1971, Autumn), "Newspapers and Urban Voters," *Journalism Quarterly*, 48:486–493; Fred Fedler, Tim Counts, and Lown-

des F. Stephens (1982, Fall), "Newspaper Endorsements and Voter Behavior in the 1980 Presidential Election," *Newspaper Research Journal*, 4:3–11.

2. James E. Gregg (1965, Autumn), "Newspaper Editorial Endorsements and California Elections, 1948–62," *Journalism Quarterly*, 42:532–538; Maxwell McCombs (1967, Autumn), "Editorial Endorsements: A Study of Influence," *Journalism Quarterly*, 44:545–548; Howard A. Scarrow with Steve Borman (1979, Fall), "The Effects of Newspaper Endorsements on Election Outcomes: A Case Study," *Public Opinion Quarterly*, 43:388–393; Jack Sean McClenghan (1973, Summer), "Effect of Endorsements in Texas Local Elections," *Journalism Quarterly*, 50:363–66; Paul L. Hain (1975, Summer), "How an Endorsement Affected a Non-Partisan Mayoral Vote," *Journalism Quarterly*, 52:337–340; Philip L. DuBois (1984), "Voting Cues in Nonpartisan Trial Court Elections: A Multivariate Assessment," *Law and Society Review*, 18:395–436.

3. Michael Hooper (1969, Summer), "Party and Newspaper Endorsement As Predictors of Voter Choice," *Journalism Quarterly*, 46:302–305; William M. Mason (1973, May), "The Impact of Endorsements on Voting," *Sociological Methods and Research*, 1:463–495.

4. Paul L. Hain (1975, Summer), "How an Endorsement Affected a Non-Partisan Mayoral Vote," *Journalism Quarterly*, 52:337–340; John E. Mueller (1970, Fall), "Choosing Among 133 Candidates," *Public Opinion Quarterly*, 34:395–402.

5. John P. Robinson (1972, Summer), "Perceived Media Bias and the 1968 Vote: Can the Media Affect Behavior After All?" *Journalism Quarterly*, 49:239–246; Maxwell McCombs (1967, Autumn), "Editorial Endorsements: A Study of Influence," *Journalism Quarterly*, 44:545–548.

6. John E. Mueller (1969, December), "Voting on the Propositions: Ballot Patterns and Historical Trends in California," *American Political Science Review*, 63:1197–1212.

7. Robert E. Hurd and Michael W. Singletary (1984, Summer), "Newspaper Endorsement Influence on the 1980 Presidential Election Vote," *Journalism Quarterly*, 61:332–338; Tim Counts (1985, Autumn), "Effects of Endorsements on Presidential Vote," *Journalism Quarterly*, 62:644–647.

Chapter Twenty-One

1. J. Zhu, J. R. Milavsky, and R. Biswas (1994), "Do Televised Debates Affect Image Perception More Than Issue Knowledge?" *Human Communication Research* 20, pp. 302–333.

Chapter Twenty-Two

1. Kiku, Adatto, (1990, May 28), "The Incredible Shrinking Soundbite," *New Republic,* p. 20.

2. Samuel L. Popkin (1991), *The Reasoning Voter* (Chicago: University of Chicago Press), p. 228.

Chapter Twenty-Three

1. An earlier version of this chapter appeared in an article authored by Daniel Romer, Kathleen H. Jamieson, and Nicole DeCoteau (1998), titled "The Treatment of Persons of Color in Local Television News: Ethnic Blame Discourse or Realistic Group Conflict," *Communication Research,* 25, 286–305.

2. For more on discourse-based explanations of ethnic tension, see Teun A. van Dijk (1993), *Elite Discourse and Racism* (Newbury Park, CA: Sage); Margaret Wetherell and Jonathan Potter (1992), *Mapping the Language of Racism: Discourse and Legitimation of Exploitation* (New York: Columbia University Press).

3. For more on realistic group conflict theory, see Lawrence Bobo (1988), "Attitudes Toward the Black Political Movement: Trends, Meaning, and Effects on Racial Policy Preferences," *Social Psychology Quarterly*, 51, 287–302; Lawrence Bobo (1988), "Group Conflict, Prejudice, and the Paradox of Contemporary Racial Attitudes," in P. A. Katz and D. A. Taylor (eds.), *Eliminating Racism: Profiles in Controversy* (New York: Plenum Press), pp. 85–116; Robert A. Levine and Donald T. Campbell (1972), *Ethnocentrism: Theories of Conflict, Ethnic Attitudes, and Group Behavior* (New York: Wiley)

4. Daniel Romer, Kathleen Hall Jamieson, Catharine Riegner, Mika Emori, and Brigette Rouson (1997), "Blame Discource versus Realistic Conflict as Explanations of Ethnic Tension in Urban Neighborhoods," *Political Communication*, 14, 273–291.

5. Robert A. Levine and Donald T. Campbell (1972), *Ethnocentrism: Theories of Conflict, Ethnic Attitudes, and Group Behavior* (New York: Wiley).

6. Teun van Dijk (1991), *Racism and the Press* (New York: Routledge); Teun A. van Dijk (1993), *Elite Discourse and Racism* (Newbury Park, CA: Sage).

7. For content analyses of the U.S. press, see Paul M. Lester and Ron Smith (1990), "African-American Photo Coverage in *Life, Newsweek,* and *Time,* 1937 to 1988," *Journalism Quarterly*, 67, 136–145; Paul M. Lester (1994), "African-American Photo Coverage in Four U.S. Newspapers, 1937–1990," *Journalism Quarterly*, 71, 380–394; Erna R. Smith (1991), *What Color Is the News? An Ethnic Content Analysis of Bay Area News Media* (San Francisco: San Francisco State University). For content analyses of television news, see Robert M. Entman (1992), "Blacks in the News: Television, Modern Racism, and Cultural Change," *Journalism Quarterly*, 69, 341–361; Robert M. Entman (1994), *Violence on Television: News and "Reality" Programming in Chicago* (Chicago: Chicago Council on Urban Affairs); Robert M. Entman (1994), "Representation and Reality in the Portrayal of Blacks on Network Television News," *Journalism Quarterly*, 71, 509–520; Paul Klite, Robert A. Bardwell, and Jason Salzman (1995), *A Day in the Life of Local TV News in America* (Denver: Rocky Mountain Media Watch); Paul Klite, Robert A. Bardwell, and Jason Salzman (1997), "Local TV News: Getting Away with Murder," *Harvard International Journal of Press/Politics*, 2, 102–112.

8. Paul Hartman and Charles Husband (1974), *Racism and the Mass Media: A Study of the Role of the Mass Media in the Formation of White Beliefs and Attitudes in Britain* (Totowa, NJ: Rowman and Littlefield), p. 164.

9. Frank D. Gilliam, Jr., and Shanto Iyengar (1997), "Prime Suspects: The Effects of Local News on the Viewing Public," paper presented at the Annual Meeting of the Western Political Science Association, Portland.

10. See Douglas S. Massey and Nancy A. Denton (1993), *American Apartheid: Segregation and the Making of the Underclass* (Cambridge, Mass.: Harvard University Press); U.S. Bureau of the Census (1992), *Poverty in the United States: 1991. Current Population Reports, Series P-60, No. 181* (Washington, DC: U.S. Government Printing Office).

11. See K. Land, P. McCall, and L. Cohen (1990), "Structural Covariates of Homicide Rates: Are There Any Invariances Across Time and Space?" *American Journal of Sociology*, 95, 922–963; D. G. Rojeck and J. L. Williams (1993), "Interracial vs. Intraracial Offenses in Terms of the Victim/Offender Relationship," in A. V. Wilson (ed.), *Homicide: The Victim/Offender Connection* (Cincinnati: Anderson Publishing), pp. 249–266.

12. The rationale for using local television news was that, on any evening, the three late-evening major local news programs are seen by over 40 percent of the television-owning households in the region; A. C. Nielsen (1994, February), *DMA Total Activity Report* (Northbrook, IL). This represents more than one million of the 2.7 million households that own televisions in the region. Furthermore, national surveys indicate that local television news is the single source of news that most Americans (over 70 percent) rely on for information; Pew Research Center (1996), *The People, the Press, and Their Leaders* (Washington, DC).

13. Paul Klite, Robert A. Bardwell, and Jason Salzman (1997), "Local TV News: Getting Away with Murder," *Harvard International Journal of Press/Politics*, 2, 102–112; Vincent C. Sacco (1995), "Media Constructions of Crime," *Annals of the American Academy of Political and Social Science*, 539, 141–154.

14. For more on the Chicago study, see Robert M. Entman (1994), *Violence on Television: News and "Reality" Programming in Chicago* (Chicago: Chicago Council on Urban Affairs). The more recent studies of stations across the country are Paul Klite, Robert A. Bardwell, and Jason Salzman (1995), *A Day in the Life of Local TV News in America* (Denver: Rocky Mountain Media Watch); Paul Klite, Robert A. Bardwell, and Jason Salzman (1997), "Local TV News: Getting Away with Murder," *Harvard International Journal of Press/Politics*, 2, 102–112.

15. If there are only two mutually exclusive groups (A and B), the proportion of victims who are members of group A is equal to

$$p(A \; A)pA \, + p(A \; B)(1{-}pA),$$

where $p(A \; A)$ is the probability that A group perpetrators victimize members of their own group;

$p(A \; B)$ is the probability that B group perpetrators victimize members of group A (intergroup victimization); and

pA and $(1{-}pA)$ are the probabilities that perpetrators are members of groups A and B respectively.

16. Homicide rates (as other official crime rates) do not isolate the contribution of Latino actors who may be classified as white in police records. However, the Latino population is less than 10 percent of Philadelphia's population, so the estimates we have should not be too different from actual rates of intergroup (that is, person of color versus white) victimization. Our use of Philadelphia county as the source of homicide rates for the media region is justified in that the county accounts for over 80 percent of the homicides in the region; Federal Bureau of Investigation (1995), *Uniform Crime Report* (Washington, DC).

17. For earlier findings that persons of color appeared more in crime news than elsewhere, see Robert M. Entman (1992), "Blacks in the News: Television, Modern Racism, and Cultural Change," *Journalism Quarterly*, 69, 341–361; Robert M. Entman (1994), *Violence on Television: News and "Reality" Programming in Chicago* (Chicago: Chicago Council on Urban Affairs).

18. For further information on the methods and other study details, see Daniel Romer, Kathleen H. Jamieson, and Nicole DeCoteau (1998), "The Treatment of Persons of Color in Local Television News: Ethnic Blame Discourse or Realistic Group Conflict," *Communication Research*, 25, 286–305.

19. For the 1993 Philadelphia statistics, see Federal Bureau of Investigation (1995), *Supplementary Homicide Report* (Washington, DC).

20. For the theories on in-group favoritism, see Henri Tajfel and John C. Turner (1986), "An Integrative Theory of Intergroup Relations," in Steven Worchel and William G. Austin (eds.), *Psychology of Intergroup Relations* (Chicago: Nelson-Hall), pp. 7–24; and John C. Turner (1987), *Rediscovering the Social Group: A Self-Categorization Theory* (Oxford: Blackwell). For theories on modern racism, see John B. McConahay (1986), "Modern Racism, Ambivalence, and the Modern Racism Scale," in S. L. Gaertner and J. Dovidio (eds.), *Prejudice, Discrimination, and Racism: Theory and Research* (New York: Academic Press); and David O. Sears (1988), "Symbolic Racism," in P. A. Katz and D. A. Taylor (eds.), *Eliminating Racism: Profiles in Controversy* (New York: Plenum Press), pp. 53–84. For theories of individually based approaches, see Susan T. Fiske (1993), "Social Cognition and Social Perception," *Annual Review of Psychology*, 44, 155–194; and David Hamilton and T. L. Rose (1980), "Illusory Correlation and the

Maintenance of Stereotypic Beliefs," *Journal of Personality and Social Psychology*, 39, 832–845.

21. On the market forces that drive TV news practices, see John H. McManus (1992), *Market-Driven Journalism: Let the Citizen Beware?* (Thousand Oaks, CA: Sage Publications).

22. On laboratory simulations of effects of receiving information, see David Hamilton and Tina Trolier (1986), "Stereotypes and Stereotyping: An Overview of the Cognitive Approach," in John Dovidio and Samuel Gaertner (eds.), *Prejudice, Discrimination, and Racism: Theory and Research* (New York: Academic), pp. 127–163.

23. On evidence that TV news helps viewers define problems, see Shanto Iyengar and Donald R. Kinder (1987), *News That Matters: Television and American Opinion* (Chicago: University of Chicago Press); that definitions have important implications for intergroup relations, see Donald R. Kinder and Lynn M. Sanders (1996), *Divided by Color: Racial Politics and Democratic Ideals* (Chicago: University of Chicago Press); Paul M. Sniderman and Thomas Piazza (1993), *The Scar of Race* (Cambridge, MA: Harvard University Press).

24. For studies indicating that coverage accentuates fear of crime, and that it activates unfavorable stereotypes, see Frank D. Gilliam, Shanto Iyengar, Adam Smith, and Oliver Wright (1996), "Crime in Black and White: The Violent, Scary World of Local News," *Harvard International Journal of Press/Politics*, 1, 6–23; Mark Peffley, Todd Shields, and Bruce Williams (1996), "The Intersection of Race and Crime in Television News Stories: An Experimental Study," *Political Communication*, 13, 309–327.

25. On white residents reporting more fear of crime the closer they live to black residents, see Wesley G. Skogan (1995), "Crime and the Racial Fears of White Americans," *Annals of the American Academy of Political and Social Science*, 539.

Chapter Twenty-Four

1. D. Giobbe (1996), "Dole Wins in Endorsements," *Editor and Publisher*, 129, p. 7.

2. P. J. Coffey (1975), "Quantitative Measure of Bias in Reporting of Political News," *Journalism Quarterly*, 52, pp. 551–553.

3. Kenneth Dautrich and Jennifer Necci Dineen (1996, October–November), "Media Bias: What Journalists and the Public Say About It," *The Public Perspective*, 7–10.

4. See S. R. Lichter and S. Rothman (1980), "Personality Development and Political Dissent: A Reassessment of the New Left," *Journal of Political and Military Sociology*, 8, pp. 191–204.

5. S. R. Lichter, S. Rothman, and L. S. Lichter (1986), *The Media Elite* (Bethesda, MD: Adler & Adler).

6. David H. Weaver and G. Cleveland Wilhoit (1992, Fall), "Journalists—Who Are They, Really?" *Media Studies Journal*, pp. 63–79.

7. David Shaw (1985, August 11), "The Times Poll: Public and Press—Two Viewpoints," *Los Angeles Times*, p. 1.

8. Michael Robinson and Margaret Sheehan (1983), *Over the Wire and on TV: CBS and UPI in Campaign '80* (New York: Russell Sage Foundation).

9. Michael J. Robinson and Austin Ranney (1985), *The Mass Media in Campaign '84: Articles from* Public Opinion *Magazine* (Washington, DC: American Enterprise Institute for Public Policy Research); Doris Graber (1987), "Kind Pictures and Harsh Words," in K. L. Schlozman (ed.), *Elections in America* (Boston: Allen & Unwin); James Glen Stovall (1988, Summer), "The Coverage of the 1984 Presidential Campaign," *Journalism Quarterly*, 65(2), p. 443.

10. Robert S. Lichter, Daniel Amundson, and Richard E. Noyes (1988), *The Video Campaign: Network Coverage of the 1988 Primaries* (Washington, DC: American Enterprise Institute for Public Policy Research; Center for Media and Public Affairs).

11. K. Kenney and C. Simpson (1993), "Was Coverage of the 1988 Presidential Race by Washington's Two Major Dailies Biased?" *Journalism Quarterly*, 70, pp. 345–355.

12. D. T. Lowry and J. A. Shidler (1995), "The Soundbites, the Biters, and the Bitten: An Analysis of Network TV News Bias in Campaign '92," *Journalism and Mass Communication Quarterly*, 72, pp. 33–44. For similar patterns in local media markets, see M. R. Just, W. R. Neuman, and A. N. Crigler (1992), *An Economic Theory of Learning from News* (Cambridge, MA: Joan Shorenstein Barone Center Press, Politics, Public Policy, Harvard University, John F. Kennedy School of Government).

13. Mark D. Watts, David Domke, Dhavan V. Shah, and David P. Fan (1999, April), "Elite Cues and Media Bias in Presidential Campaigns," *Communication Research*, 26(2), p. 167.

14. G. H. Stempel and J. W. Windhauser (1989), "Coverage of the Prestige Press of the 1988 Presidential Campaign," *Journalism Quarterly*, 66, pp. 894–896.

15. Times Mirror Center for People and the Press (1989), *Polling the Nation 1986–1995*, CD-ROM, ORS Publishing.

16. Public Opinion Online, November 5, 1996, survey conducted for Institute for Social Inquiry, September 6–14, 1996.

17. J. W. Mashek, L. T. McGill, and A. C. Powell III (1997), *Lethargy '96: How the Media Covered a Listless Campaign*. (Arlington, VA: Freedom Forum).

18. R. P. Vallone, L. Ross, and M. R. Lepper (1985), "The Hostile Media Phenomenon: Biased Perception and Perceptions of Media Bias in Coverage of the Beirut Massacre," *Journal of Personality and Social Psychology*, 49, pp. 577–585.

19. Mashek, et al., *Lethargy '96*.

20. Watts, et al., "Elite Cues," p. 167.

21. Kathleen Hall Jamieson (1992), *Dirty Politics* (New York: Oxford University Press), pp. 165ff.

22. For example, "White House Releases Data to Defend Indonesian Policy" (October 17, 1996); "Democrats Curb Raising of Funds by a Top Official" (October 19, 1996); "Fund Raiser for Democrats Now Faces Harsh Spotlight" (October 21, 1996); "Democrats Return Drug Trafficker's $20,000 Gift (October 26, 1996); "Reno Makes Move Toward an Inquiry into Fund-Raising" (November 1).

23. Jamieson, *Dirty Politics*.

Chapter Twenty-Five

1. M. Gurevitch and J. Blumler (1995), "The Formation of Campaign Agendas in the United States and Britain," in *The Crisis of Public Communication* (New York: Routledge).

2. The data for this study were obtained from the archive created by the Campaign Discourse Mapping Project, which contains 112 Clinton speeches and 74 Dole speeches from the 1996 general election. We located 510 stories about the campaign in the *New York Times*.

Chapter Twenty-Seven

1. Scholars have shown that polls can affect voter turnout—see J. C. Petrocik (1991), "An Algorithm for Estimating Turnout as a Guide to Predicting Elections," *Public Opinion Quarterly*, 55, 643–647; vote intention—see A. Mehrabian (1998), "Effects of Poll Reports on Voter Preferences," *Journal of Social Psychology*, 28, 2119–2130; and V. G. Morwitz and C. Pluzinski (1996), "Do Polls Reflect Opinions or Do Opin-

ions Reflect Polls? The Impact of Political Polling on Voters' Expectations, Prefer-ences, and Behavior," *Journal of Consumer Research,* 23, 53–67; and can frame who is winning and losing for strategy-oriented coverage—see J. W. Rhee (1996), "How Polls Drive Campaign Coverage: The Gallup/CNN/*USA Today* Tracking Poll and *USA Today's* Coverage of the 1992 Presidential Campaign," *Political Communication,* 13, 213–229. Experimental research on the effect of poll coverage in the media has generally un-covered only slight or null effects—see S. Ansolabehere and S. Iyengar (1994), "Of Horseshoes and Horse Races: Experimental Studies of the Impact of Poll Results on Electoral Behavior," *Political Communication,* 11, 413–430.

Conclusion

1. Katherine Q. Seelye and James Dao (2000, January 9), "Gore Attacks Bradley on Agriculture Votes and Medicare," *New York Times,* p. 12.

2. Jonathan Roos (2000, January 9), "Farm Fight Democrats Compare Their Com-passion," *Des Moines Register,* p. 1.

3. Katherine Q. Seelye and John M. Broder (2000, February 17), "The Vice Presi-dent: Questions over Veracity Have Long Dogged Gore," *New York Times.*

4. Ibid.

5. See Adam Clymer (2000, February 26), "McCain Factor Quiets Talk of Dwindling Turnout," *New York Times,* p. A13.

6. Peter Marks (2000, February 21), "Bush Barked, but Voters Felt Only McCain's Bite," *New York Times,* p. A13.

7. Stephen Seplow (2000, February 20), "In Campaign 2000, Attack Ads Require a Gentle Touch," *Philadelphia Inquirer,* pp. D1, D3.

8. Carey Goldberg (2000, February 26), "Advising McCain, Rudman Is Happily Back in the Fray," *New York Times,* p. A9.

9. In Jake Topper (2000, February 22), "Mud-Slinging with a Spin," Salon.com.

10. Dick Polman (2000, February 24), "Catholic Question Is Shadowing Bush," *Philadelphia Inquirer,* pp. A1, A17.

11. Ibid., p. 1. Polman is reporting results of a survey by Michigan pollster Ed Sar-polus.

12. "Poll Results," *New York Times* , February 21, 2000, p. A13.

13. "Poll: The Voters in Michigan," *New York Times,* February 24, 2000, p. A22.

Appendix 1

1. Definitions are from *Webster's New World Dictionary of Media Communications* (New York: Macmillan, 1996).

2. Robert N. Reed and Maxine K. Reed (1992), *The Encyclopedia of Television, Cable, and Video* (New York: Van Nostrand Reinhold).

Selected References

Abelson, R. P., D. R. Kinder, S. T. Fiske, and M. D. Peters (1982). "Affective and Semantic Components in Political Person Perception." *Journal of Personality and Social Psychology* 42:619–630.

Abernathy, E. (1964). *The Advocate: A Manual of Persuasion*. New York: Mckay.

Andrews, F. M. (1982). "The Influence of Evidenciary [*sic*] and Extraevidenciary [*sic*] Factors on Decisions in a Simulated Rape Trial." *Dissertation Abstracts International*, 43, 516B–517B.

Ansolabehere, S., R. Behr, and S. Iyengar (1991). "Mass Media and Elections: An Overview." *American Politics Quarterly* 19, pp. 109–139.

Ansolabehere, Stephen, and Shanto Iyengar (1994). "Of Horseshoes and Horse Races: Experimental Studies of the Impact of Poll Results on Electoral Behavior." *Political Communication*, 11, 413–430.

_____(1995). *Going Negative: How Political Advertisements Shrink and Polarize the Electorate*. New York: Free Press.

_____(1996). "Can the Press Monitor Campaign Advertising?" *Press/Politics* 1(1):72–86.

Ansolabehere, Stephen, Shanto Iyengar, Adam Simon, and Nicholas Valentino (1994). "Does Attack Advertising Demobilize the Electorate?" *American Political Science Review* 88:829–838.

Arendt, Hannah (1968). *Between Past and Future, Eight Exercises in Political Thought*. New York: Viking Press.

Aristotle. *Nicomachean Ethics*, 1141b.

Austin, Erica, and Bruce Pinkleton (1995). "Positive and Negative Effects of Political Disaffection on the Less Experienced Voter." *Journal of Broadcasting and Electronic Media* 39:215–235.

Bacon, Francis (1620). *The New Organon* [Novum Organum], *Aphorisms Concerning the Interpretation of Nature and the Kingdom of Man*, XLIII.

Bartels, Larry M. (1992). "The Impact of Electioneering in the United States." In D. Butler and A. Ranney (eds.), *Electioneering: A Comparative Study of Continuity and Change*. Oxford: Clarendon Press, p. 267.

_____(1993). "Messages Received: The Political Impact of Media Exposure." *American Political Science Review*, 87(2):267.

_____(1997). "How Campaigns Matter." Unpublished manuscript.

Bartels, Larry M., et al. (1998). "Campaign Reform: Insights and Evidence." Report of the Task Force on Campaign Reform Sponsored by the Pew Charitable Trusts, Princeton University, Woodrow Wilson School of Public and International Affairs.

Beck, D., P. Taylor, J. Stanger, and D. Rivlin (1997). *Issue Advocacy Advertising During the 1996 Campaign*. The Annenberg Public Policy Center of the University of Pennsylvania.

Becker, L. B., M. A. McCombs, and J. M. McLeod (1975). "The Development of Political Cognitions." In S. Chaffee (ed.), *Political Communication*. London: Sage.

Selected References

Bennett, Linda L. M., and Stephen Earl Bennett. (1989). "Enduring Gender Differences in Political Interest: The Impact of Socialization and Political Dispositions." *American Politics Quarterly*, 17(1), 105–122.

Berelson, B., P. Lazarsfeld, and W. McPhee (1954). *Voting*. Chicago: University of Chicago Press.

Berlo, David, James Lemert, and Robert Mertz (1969). "Dimensions for Evaluating the Acceptability of Message Sources." *Public Opinion Quarterly*, 33(4):563–576.

Bobo, Lawrence (1988). "Attitudes Toward the Black Political Movement: Trends, Meaning, and Effects on Racial Policy Preferences." *Social Psychology Quarterly*, 51, 287–302.

_____(1988). "Group Conflict, Prejudice, and the Paradox of Contemporary Racial Attitudes." In P. A. Katz and D. A. Taylor (eds.), *Eliminating Racism: Profiles in Controversy*. New York: Plenum Press, pp. 85–116.

Bradley, P. H. (1981). "The Folk-Linguistics of Women's Speech: An Empirical Examination." *Communication Monographs*, 48, pp. 73–90.

Broder, David (1997). "Interview." *Miller Center Journal*, Spring.

Bryce, James (1888; 1995). *The American Commonwealth*. Vol. II. London: Macmillan, Vol. II, p. 208.

Buchanan, Bruce (1996). *Renewing Presidential Politics: Campaigns, Media, and the Public Interest*. Lanham, MD: Rowman and Littlefield, p. 105.

Buckley v. Valeo, 424 U.S. 1 (1976).

Burgoon, M., M. Pfau, and T. S. Birk (1995). "An Inoculation Theory Explanation of the Effects of Corporate Issue Advocacy Advertising Campaigns." *Communication Research* 22(4):485–505, August.

Burnham, W. D. (1970). *Critical Elections and the Mainsprings of American Politics*. New York: W. W. Norton.

Cacioppo, J. T., R. E. Petty, and K. J. Morris (1983). "Effects of Need for Cognition on Message Evaluation, Recall, and Persuasion." *Journal of Personality and Social Psychology*, 45, pp. 805–818.

Campbell, Angus, Philip E. Converse, Warren E. Miller, and Donald Stokes (1960). *The American Voter*. New York: Wiley.

Cappella, Joseph N., and Kathleen Hall Jamieson (1994). "Broadcast Adwatch Effects: A Field Experiment." *Communication Research* 21(3):342–365.

_____(1996). "News Frames, Political Cynicism, and Media Cynicism." *Annals of the American Academy of Political and Social Science*, 546:71–84.

_____(1997). *Spiral of Cynicism: The Press and the Public Good*. Oxford: Oxford University Press.

Cathcart, R. S. (1955). "An Experimental Study of the Relative Effectiveness of Four Methods of Presenting Evidence." *Speech Monographs*, 22, pp. 227–233.

Chaffee, Steven H., Xinshu Zhao, and Glenn Leshner (1994). "Political Knowledge and the Campaign Media of 1992." *Communication Research* 21(3):305–324.

Christ, William, Esther Thorson, and Clarke Caywood (1994). "Do Attitudes Toward Political Advertising Affect Information Processing of Televised Political Commercials?" *Journal of Broadcasting and Electronic Media* 38:251–270.

Cigler, A. J., and B. A. Loomis (1995). "Contemporary Interest Group Politics: More Than 'More of the Same.'" In A. J. Cigler and B. A. Loomis (eds.), *Interest Group Politics*, 4th ed. Washington: CQ Press, 393–406.

Coffey, P. J. (1975). "Quantitative Measure of Bias in Reporting of Political News." *Journalism Quarterly*, 52, pp. 551–553.

Cohen, B. (1963). *The Press and Foreign Policy*. Princeton: Princeton University Press.

Corrado, A., T. Mann, D. Ortiz, T. Potter, and F. Sorauf (1997). *Campaign Finance Reform: A Sourcebook*. Washington: Brookings Institution Press.

Counts, Tim (1985)."Effects of Endorsements on Presidential Vote." *Journalism Quarterly*, 62:644–647, Autumn.

Craig, S. (1993). *The Malevolent Leaders: Popular Discontent in America*. Boulder, CO: Westview Press, p. 13.

Cronin, M. W. (1973). "An Experimental Study of the Effects of Authoritative Testimony of Small Group Problem-Solving Discussions." *Dissertation Abstracts International*, 33, 6485A.

Delli Carpini, Michael X., and Ester R. Fuchs (1993). "The Year of the Woman? Candidates, Voters, and the 1992 Election." *Political Science Quarterly*, 108(1):29–36.

Delli Carpini, Michael X., and Scott Keeter (1991). "Stability and Change in the U.S. Public's Knowledge of Politics." *Public Opinion Quarterly*, 55:583–612.

_____(1993). "Measuring Political Knowledge: Putting First Things First." *American Journal of Political Science*, 37(4):1179–1206.

_____(1996). *What Americans Know About Politics and Why It Matters*. New Haven: Yale University Press.

de Sola Pool, Ithiel (1971). "What Will Be New in the New Politics?" In Ray Hiebert, Robert Jones, John Lorenz, and Ernest Lotito, *The Political Image Merchants*. Washington, DC: Acropolis, p. 256.

Dionne, E. J., Jr. (1991). *Why Americans Hate Politics*. New York: Simon & Schuster, p. 16.

DuBois, Philip L. (1984). "Voting Cues in Nonpartisan Trial Court Elections: A Multivariate Assessment." *Law and Society Review*, 18:395–436.

Entman, Robert M. (1992). "Blacks in the News: Television, Modern Racism, and Cultural Change." *Journalism Quarterly*, 69, 341–361.

_____(1994). *Violence on Television: News and "Reality" Programming in Chicago*. Chicago: Chicago Council on Urban Affairs.

_____(1994). "Representation and Reality in the Portrayal of Blacks on Network Television News." *Journalism Quarterly*, 71, 509–520.

Erikson, Robert S. (1976). "The Influence of Newspaper Endorsements in Presidential Elections: The Case of 1964." *American Journal of Political Science*, 20:207–233, May.

Faber, Ronald, Albert Tims, and Kay Schmitt (1993). "Negative Political Advertising and Voting Intent: The Role of Involvement and Alternative Information Sources." *Journal of Advertising* 22(4):67–76.

Fedler, Fred, Tim Counts, and Lowndes F. Stephens (1982). "Newspaper Endorsements and Voter Behavior in the 1980 Presidential Election." *Newspaper Research Journal*, 4:3–11, Fall.

Finkel, S. (1993). "Reexamining the 'Minimal Effects' Model in Recent Presidential Campaigns." *Journal of Politics* 55(1):1–21.

Finkel, S., and J. Geer (1998). "A Spot Check: Casting Doubt on the Demobilizing Effect of Attack Advertising." *American Journal of Political Science* 42:573–595.

Fishel, J. (1985). *Presidents and Promises*. Washington, DC: Congressional Quarterly Press, pp. 37–38.

Fiske, Susan T. (1993). "Social Cognition and Social Perception." *Annual Review of Psychology*, 44, 155–194.

Fleshler, H., J. Ilardo, and J. Demoretcky (1974). "The Influence of Field Dependence, Speaker Credibility Set, and Message Documentation on Evaluations of Speaker and Message Credibility." *Southern Speech Communication Journal*, 39, pp. 389–402.

Francis, Joe D., and Lawrence Busch (1975). "What We Now Know About 'I Don't Knows.'" *Public Opinion Quarterly*, 39(2):207–218.

Franklin, Benjamin (n.d.). *The Complete Works in Philosophy, Politics, and Morals of the Late Dr. Benjamin Franklin*. Vol. I. London.

Franklin, Charles H. (1991). "Eschewing Obfuscation? Campaigns and the Perception of U.S. Senate Incumbents." *American Political Science Review*, 85(4):1193–1214.

Friedman, T., with Elaine Sciolino (1993). "Clinton and Foreign Issues: Spasms of Attention." *New York Times,* March 22.

Garramone, Gina (1984). "Voter Responses to Negative Political Ads." *Journalism Quarterly* 61:250–259.

_____(1985). "Effects of Negative Political Advertising." *Journal of Broadcasting and Electronic Media* 29:147–159.

Gelman, A., and G. King (1993). "Why Are American Presidential Election Campaign Polls So Variable When Votes Are So Predictable?" *British Journal of Political Science* 23.

Germond, Jack, and J. Witcover (1996). "Why Americans Don't Go to the Polls." *National Journal* 28:2562.

Gilliam, Frank D., Jr., and Shanto Iyengar (1997). "Prime Suspects: The Effects of Local News on the Viewing Public." Paper presented at the Annual Meeting of the Western Political Science Association, Portland.

Gilliam, Frank D., Shanto Iyengar, Adam Smith, and Oliver Wright (1996). "Crime in Black and White: The Violent, Scary World of Local News." *Harvard International Journal of Press/Politics,* 1, 6–23.

Goldstein, Kenneth (1997). "Political Advertising and Political Persuasion in the 1996 Presidential Campaign." Paper submitted to the American Political Science Association, August 28–31.

Graber, Doris A. (1987) "Kind Pictures and Harsh Words." In K. L. Schlozman (ed.), *Elections in America.* Boston: Allen & Unwin.

_____(1988). *Processing the News: How People Tame the Information Tide.* New York: Longman.

_____(1989). *Mass Media and American Politics.* 3d ed. Washington, DC: Congressional Quarterly Press.

Gregg, James E. (1965). "Newspaper Editorial Endorsements and California Elections, 1948–62." *Journalism Quarterly,* 42:532–538, Autumn.

Gregory, Dick (1972). *Dick Gregory's Political Primer.* Ed. James R. McGraw. New York: Harper & Row.

Gurevitch, M., and J. Blumler (1995). "The Formation of Campaign Agendas in the United States and Britain." In *The Crisis of Public Communication.* New York: Routledge.

Hain, Paul L. (1975). "How an Endorsement Affected a Non-Partisan Mayoral Vote." *Journalism Quarterly,* 52:337–340, Summer.

Hamburger, M. (1998). "Political Advertising, Issue Advocacy, and Our Grim Future." Paper presented at the Conference on Political Advertising in Election Campaigns, American University, Washington, DC, April 17.

Hamill, R., T. D. Wilson, and R. E. Nesbett (1980). "Insensitivity to Sample Bias: Generalizing from Atypical Cases." *Journal of Personality and Social Psychology,* 39, pp. 578–589.

Hamilton, David, and T. L. Rose (1980). "Illusory Correlation and the Maintenance of Stereotypic Beliefs." *Journal of Personality and Social Psychology,* 39, 832–845.

Hamilton, David, and Tina Trolier (1986). "Stereotypes and Stereotyping: An Overview of the Cognitive Approach." In John Dovidio and Samuel Gaertner (eds.), *Prejudice, Discrimination, and Racism: Theory and Research.* New York: Academic, pp. 127–163.

Hample, D. (1985). "Refinements on the Cognitive Model of Argument: Concreteness, Involvement, and Group Scores." *Western Journal of Speech Communication,* 49, pp. 267–285.

Hartman, Paul, and Charles Husband (1974). *Racism and the Mass Media: A Study of the Role of the Mass Media in the Formation of White Beliefs and Attitudes in Britain.* Totowa, NJ: Rowman and Littlefield, p. 164.

Herrnson, Paul (1995). *Congressional Elections: Campaigning at Home or in Washington.* Washington, DC: Congressional Quarterly Press.

Hershey, M. (1989). "The Campaign and the Media." In Gerald M. Pomper (ed.), *The Election of 1988.* Chatham, NJ: Chatham House, p. 99.

Hetherington, M. (1996). "The Media's Role in Forming Voters' National Economic Evaluations in 1992." *American Journal of Political Science* 40, pp. 372–395.

Holbrook, T. (1996). *Do Campaigns Matter?* Thousand Oaks, CA: Sage.

Hooper, Michael (1969). "Party and Newspaper Endorsement As Predictors of Voter Choice." *Journalism Quarterly*, 46:302–305, Summer.

Hovland, C. (1959). "Reconciling Conflicting Results Derived from Experimental and Survey Studies of Attitude Change." *American Psychologist* 14.

Hume, B. (1993). "Campaign Mode: Bill Clinton's Travels and Campaign-Style Tactics Geared to Protect His Problems with the Press." *National Review,* August 23.

Hurd, Robert E., and Michael W. Singletary (1984). "Newspaper Endorsement Influence on the 1980 Presidential Election Vote." *Journalism Quarterly*, 61:332–338, Summer.

Iyengar, Shanto (1991). *Is Anyone Responsible?* Chicago: University of Chicago Press.

Iyengar, Shanto, and Donald R. Kinder (1987). *News That Matters: Television and American Opinion.* Chicago: University of Chicago Press.

Jacobson, Gary (1983). *The Politics of Congressional Elections.* Boston: Little, Brown.

_____(1989). "Strategic Politicians and the Dynamics of U.S. House Elections, 1946–86." *American Political Science Review,* 83(3), 773, September.

_____(1990). "The Effects of Campaign Spending in House Elections: New Evidence for Old Arguments." *American Journal of Political Science* 34(2), 334, May.

Jamieson, Kathleen Hall (1988). *Eloquence in an Electronic Age.* New York: Oxford University Press.

_____(1992). *Dirty Politics.* New York: Oxford University Press.

_____(1994). *The Role of Advertising in the Health Care Debate.* Parts 1–3. University of Pennsylvania releases.

_____(1998). *Annenberg Public Policy Center Survey Shows Influence of Ads by Tobacco Industry.* The Annenberg Public Policy Center of the University of Pennsylvania.

_____(1998). *Tax and Spend vs. Little Kids: Advocacy and Accuracy in the Tobacco Settlement Ads of 1997–98.* Annenberg Public Policy Center of the University of Pennsylvania.

Jamieson, K. H., and D. Birdsell (1988). *Presidential Debates: The Challenge of Creating an Informed Electorate.* Oxford: Oxford University Press.

Jamieson, Kathleen Hall, Paul Waldman, and Susan Sherr (2000). "Eliminate the Negative? Categories of Analysis for Political Advertising." In James A. Thurber, Candice Nelson, and David Dulio (eds.), *Crowded Airwaves: Campaign Advertising in Modern Elections.* Washington, DC: Brookings Institution Press.

Jay, John. "An Address to the People of the State of New York on the Subject of the Constitution." In P. L. Ford (ed.) (1888), *Pamphlets on the Constitution of the United States.* Brooklyn.

Jennings, M. Kent (1996). "Political Knowledge over Time and Across Generations." *Public Opinion Quarterly*, 60, 228–252.

Johnson-Cartee, Karen, and Gary Copeland (1991). *Negative Political Advertising: Coming of Age.* Hillsdale, NJ: Lawrence Erlbaum Associates.

Johnston, Richard, André Blais, Henry E. Brady, and Jean Crête (1992). *Letting the People Decide.* Palo Alto, CA: Stanford University Press.

Joslyn, Richard A. (1986). "Political Advertising and the Meaning of Elections." In Lynda Kaid, Dan Nimmo, and K. R. Sanders (eds.), *New Perspectives on Political Advertising.* Carbondale, IL: Southern Illinois University Press.

271

_____(1991). "Candidate Appeals and the Meaning of Elections." In Benjamin Ginsberg and Alan Stone (eds.), *Do Elections Matter?* Armonk, NY: M. E. Sharpe.

Just, M. R., W. R. Neuman, and A. N. Crigler (1992). *An Economic Theory of Learning from News.* Cambridge, MA: Joan Shorenstein Barone Center Press, Politics, Public Policy, Harvard University, John F. Kennedy School of Government.

Kaid, Lynda Lee, and John Boydston (1987). "An Experimental Study of the Effectiveness of Negative Political Advertisements." *Communication Quarterly* 35:193–201.

Kaid, Lynda Lee, and Anne Johnston (1991). "Negative Versus Positive Television Advertising in U.S. Presidential Campaigns, 1960–1988." *Journal of Communication,* 41, p. 53, Summer.

Kant, Immanuel. 11 "Of Aesthetic Judgment," Section 53.

Keith, Bruce, David Magleby, and Candice Nelson (1992). *The Myth of the Independent Voter.* Berkeley: University of California Press.

Kenney, K., and C. Simpson (1993). "Was Coverage of the 1988 Presidential Race by Washington's Two Major Dailies Biased?" *Journalism Quarterly,* 70, pp. 345–355.

Key, V. O. (1966). *The Responsible Electorate.* Cambridge: Harvard University Press.

Kinder, Donald, and D. R. Kiewiet (1981). "Sociotropic Politics: The American Case." *British Journal of Political Science* 11, pp. 129–161.

Kinder, Donald R., and Lynn M. Sanders (1996). *Divided by Color: Racial Politics and Democratic Ideals.* Chicago: University of Chicago Press.

Kirkpatrick, S., W. Lyons, and M. Fitzgerald (1975). "Candidates, Parties, and Issues in the American Electorate." *American Politics Quarterly* 3, pp. 247–283.

Klapper, J. (1960). *The Effects of Mass Communication.* Glencoe, IL: Free Press.

Klein, J. (1991). "Negativity Effects in Impression Formation: A Test in the Political Arena." *Personality and Social Psychology Bulletin* 17:412–418.

Kleinnijehuis, J., and J. de Ridder (1997). "Effects of Strategy News Framing on Party Preferences." Paper presented at the meeting of the American Political Science Association, Washington, DC, August.

Klite, Paul, Robert A. Bardwell, and Jason Salzman (1995). *A Day in the Life of Local TV News in America.* Denver: Rocky Mountain Media Watch.

_____(1997). "Local TV News: Getting Away with Murder." *Harvard International Journal of Press/Politics,* 2, 102–112.

Ladd, E. (1978). *Where Have All the Voters Gone?* New York: W. W. Norton.

Land, K., P. McCall, and L. Cohen (1990). "Structural Covariates of Homicide Rates: Are There Any Invariances Across Time and Space?" *American Journal of Sociology,* 95, 922–963.

Lane, Robert E., and David O. Sears (1964). *Public Opinion.* Englewood Cliffs, NJ: Prentice-Hall.

Lang, A. (1991). "Emotion, Formal Features, and Memory for Televised Political Advertisements." In F. Biocca (ed.), *Television and Political Advertising.* Vol. 1: Psychological Processes, pp. 221–243. Hillsdale, NJ: Erlbaum.

Lau, R. R. (1982). "Negativity in Political Perception." *Political Behavior* 4:353–377.

Lazarsfeld, P., B. Berelson, and H. Gaudet (1948). *The People's Choice.* New York: Columbia University Press.

Lester, Paul M. (1994). "African-American Photo Coverage in Four U.S. Newspapers, 1937–1990." *Journalism Quarterly,* 71, 380–394.

Lester, Paul M., and Ron Smith (1990). "African-American Photo Coverage in *Life, Newsweek, and Time,* 1937 to 1988." *Journalism Quarterly,* 67, 136–145.

Levine, Robert A., and Donald T. Campbell (1972). *Ethnocentrism: Theories of Conflict, Ethnic Attitudes, and Group Behavior.* New York: Wiley.

Lewis-Beck, M., and T. Rice (1992). *Forecasting Elections.* Washington, DC: Congressional Quarterly Press.

Lichter, S. R., and S. Rothman (1980). "Personality Development and Political Dissent: A Reassessment of the New Left." *Journal of Political and Military Sociology*, 8, pp. 191–204.

Lichter, S. R., S. Rothman, and L. S. Lichter (1986). *The Media Elite*. Bethesda, MD: Adler & Adler.

Lippmann, Walter (1955). *Essays in the Public Philosophy*. Boston: Little, Brown.

Loomis, B. (1995). "Organized Interests, Paid Advocacy, and the Scope of Conflict." Paper presented at the Midwest Political Science Association Meeting, Chicago, April 6–8.

——— (1996). "Narratives and Networks: Telecommunications Lobbying, 1992–1996." Paper presented at the Midwest Political Science Association Meeting, Chicago, April 18–20.

_____(1996). "Interests, Narratives, and Deliberation: 'Saving Medicare' and Passing Kennedy-Kassebaum." Paper presented at the American Political Science Association Meeting, San Francisco, August 29–September 1.

Loomis, B. A., and E. Sexton (1995). "Choosing to Advertise: How Interests Decide." In A. J. Cigler and B. A. Loomis (eds.), *Interest Group Politics*. 4th ed. Washington, DC: CQ Press, pp. 193–213.

Lowry, D. T., and J. A. Shidler (1995). "The Soundbites, the Biters, and the Bitten: An Analysis of Network TV News Bias in Campaign '92." *Journalism and Mass Communication Quarterly*, 72, pp. 33–44.

Markus, G. (1988). "The Impact of Personal and National Economic Conditions on the Presidential Vote." *American Journal of Political Science* 32:137–154.

Mashek, J. W., L. T. McGill, and A. C. Powell III (1997). *Lethargy '96: How the Media Covered a Listless Campaign*. Arlington, VA: Freedom Forum.

Mason, William M. (1973). "The Impact of Endorsements on Voting." *Sociological Methods and Research*, 1:463–495, May.

Massey, Douglas S., and Nancy A. Denton (1993). *American Apartheid: Segregation and the Making of the Underclass*. Cambridge, MA: Harvard University Press.

Matthews, D. (1978). "Winnowing." In J. D. Barber (ed.), *The Race for the Presidency*. Englewood Cliffs, NJ: Prentice-Hall.

McClenghan, Jack Sean (1973). "Effect of Endorsements in Texas Local Elections." *Journalism Quarterly*, 50:363–366, Summer.

McCombs, Maxwell (1967). "Editorial Endorsements: A Study of Influence." *Journalism Quarterly*, 44:545–548, Autumn.

McCombs, M., and D. Shaw (1972). "The Agenda-Setting Function of the Mass Media." *Public Opinion Quarterly* 36, pp. 176–187.

McConahay, John B. (1986). "Modern Racism, Ambivalence, and the Modern Racism Scale." In S. L. Gaertner and J. Dovidio (eds.), *Prejudice, Discrimination, and Racism: Theory and Research*. New York: Academic Press.

McGill, Lawrence, Andras Szanto, and Marianne Johnston (1997). In John W. Mashek, with Lawrence McGill and Adam Clayton Powell III, *Lethargy '96: How the Media Covered a Listless Campaign*. New York: Freedom Forum.

McGuire, W. (1986). "The Myth of Massive Media Impact: Savagings and Salvagings." *Public Communication and Behavior* 1, pp. 173–257.

McManus, John H. (1992). *Market-Driven Journalism: Let the Citizen Beware?* Thousand Oaks, CA: Sage.

Mehrabian, A. (1998). "Effects of Poll Reports on Voter Preferences." *Journal of Social Psychology*, 28, 2119–2130.

Mendelsohn, M. (1996). "The Media and Interpersonal Communications: The Priming of Issues, Leaders, and Party Identification." *Journal of Politics* 58, pp. 112–125.

Merritt, Sharyne (1984). "Negative Political Advertising: Some Empirical Findings." *Journal of Advertising* 13:27–38.

273

Miller, M. M. (1916). *American Debate.* New York: G. P. Putnam's and Sons.

Miller, M. M. (ed.) (1913). *Great Debates in American History.* New York: Current Literature.

Miller, W., and J. M. Shanks (1996). *The New American Voter.* Cambridge: Harvard University Press.

Morley, D. D. (1987). "Subjective Message Constructs: A Theory of Persuasion." *Communication Monographs,* 54, pp. 183–203.

Morwitz, V. G., and C. Pluzinski (1996). "Do Polls Reflect Opinions or Do Opinions Reflect Polls? The Impact of Political Polling on Voters' Expectations, Preferences, and Behavior." *Journal of Consumer Research,* 23, 53–67.

Mueller, John E. (1969). "Voting on the Propositions: Ballot Patterns and Historical Trends in California." *American Political Science Review,* 63:1197–1212, December.

_____(1970). "Choosing Among 133 Candidates." *Public Opinion Quarterly,* 34:395–402, Fall.

Murray, F. S. (1968). "Judgment of Evidence." *American Journal of Psychology,* 81, pp. 319–333.

Nadeau, Richard, and Richard G. Niemi (1995). "Educated Guesses: The Process of Answering Factual Knowledge Questions in Surveys." *Public Opinion Quarterly,* 59, 323–346.

Nie, Norman H., Sidney Verba, and John R. Petrocik (1979). *The Changing American Voter.* Cambridge: Harvard University Press.

Nilsen, Thomas R. (1958). "Free Speech, Persuasion, and the Democratic Process." *Quarterly Journal of Speech,* October, pp. 235–243.

O'Keefe, D. J. (1977). "Two Concepts of Argument." *Journal of the American Forensic Association* 13, pp. 121–128.

Page, Benjamin (1978). *Choices and Echoes in Presidential Elections: Rational Man and Electoral Democracy.* Chicago: University of Chicago Press.

Pan, Z., and G. Kosicki (1993). "Framing Analysis: An Approach to News Discourse." *Political Communication* 10, pp. 55–75.

Patterson, Thomas (1993). *Out of Order.* New York: Alfred A. Knopf.

Patterson, Thomas, and Robert McClure (1976). *The Unseeing Eye: The Myth of Television Power in National Elections.* New York: Putman.

Peffley, Mark, Todd Shields, and Bruce Williams (1996). "The Intersection of Race and Crime in Television News Stories: An Experimental Study." *Political Communication,* 13, 309–327.

Pentony, J. F. (1995). "The Effect of Negative Campaigning on Voting, Semantic Differential and Thought Listing." *Journal of Social Behavior and Personality* 10:631–644.

Petrocik, J. C. (1991). "An Algorithm for Estimating Turnout as a Guide to Predicting Elections." *Public Opinion Quarterly,* 55, 643–647.

_____(1996). "Issue Ownership in Presidential Elections, with a 1980 Case Study." *American Journal of Political Science,* 40(3):825, August.

Petty, R. E., and J. T. Cacioppo (1984). "The Effects of Involvement on Responses to Argument Quantity and Quality." *Journal of Personality and Social Psychology,* 46, pp. 69–81.

Petty, R. E., J. T. Cacioppo, and R. Goldman (1981). "Personal Involvement as a Determinant of Argument Based Persuasion." *Journal of Personality and Social Psychology,* 41, pp. 847–855.

Petty, R. E., S. E. Harkins, and K. D. Williams (1980). "The Effects of Group Diffusion or Cognitive Effort on Attitudes." *Journal of Personality and Social Psychology,* 38, pp. 81–92.

Pew Research Center for the People and the Press (1996). *Fewer Happy with Clinton Victory Than with GOP Congressional Win.* Washington, DC, November.

Pinkelton, Bruce (1997). "The Effects of Negative Comparative Political Advertising on Candidate Evaluations and Advertising Evaluations: An Exploration." *Journal of Advertising* 26:19–29.

Polsby, N., and A. Wildavsky (1996). *Presidential Elections*. Chatham, NJ: Chatham House Publishers, pp. 299–300.

Pomper, G. (1980). *Elections in America*. New York: Longman.

Popkin, Samuel L. (1991). *The Reasoning Voter*. Chicago: University of Chicago Press.

Public Opinion Online (November 5, 1996). Survey conducted for Institute for Social Inquiry, September 6–14, 1996.

Quirk, P., and S. Matheson (1997). "The Presidency: Elections and Presidential Governance." In Michael Nelson (ed.), *The Elections of 1996*. Washington, DC: Congressional Quarterly Press, p. 121.

Rapoport, Ronald B. (1981). "The Sex Gap in Political Persuading: Where the 'Structuring Principle' Works." *American Journal of Political Science*, 25(1):32–48.

Reid, L. N., L. C. Soley, and B. G. Vanden Bergh (1981). "Does Source Affect Response to Direct Advocacy Print Advertisements?" *Journal of Business Research*, 9:309–319.

Reynolds, R. A., and M. Burgoon (1983). "Belief Processing, Reasoning, and Evidence." In R. N. Bostrom (ed.), *Communication Yearbook 7*. Beverly Hills, CA: Sage, pp. 83–104.

Rhee, J. W. (1996). "How Polls Drive Campaign Coverage: The Gallup/CNN/*USA Today* Tracking Poll and *USA Today*'s Coverage of the 1992 Presidential Campaign." *Political Communication*, 13, 213–229.

Roberts, M., and M. McCombs (1994). "Agenda Setting and Political Advertising: Origins of the News Agenda." *Political Communication*, 11, pp. 249–263.

Robinson, John P. (1972). "Perceived Media Bias and the 1968 Vote: Can the Media Affect Behavior After All?" *Journalism Quarterly*, 49:239–246, Summer.

_____(1974). "The Press as King-Maker: What Surveys from Last Five Campaigns Show." *Journalism Quarterly*, 51:587–594, Winter.

_____(1976). "The Press and the Voter." *Annals of the American Academy of Political and Social Science*, 427:95–103, September.

Robinson, Michael J., and Austin Ranney (1985). *The Mass Media in Campaign '84: Articles from* Public Opinion *Magazine*. Washington, DC: American Enterprise Institute for Public Policy Research.

Robinson, Michael, and Margaret Sheehan (1983). *Over the Wire and on TV: CBS and UPI in Campaign '80*. New York: Russell Sage Foundation.

Roddy, Brian, and Gina Garramone (1988). "Appeals and Strategies of Negative Political Advertising." *Journal of Broadcasting and Electronic Media* 32:415–427.

Roese, W. J., and G. N. Sande (1993). "Backlash Effects in Attack Politics." *Journal of Applied Social Psychology* 23:632–653.

Rojeck, D. G., and J. L. Williams (1993). "Interracial vs. Intraracial Offenses in Terms of the Victim/Offender Relationship." In A. V. Wilson (ed.), *Homicide: The Victim /Offender Connection*. Cincinnati: Anderson Publishing, pp. 249–266.

Romer, Daniel, Kathleen H. Jamieson, and Nicole DeCoteau (1998). "The Treatment of Persons of Color in Local Television News: Ethnic Blame Discourse or Realistic Group Conflict." *Communication Research*, 25, 286–305.

Romer, Daniel, Kathleen Hall Jamieson, Catharine Riegner, Mika Emori, and Brigette Rouson (1997). "Blame Discourse Versus Realistic Conflict as Explanations of Ethnic Tension in Urban Neighborhoods." *Political Communication*, 14, 273–291.

Rosenstone, S. (1983). *Forecasting Presidential Elections*. New Haven: Yale University Press.

Sacco, Vincent C. (1995). "Media Constructions of Crime." *Annals of the American Academy of Political and Social Science*, 539, 141–154.

Salmon, C. T., L. N. Reid, J. Pokrywczynski, and R. W. Willett (1985). "The Effectiveness of Advocacy Advertising Relative to News Coverage." *Communication Research*, 12(4):546–567, October.

Sanchez, Maria Elena, and Giovanna Morchio (1992). "Probing 'Don't Know' Answers: Effects on Survey Estimates and Variable Relationships." *Public Opinion Quarterly*, 56, 454–474.

Scarrow, Howard A., with Steve Borman (1979). "The Effects of Newspaper Endorsements on Election Outcomes: A Case Study." *Public Opinion Quarterly*, 43:388–393, Fall.

Sears, David O. (1988). "Symbolic Racism." In P. A. Katz and D. A. Taylor (eds.), *Eliminating Racism: Profiles in Controversy*. New York: Plenum Press, pp. 53–84.

Shapiro, Robert Y., and Harpreet Mahajan (1986). "Gender Differences in Policy Preferences: A Summary of Trends from the 1960s to the 1980s." *Public Opinion Quarterly*, 50, 42–61.

Shaw, C. (1996). "Has President Clinton Fulfilled His 1992 Campaign Promises?" Department of Government, University of Texas, paper presented at the 1996 Annual Meeting of the American Political Science Association, San Francisco, CA, pp. 19, 22.

Shaw, Daron (1999). "The Effect of TV Ads and Candidate Appearances on Statewide Presidential Votes, 1988–96." *American Political Science Review*, 93:345–362, June.

Skogan, Wesley G. (1995). "Crime and the Racial Fears of White Americans." *Annals of the American Academy of Political and Social Science*, 539.

Smith, Erna R. (1991). *What Color Is the News? An Ethnic Content Analysis of Bay Area News Media*. San Francisco: San Francisco State University.

Sniderman, Paul M., and Thomas Piazza (1993). *The Scar of Race*. Cambridge: Harvard University Press.

Stanger, J., and D. Rivlin (1998). *Issue Advocacy Advertising During the 1997–1998 Election Cycle*. The Annenberg Public Policy Center of the University of Pennsylvania.

Stempel, G. H., and J. W. Windhauser (1989). "Coverage of the Prestige Press of the 1988 Presidential Campaign." *Journalism Quarterly*, 66, pp. 894–896.

Stiff, J. B. (1986). "Cognitive Processing of Persuasive Message Cues: A Meta-Analytic Review of the Effects of Supporting Information on Attitudes." *Communication Monographs*, 53, pp. 75–89.

Stovall, James G. (1988). "The Coverage of the 1984 Presidential Campaign." *Journalism Quarterly*, 65:443, Summer.

Tajfel, Henri, and John C. Turner. (1986). "An Integrative Theory of Intergroup Relations." In Steven Worchel amd William G. Austin (eds.), *Psychology of Intergroup Relations*. Chicago: Nelson-Hall, pp. 7–24.

Thoreau, Henry David. *Life Without Principle*, Number 37, as reflected in the 1906 Houghton Mifflin edition. Found on Web site http://www.walden.org/thoreau/writings/essays/reform/Life-without-Principle.htm.

Times Mirror Center for People and the Press (1989). *Polling the Nation 1986–1995*. (CD-ROM). ORS Publishing.

Toulmin, Stephen (1990). *The Uses of Argument*. Cambridge: Cambridge University Press.

Toulmin, S. E., R. Rieke, and A. Janik (1979). *An Introduction to Reasoning*. New York: Macmillan.

Truman, D. (1981). *The Governmental Process: Political Interests and Public Opinion*. Westport, CT: Greenwood Press, pp. 282–283.

Tufte, E. (1978). *Political Control of the Economy*. Princeton: Princeton University Press.

Turner, John C. (1987). *Rediscovering the Social Group: A Self-Categorization Theory*. Oxford: Blackwell.

U.S. Bureau of the Census (1992). *Poverty in the United States: 1991. Current Population Reports, Series P–60, No. 181*. Washington, DC: U.S. Government Printing Office.

Vallone, R. P., L. Ross, and M. R. Lepper (1985). "The Hostile Media Phenomenon: Biased Perception and Perceptions of Media Bias in Coverage of the Beirut Massacre." *Journal of Personality and Social Psychology*, 49, pp. 577–585.

van Dijk, Teun A. (1991). *Racism and the Press*. New York: Routledge.

_____(1993). *Elite Discourse and Racism*. Newbury Park, CA: Sage.

Vinyard, Dale, and Roberta S. Sigel (1971). "Newspapers and Urban Voters." *Journalism Quarterly*, 48:486–493, Autumn.

Wallace, Karl (1955). "An Ethical Basis of Communication." *Speech Teacher* 4:1–9, January.

Wattenberg, M. (1991*). The Rise of Candidate-Centered Politics*. Cambridge: Harvard University Press, p. 34.

_____(1996). *The Decline of American Political Parties, 1952–1994*. Cambridge: Harvard University Press.

Watts, Mark D., David Domke, Dhavan V. Shah, and David P. Fan (1999). "Elite Cues and Media Bias in Presidential Campaigns." *Communication Research*, 26(2):144–175, April.

Weaver, David H., and G. Cleveland Wilhoit (1992). "Journalists—Who Are They, Really?" *Media Studies Journal*, pp. 63–79, Fall.

West, Darrell M. (1997). *Air Wars*. 2d ed. Washington, DC: Congressional Quarterly Press.

_____(1998). "How Issue Ads Have Reshaped American Politics." Paper presented at the Conference on Political Advertising in Election Campaigns, American University, Washington, DC, April 17.

West, Darrell M., and Richard Francis (1996). "Electronic Advocacy: Interest Groups and Public Policy Making." *PS: Political Science and Politics*, 29(1):25–32, March.

Wetherell, Margaret, and Jonathan Potter (1992). *Mapping the Language of Racism: Discourse and Legitimation of Exploitation*. New York: Columbia University Press.

Willard, Charles Arthur (1989). *A Theory of Argumentation*. Tuscaloosa and London: University of Alabama Press.

Wirl, Daniel (1986). "Reinterpreting the Gender Gap." *Public Opinion Quarterly*, 50, 316–330.

Zaller, J. (1996). "The Myth of Massive Media Impact Revived." In D. Mutz, P. Sniderman, and R. Brody (eds.), *Political Persuasion and Attitude Change*. Ann Arbor, MI: University of Michigan Press.

Zhu, J., J. R. Milavsky, and R. Biswas (1994). "Do Televised Debates Affect Image Perception More Than Issue Knowledge?" *Human Communication Research* 20, 302–333.

Index

Index